RICHARD III & BUCKINGHAM'S REBELLION

LOUISE GILL

SUTTON PUBLISHING

First published in the United Kingdom in 1999 by
Sutton Publishing Limited · Phoenix Mill
Thrupp · Stroud · Gloucestershire · GL5 2BU

Paperback edition first published in 2000

British Library Cataloguing in Publication Data
A catalogue record for this book is available from the British Library.

ISBN 0-7509-2468-3

Cover illustrations courtesy of Geoffrey Wheeler

Typeset in 11/14pt Erhardt.
Typesetting and origination by
Sutton Publishing Limited.
Printed in Great Britain by
Redwood Books, Trowbridge, Wiltshire.

Contents

Acknowledgements

This book has been in progress for a number of years. It began with my PhD thesis for the University of Tasmania, whose topic was suggested by Professor Michael Bennett. To him I owe a special debt of gratitude, for his insight, wit and wisdom, and for his guidance and support throughout this project. To the History Departments of the University of Tasmania and the University of Melbourne for making available their resources, I am also indebted. To those archivists and librarians on both sides of the globe who have shown me great kindness and patience, and to my family and friends who have laboured on my behalf, especially Dr Em Underwood, my heartfelt thanks. I dedicate this book to my favourite people, Mark, Michelle and Simone, whose support for my work has always been unconditional.

Louise Gill
Melbourne
January 1999

List of Illustrations

Introduction

Less than four months after his usurpation of the throne in late June 1483, Richard III was confronted with a major uprising from within his own household which aimed at replacing him with the little-known Lancastrian exile, Henry Tudor. The revolt was led by Edward IV's closest servants who were outraged at Richard of Gloucester's coup after his brother's death and appalled at the disappearance and presumed murder of the young king, Edward V. Buckingham's rebellion, as it is known, capped the most dramatic period in English political history: three weeks after Edward IV's death on 9 April, Gloucester seized control of Edward V who had been in the care of the queen's kin, the Woodvilles, and dismantled their power base at Ludlow. Newly appointed protector of the realm, Richard then smashed an alleged plot against his life; declared his nephews illegitimate and ineligible to succeed to the thone; and in late June began to call himself king. Throughout this activity Henry, Duke of Buckingham, gave him unqualified support for which he received unprecedented rewards. Yet within weeks of Richard's coronation Buckingham became involved in the plot to overthrow Richard, install Henry Tudor at Westminster, and unite the Houses of York and Lancaster through Henry Tudor's marriage with Edward IV's eldest daughter, Elizabeth.

Buckingham's astounding defection from Richard to lead the rebellion for a political unknown, in view of all he had gained and all he stood to lose, is a fascinating topic that begs discussion. Nevertheless, the most significant aspect of Buckingham's rebellion was the united and unique opposition of the royal affinity to the crown, particularly as it followed a period of internal peace and nation-building from 1471 when Edward IV was able to unite the polity behind his régime. Revolt against the crown was not new in Yorkist England and Edward's first rule from 1461 to 1470 was marked by treason and betrayal which sometimes engulfed members of the royal household. Indeed Edward's own accession had followed a period of feckless kingship and aristocratic feuding when dynastic tensions encouraged blood-letting and revolt. Edward's father, Richard of York, chosen to lead the government twice in the 1450s during two episodes of mental illness suffered by the Lancastrian king, Henry VI, was virtually excluded from power when the king regained his faculties. And during a period of social and economic malaise compounded by England's failure abroad, York formalized his claim to the throne in 1460 and set the scene for the Yorkist usurpation of 1461. This, in turn, ushered in a decade of two crowned kings.

During the 1460s the leading magnate, Richard Neville, Earl of Warwick, jostled with Edward's kinsmen, the Woodvilles, for patronage and power. Feeling decidedly second-best in the contest, Warwick, who had been the power behind the Yorkist accession in 1461, switched sides to mastermind the Lancastrian *coup d'état* of 1470, taking with him Edward's brother George, Duke of Clarence. The readeption of Henry VI lasted just six months and ended violently with the deaths of Warwick and Henry's son, slaughtered in the field, and of Henry himself in obscure circumstances in the Tower of London. Thus the Lancastrians' hopes were thwarted, and for twelve years peace replaced the civil strife that had polarized the nation. Edward IV used the period to recast many of his policies which greatly strengthened his rule, the only ripples being the Earl of Oxford's revolt, the alleged treason and execution of Clarence in 1478, and the well-publicized hostility between the king's chamberlain, Lord Hastings, and Edward's brother-in-law, Earl Rivers. The period inflicted some casualties, however, most significantly the Duke of Buckingham who, as a prince of the blood and the scion of one of the oldest magnate families, had cause to resent his exclusion from his property entitlements and from serious political office by the king. He was thus ripe for intrigue following Edward's death. Though his support for Richard III in 1483 is a topic of interest, his defection from the king is more important, rather for what it says about the polity than about the duke himself. In this context the political culture of the south merits attention, not least the role of the royal affinity, and their activity and allegiance through the Wars of the Roses.

A sample of fifty-five of the leaders of Buckingham's rebellion has been selected for the following study; all of them were prominent royal servants. Much of the discussion turns on eighteen of Edward IV's southern knights and squires of the body whose position at court and power in the country enabled them to orchestrate the movement against the crown in 1483.*

* See appendix 4 for the sample of rebels, and Edward IV's knights and squires of the body.

CHAPTER 1
Tales of Rebellion

It had been a period of high drama. The events unleashed by Edward IV's death on 9 April 1483 were unprecedented in English political history. Through late spring and early summer the tension in the capital must have been palpable. By mid-autumn, though, perhaps a different mood prevailed in which the new king could enjoy the success of his northern progress. While most kings after their accession were keen to display their royal magnificence and to delight as well as overawe their subjects, Richard III had a more pressing concern. With memories of his usurpation of the throne fresh in people's minds, he needed to win over the south; to reassure both royal servants and ruling élites that continuity rather than dysfunction was to be the keynote of his rule. Eager to display his magnificence, he was anxious to secure their loyalty, which was essential for effective government. The king's progress began with a flourish, each centre providing lavish displays and ceremonials that had been carefully selected and artfully orchestrated in what was essentially a huge propaganda campaign. Wending his way north in late July just two weeks after his coronation, Richard spent several weeks in the Home Counties visiting Oxford University and staying briefly at his estates at Windsor and Woodstock, and later at Minster Lovell, the seat of his new chamberlain Francis, Viscount Lovell. Threading up through the Thames Valley as far as Gloucester, where the Duke of Buckingham left the royal party for Brecon, Richard, having veered north-east, paused at Warwick, Coventry, Leicester and Nottingham, arriving in York on 29 August. There he stayed for three-and-a-half splendid weeks full of pomp and pageantry which saw his son inaugurated as Prince of Wales. This was the apogee of his reign. Despite persistent rumours of disaffection in the south, the new king had cause to be well-pleased at Lincoln on the first leg of his return journey to Westminster. His pleasure, though, would have been short-lived. It was in Lincolnshire in early October that he received firm news of incipient rebellion, and of Buckingham's role in it.

While trouble was not entirely unexpected, for a short time it must have seemed to Richard as if all roads in southern England led to rebellion. The series of risings referred to by latter-day historians as 'Buckingham's Rebellion' was

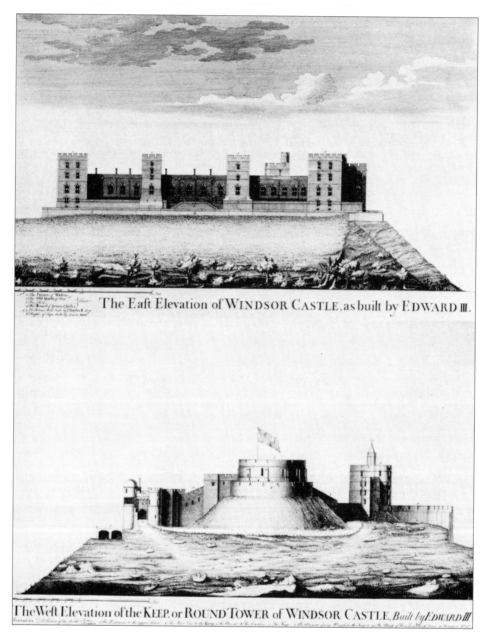

The Eaſt Elevation of WINDSOR CASTLE, as built by EDWARD III.

The Weſt Elevation of the KEEP, or ROUND TOWER of WINDSOR CASTLE, Built by EDWARD III

Top: the east elevation of Windsor Castle, built by Edward III; below: the west elevation of the keep or round tower of Windsor Castle.

planned across the south for 18 October 1483.[1] Led by a sprinkling of nobles and prelates, it was a gentry-driven revolt whose aim was to replace Richard III with Edward IV's eldest daughter, uniting her in marriage with the Lancastrian exile Henry Tudor, thus joining the dynasties of York and Lancaster. On paper at least it must have appeared a sound strategy. In terms of organization there was much to commend it, with five main theatres of revolt: south-east Wales, Exeter, Newbury, Salisbury and Kent. Rebels from Kent, Surrey and Sussex planned to take the capital and free Edward IV's queen and the princesses from captivity. In the central-south men would group at Newbury and Salisbury, linking up with forces raised by the Duke of Buckingham and the Marquess of Dorset in Wales and the west respectively. This assembly was planned in support of Henry Tudor, sailing from Brittany and set to land off the Devon coast at Plymouth, or further east at Poole or perhaps Weymouth in Dorset, allegedly around 18 October. Having raised the south, the rebels would then join forces and mount a major assault on London, the administrative heart of the kingdom; Richard III would be captured and overthrown, and Henry Tudor installed at Westminster as King Henry VII.

Despite its careful planning the revolt had little chance of success; errors of judgement, disaffection and inclement weather were all factors in its collapse. On the other hand Richard displayed spirited and united leadership indicating both a clarity of focus and sound intelligence in the royal camp. The rebels lost the initiative when some over-zealous Kentishmen alerted the crown to sedition over a week earlier than anticipated. The speedy response of the king's agents soon ended the Kentishmen's hopes of raising the region and taking the capital. The rebels' problems in Kent were matched elsewhere. The king had dispatched throughout the south spies whose intelligence enabled him to stay one step ahead of the dissidents. In the west Buckingham struggled against disloyalty, foul conditions and the guerrilla-like tactics of Richard's allies who easily scattered the insurgents. Desperate for a safe haven, and with a hefty price on his head, he made for the home of his childhood servant, Ralph Bannaster, who in the event turned him over to the king's men. Around the time of Buckingham's capture the central-southern sectors of Newbury and Salisbury crumbled before the royal host as Richard sped down through the region and then moved west towards Exeter. There the rebels fared no better. As the days passed and neither Henry Tudor nor Buckingham appeared it was clear that the revolt had failed. While Dorset had raised his standard on 18 October, the Exeter contingent was forced to disperse, many falling back to Bodmin in Cornwall to make a last-ditch attempt to rally support before they, too, took flight, a number making for exile overseas. For all its daring and originality the revolt was crushed by Richard within three weeks.

Tomb chest allegedly of Henry Stafford, Duke of Buckingham.

Given the nature and size of the rebellion, most people in the south must have sensed what was afoot well before it began. Since August the roads connecting the disaffected areas had been well travelled by couriers who relayed early intelligence around the south; by the rebels making for their rallying points; by royal agents and spies following hard on their heels; by Richard's deputies sent to round up the dissidents; and in the Home Counties and the west, by the king himself and his royal entourage. Needless to say, the heavy traffic would have made communications between the sectors difficult and as the official date for the rising approached, intelligence must have been sketchy and confused. News from the rebels' camp in the west was hampered by the worst weather for a generation. Termed 'Buckingham's water', the storms that lashed the coast were remembered long after their devastation. They may have been regarded as a portent, and perhaps even before standards were raised some had already sensed defeat and fled. Whatever else, there can have been no tales of daring in battle to boost morale and thrill the local communities; but as the days passed and men trundled home, there were ample reports of flight before the royal host, and later of miserable skirmishes in grim conditions as the king's men 'mopped up' stubborn and worrying pockets of resistance. None the less, with so much activity the south must have been rife with all manner of news, with fact difficult to distinguish from fiction. The earliest verbal accounts – probably partisan, embellished and contradictory – would certainly have entertained folk; fashioned as they were from gossip and hearsay, eye-witness observations and slivers of official news, they would have circulated through the local communities and the larger cities in England within days of the events.

Despite rich layers of anecdotal material in 1483, very little information which was actually set down has survived, offering slim pickings for historians on the rising itself. However, using the three main sources of contemporary historical information, central and local government records and private letters and papers, it is possible to collate and interpret key evidence in order to reconstruct the episode. Of the official material the chancery and exchequer records are invaluable, along with British Library Harleian Manuscript 433.[2] Comprising material that passed under the great and privy seals and the signet, much of which is recorded in the patent, close and pardon rolls, these records yield crucial detail on the king's movements and those of his enemies prior to the revolt, Richard's response to the rising, his military preparations, and the rebels' punishment in terms of fines, bonds and forfeitures, and in some cases pardons. In the aftermath of the rebellion they record dissent, disturbance and the threat to the régime of the Lancastrian pretender, Henry Tudor. In this context the pardon roll offers telling insights into the numbers, categories and calibre of the disaffected, or at least those who felt it wise to indemnify themselves as a precautionary measure. Sought after by a wide range of royal subjects including an archbishop, aristocrats and high-flyers such as the famous printer-publisher, William Caxton, the pardons help to bring home the significance of the rising as viewed by the recipients and undoubtedly the crown.[3] Generally speaking, the official documents give a public face to the principal gentry as the critical component in the rising, with rich evidence of their role in public life. For the fossickers, a culture of royal service in the south can be identified among the weightiest families whose employment from the crown often involved hereditary positions. The official documents also illustrate the crown's efforts to fill the political vacuum created by their loss in the aftermath of the rebellion. The records are thus invaluable in assessing both the immediate and the longer-term consequences of the revolt, and Richard's success in managing the south in its wake. Hard detail on the rising itself is thin on the ground. The main source is the four-part Act of Attainder of January and February 1484 which lists the leading rebels in the various sectors of revolt, some one hundred traitors to the new régime, offers a commentary on the rising and provides its official date. Interestingly the attainder also contains Richard's allegation against Buckingham for inviting Henry Tudor to invade England on 24 September.[4] Detail is also furnished by royal proclamations and letters, and by two indictments taken after the rising in the west, at Torrington and Bodmin, before Lord Scrope of Bolton. Both provide names of rebels and are important in their own right as they are apparently the only surviving inquisitions from the revolt.[5] Private papers, especially those of the Duke of Norfolk, giving details on the south-east sector, also assist the sleuth, while the family letters of the Celys, Plumptons, Pastons and Stonors contain pertinent offerings on the rising itself and surrounding events.

Generally speaking, documents of state provide the most reliable (if dull) information, divulging fact rather than context or atmosphere. None the less they provide the historian with some sort of grip on the period and a touchstone in regard to the chronicles and histories; they have all the more appeal in the light of the charge of partisanship attached to the sources for Richard III's reign. Certain classes of material, though, especially royal letters and proclamations, can offer both inference and insight, and on occasion real drama as well as hard fact. Much can be inferred from them in regard to Richard's response, his priorities, preparations and punishments. The king's itinerary, for example, from Lincoln on 11 October until his return to Westminster on 25 November, tells us as much about the rebels' failure as it does the king's success. Then again, with widespread revolt incipient, his first priority was to order up the great seal from John Russell, Bishop of Lincoln, his chancellor in London; this was an unusual step which virtually put full control of the government in his hands. This may point to Richard's mistrust of his chancellor, so recently appointed by him; though Russell remained in office, he nevertheless again lost the great seal almost two years later when Henry Tudor invaded the kingdom. The drama is played out, however, in the king's official response to Buckingham's defection which is revealed in two royal letters, the first recorded in the minutes of the proceedings of York City Council, and the second in the letter from Richard requesting the great seal.[6] Significantly, the minutes record Richard's request for help against Buckingham on the eve of revolt, when a few months earlier they had documented his plea for aid against the Woodvilles who intended his murder, together with 'his cousin the Duke of Buckingham'.[7] Letters from nobles and gentry alike are also often forthcoming. The Duke of Norfolk, for instance, in alarmist fashion informed his client John Paston on 10 October that the Kentishmen were poised 'to come and rob the city'.[8] The more colourful the material, however, the more care is required by historians in its use. According to one Yorkshire squire, for example, Buckingham had 'so many men' at Brecon on 18 October that he was able 'to go where he will'.[9] The reality, of course, was quite different.

While few outside official circles were privy to most aspects of the royal response, for the more astute and politically informed subjects the king's proclamations were a constant source of news as well as a revelation. Given their obvious partisan bent, they none the less informed the public of the crown's concern over what was clearly not a small-scale and localized revolt in the traditional lord-follower mould, evident in the absence of nobles and the prominence of leading gentry. Apart from 'naming names', the proclamations from mid-October to early November contain some stinging personal attacks and emphasize the speed of Richard's very public and vitriolic response to Buckingham's betrayal. Driven by an overwhelming need to bring his former ally – a prince of the blood – to account, Richard used the full weight of the royal publicity machine to damn the duke. Even before 18 October Buckingham's leadership of the rebellion was common knowledge. Certain of his defection by 11 October, the king had issued a proclamation denouncing him on the 15th which was published at York on the 16th and at Hull on the 17th. When Buckingham's sector seemed doomed and the formidable coalition Richard had feared failed to materialize, a second royal proclamation was published at Leicester on the 23rd and circulated to the sheriffs in southern and central England. The charge was repeated four weeks later in the commission of arrest before Scrope at Bodmin, where it was alleged that some of the most powerful gentry in the land had arrayed in order to 'overthrow' and to 'utterly destroy the king' and to 'set up another . . . in his place, by the command and order of Henry, Duke of Buckingham'.[10]

The news of the rebellion travelled quickly in England, spreading out through the localities and the major centres, though France and other parts of western Europe were not far behind. In fact the first verbal accounts crossed the Channel with the rebels themselves, reaching the courts of France, Brittany and the Low Countries within weeks of the débâcle. Seeking a grant of safe conduct from the new French king, Charles VIII, to reach Brittany by way of Normandy, Henry Tudor's envoys no doubt recounted their ordeal at sea: already overdue, the appalling conditions which further delayed them; their inability to land off the Dorset coast because of Richard's presence; the obvious failure of the other sectors of revolt; and Buckingham's execution before the king at Salisbury on 2 November. Henry Tudor himself had first heard of the duke's death on 8 or 9 November while moored off the Devon coast outside Plymouth Harbour, where he was anxiously awaiting a sign from Buckingham or Dorset as to how matters stood onshore and whether or not it was safe to land. Once apprised of the duke's death, Henry fled back across the Channel making landfall on the north coast of France, east of Brittany, his destination. There he stayed for three days before returning to Brittany, having secured a grant of safe conduct from Charles VIII. Francis, Duke of Brittany, Henry's custodian since 1471, had almost certainly been informed of events before Henry arrived. The news was carried further afield by other members of Henry Tudor's expedition, some of whom docked at Dieppe, Calais and as far north as Flanders. Still other accounts of the rebellion were broadcast by the political exiles themselves, around 500 or so, most of whom fled from the royal host in the west and soon joined Henry Tudor at Vannes in Brittany. Others escaped to the Low Countries where their tales of rebellion were doubtless related to sympathetic company. In little time the news would have been circulated more widely by merchants travelling along the trade-routes of northern Europe.

While stories of the revolt certainly reached foreign courts before the end of 1483, the first written accounts to circulate abroad were begun around six years later by Philippe de Commynes and Jean Molinet. Commynes, a Flemish-born but French-based diplomat and historian, provides real insights into Henry Tudor's Breton-backed expedition. He was already acquainted with Henry through his diplomatic work in Brittany in 1471, and the two met again shortly before Henry's journey to Bosworth in 1485. Dispassionate yet clearly informed, Commynes stresses the welcome assistance of the Duke of Brittany in supporting Henry's expedition which nevertheless failed owing to 'a great storm' and 'contrary winds'. Noting also the 'co-operation' of Buckingham 'who later died for his part', Commynes highlights the number of refugees with Henry and the latter's fear of straining the duke's purse-strings.[11] Acclaimed by Lord Macaulay, the great Victorian statesman, as one of the most gifted men of his age, Commynes's work displays neither anti-Ricardian nor Breton prejudice.[12] Given the fluctuating state of affairs in 1483 between England, Brittany and France and the recently deceased Louis XI's inability to secure Henry from the Bretons, he may perhaps have had reason for partisanship, but none the less he speaks well of Duke Francis, and is not blind to Henry Tudor's pretensions, though he was clearly impressed by him. Historians have pointed to his interpretation of Richard's coup and Buckingham's role in it, and in the fate of the princes, as muddled and contradictory; nevertheless Commynes accurately captured public opinion which was at best confused. His Burgundian contemporary, the erudite historian and bibliophile Jean Molinet, even less open to the charge of Tudor prejudice, offers some acute political observations on 1483, stressing the outrage of the people over Richard's actions following Edward's death, not least over the disappearance of the princes who it was widely believed had been murdered. Molinet condemns Richard, although he mentions and then quickly dismisses Buckingham as the instigator of the crime. While factual and chronological errors mar this part of his work (for a coalition of prelates, nobles and gentry who rose against Richard of Gloucester, found and buried the bodies of Edward IV's sons before Richard's coronation), like Commynes, Molinet represents the broad range of public opinion and, moreover, provides by implication at least a rationale for rebellion.[13]

For those in England keen to winnow out the evidence, Dominic Mancini's *The Usurpation of Richard III*, written up before the end of 1483 from evidence obtained while he was a guest in England, unfortunately ends shortly after Richard's coronation.[14] Before long though, the most important account of the rising appeared as part of a work known as the 'second continuation' of the Crowland Abbey chronicle, itself attached to a 'first continuation' of 'Ingulph's' chronicle. Penned in 1486 by a scholarly and knowledgeable hand, possibly that of the king's chancellor John Russell, the chronicle traces the upheavals of English political life from 1459 to 1485. Infuriatingly terse on important events between May and November 1483, the author's acuity is yet remarkably instructive. Importantly, the chronicle focuses on the revolt as a gentry movement whose motivation was quite independent of the central intrigue. According to the chronicler men had already met to consider strategies to restore Edward IV's sons well before Buckingham joined the rebellion. While the duke, allegedly contrite over his activity with Richard, was proclaimed 'chief mover' of the revolt and, at John Morton's behest, wrote to Henry Tudor inviting him to rebel, his role as figure-head is implied. Curiously his 'leadership' coincided with a rumour that the princes had 'died a violent death'. With authority the continuator stresses the discontent of the people in the south and accurately names the counties involved: 'Kent, Essex, Sussex, Hampshire, Dorsetshire, Somersetshire, Wiltshire and Berkshire as well as some others of the southern counties . . .'.[15] He also notes Richard's network of

Yorkist livery collar of suns and roses.

spies who informed him of sedition. While this information had been well publicized by 1486, no other contemporary account is as informative or displays the same bureaucratic thoroughness of the listing. Though the author clearly had inside information, his treatment of the revolt suggests more than an official interest. Whatever else, the chronicle is by far the most informed, if circumspect, source for the rebellion.

While most other contemporary accounts diminish by comparison, they do yield points of interest, such as material found in the chronicles of London, which were compiled between the late thirteenth and sixteenth centuries, probably on a yearly basis, and then reworked by redactors. The project of civic-minded citizens, most notably Robert Fabian, news was obtained first-hand and from hearsay, newsletters, and occasionally from official documents. The three relevant London chronicles for the rising are known as 'Vitellius A XVI', *Fabian's Chronicle* and *The Great Chronicle of London*. In addition a chronicle known as 'College of Arms Ms 2M6', first discovered in 1981 and probably compiled around 1485, is of interest because of its focus on Buckingham's alleged involvement in the deaths of the princes. The chronicles are, however, guilty of some serious factual errors. For example *The Great Chronicle* states that the rebellion occurred not only because it was strongly rumoured that Richard had murdered the princes, but also that he had poisoned Anne Neville his queen and intended to marry Elizabeth of York, Edward IV's eldest daughter, thus placing the rebellion in 1485.[16] None the less, while it accents Buckingham's leadership, like the Crowland chronicle it also records the independent action of the gentry and provides names. 'Many knights and men of worship' rose 'with all the power that they could make'; they included Thomas St Leger, George Brown, William Clifford and Thomas Rameney 'with many others'.[17] Ducal cowardice and an inability to muster his followers forced the rebels to disband their retinues and fend 'for themselves in the best wise that they might'.[18] Despite their flaws the chronicles are important contemporary records of events which reflect to a degree the popular opinion of London. Thus may be viewed the addled jottings of the Warwickshire priest, John Rous, *Historia Regum Anglia* (1490), and points of interest verified from other sources.[19] In this context a memoir written around 1503 by Elizabeth Mores, a servant in the household of her future husband, Sir Richard de la Bere of Kinnersley, Herefordshire, expands on the duke's weakness at the muster noted in *The Great Chronicle*. Though not discovered until 1579, the memoir provides interesting detail of the pillaging spree of Buckingham's retainers at Brecon under Sir Thomas Vaughan, following his flight across the border to Weobley with his wife and sons, Bishop Morton and his closest servants. It records his unsuccessful bid to recruit the gentlemen of Herefordshire to his cause, Richard's proclamation of 23 October with its offer of a reward for the duke's capture (wrongly stated as £4000 rather than £1000), and his subsequent betrayal.[20]

Little of real merit reached the general public until the work of the gifted Renaissance historian Polydore Vergil went to the press in 1534. From Urbino, Vergil began his *Anglica Historia* in 1502 at the behest of Henry VII. Offering the last contemporary and the fullest account of the rising, Vergil's history contrasts with most earlier works on the period and is viewed by many as a harbinger in historical writing. While the work of his contemporary, Sir Thomas More, *History of Richard III*, was acknowledged as a literary masterpiece, it was Vergil who stamped his writing with the authority of a real historian.[21] Because of his perceived anti-Ricardian prejudice and his popularity among later writers, his role in developing the Tudor tradition has long been contentious. While Vergil did not invent the Tudor tradition but simply reflected a widely held view of Richard III, his role in its development was large. Expanding on the notion of 'God's judgement' put forward by Commynes, Vergil's portrait of Richard fits into a schematic framework in which all fifteenth-century kings were subject to divine justice. The rulers both Lancaster and York were agents of destruction who in turn paid horribly for their crimes. In 1485 Henry Tudor broke the 'crime and punishment' cycle and restored peace to the realm when he defeated Richard at Bosworth, married Elizabeth of York and produced a son who acceded to the throne in Vergil's own time.[22] Buckingham's rebellion fits neatly into this cycle. Polydore developed a rationale for the duke's disaffection which he used as a device to accent Richard's wickedness and Buckingham's moral rehabilitation. Through the sixteenth and seventeenth centuries Buckingham's behaviour was thus interpreted and embellished by a number of writers in the same tradition.

Focusing on the luminaries in the rebellion, Vergil unravels two plots: the first centres on Buckingham and John Morton at Brecon. Piqued over Richard's hold on his hereditary lands (which in reality the king had granted him) and repentant for having 'done many things against his own conscience', the duke told Morton of his plan to replace Richard with Henry Tudor and unite the Houses of York and Lancaster through marriage. The second, connected, plot features Margaret Beaufort, Henry Tudor's mother, Elizabeth Woodville, Edward IV's widow, and their go-between, the physician Lewis Caerleon. Lady Margaret sent Hugh Conway to apprise her son in Brittany of events in England, while the conspirators in London and at Brecon made common ground. Despite the second intrigue, Buckingham was the acknowledged leader of the rebellion, of which Richard had some knowledge. Vergil's role in developing the Tudor tradition is evident in the first plot which contains three main elements: Richard's manipulative powers and treachery, which seduced one of the leading nobles of the realm; Buckingham's about-face and repentance at having been a party to such treachery; and finally the duke's determination to expiate his sins by helping Henry Tudor attain both the crown and Elizabeth of York.[23]

With few sources available to him Vergil scoured the halls and chambers at court, hunting down and probably badgering men who had been participants in the events and were still alive in 1502; they included Richard Fox, Bishop of Winchester, Reginald Bray and Christopher Urswick, Henry's confessor, as well as power-brokers such as Thomas, Lord Stanley. His methods paid off, and he developed a reasoned account of the rising, spiced with snippets that do not

Sir Reginald Bray (d. 1503) from the stained-glass window at Malvern Priory.

appear in earlier records. He notes, for instance, that Margaret Beaufort appointed her servant Reginald Bray to recruit 'noble or worshipful men . . . able to make help in the cause'; he also has news of the Marquess of Dorset who had fled sanctuary, and prior to the rising was allegedly busy recruiting in Yorkshire with the aid of Thomas Lovell.[24] He provides the names of gentry leaders: Edward Courtenay in the west and Richard Guildford in the east; and lists some of the refugees in Brittany with Henry Tudor, including Dorset himself, Sir Giles Daubenay, Sir William Berkeley, William Brandon, Richard Edgecombe, John Halwell, Thomas Arundel and John Cheyne. He also augments the list of refugees with the names of John Bourchier and Evan Morgan, and records the flight of Bishop Morton to Flanders. Again, much of his detail of 1483 is original and demonstrates his use of oral sources including Stanley and others of like mind.[25]

Vergil's history was plundered and embellished by the next generation of writers, most notably the chronicler Edward Hall, *The Union of the Two Noble and Illustre Families of Lancastre and York* (1548). Adding some insights, Hall uses the same schematic framework as Vergil, in which Henry Tudor's overthrow of a tyrant fitted into a scheme of divine providence that ended a long period of suffering. Like Vergil, only by making Richard III an exception was he able to work around the notion implicit in Tudor tradition that all kings must be obeyed. Historically, Buckingham's rebellion, like Henry Tudor's usurpation in 1485, could only be justified because the king was a monster whom the duke tried but failed to overthrow in 1483, but whose tyranny finally ended two years later. Closely following Vergil, Hall includes a new item from an unknown source concerning a chance meeting before the rising between Buckingham and Margaret Beaufort on the road between Worcester and Bridgnorth; the duke was on his way to Brecon, Lady Margaret to her Stafford manor in Shropshire.[26] Such an encounter is quite plausible: in August and September 1483 Buckingham's manor of Thornbury was at the centre of a conspiracy involving the duke, Morton, Bishop Lionel Woodville, a guest at the manor, and more than likely Margaret Beaufort at Bridgnorth.[27] Thornbury was well positioned as a centre for conspiracy between London and Brecon. Close to the Severn and to Bristol, it was also in line for communications with the other centres of rebellion. Importantly, if as Hall suggests Lady Beaufort was at Bridgnorth then the conspirators were indeed nicely placed to send and receive information around various parts of the Stafford estates, before dispatching it further afield. By this stage the theatres of revolt were clearly delineated and it seems likely that the earlier Woodville plot laid the organizational pattern for the autumn risings. Hall also reworks Vergil's account of Buckingham's downfall in which Ralph Bannaster 'in great haste and evil speed conveyed him to the city of Salisbury'. Thus he presents the duke as a genuinely sympathetic character who has come full circle in his moral rehabilitation from the disingenuous lord with Morton at Brecon to the victim of Bannaster in the 'Buckingham tragedy'.[28]

Most writers who followed Hall augmented the list of refugees, though added little to the Tudor tradition. Richard Grafton's *Chronicle* (1568) notes Robert Poyntz as a captain in the revolt and adds the name of Humphrey Cheyne to Vergil's list of exiles; while Raphael Holinshed's *Chronicles of England, Scotland and Ireland* (1578) furnishes interesting detail taken from an Exeter antiquarian, John Hooker, concerning a list of five hundred rebels indicted for 'high treason' before Lord Scrope at Torrington in November 1483.[29] A sliver of information, probably gleaned from the official sources, is provided by the Elizabethan antiquarian John Stow, *The Annales of England* (1592), who wrote of trouble at Gravesend in Kent in early October and at Canterbury in early November 1483 which 'collapsed' only when news of Buckingham's execution became known. In addition, he names Sir John Scott among the rebels.[30]

The traditional view of Buckingham's rebellion, with its origins in the earliest verbal and written accounts, was enhanced by Vergil, amplified by Hall and then immortalized by William Shakespeare, whose *King Richard III* (1597) made for fascinating and vibrant if distorted theatre. As for the duke himself, with time his image altered from the repentant lord under Vergil and Hall to the arrogant self-server in Shakespeare's hands. Both views are expounded in the oral tradition which found an outlet in ballad and verse, and kept alive through the years such topics as Buckingham's moral awakening, revolt and treachery. Thus the stories surrounding the events of 1483 provided generations with ample material to weave into verse and song, and among a largely illiterate population they commanded a ready audience. While the medium encouraged exaggerations, additions and distortions, its contribution to the themes in question cannot be ignored. Ballads such as 'Buckingham Betrayd by Banaster', 'Murdering of Edward the Fourth his Sons' and 'The Song of Lady Bessy' reinforce information contained in the primary sources and add insights into Tudor and Jacobean attitudes to, and perceptions of, Richard's reign.[31]

This is evident in the mid-seventeenth century ballad, 'Murdering of Edward the Fourth his Sons', probably based on a 1612 version, which portrays Buckingham as Richard's accomplice after Edward IV's death, though it is Richard who finds the means 'to work . . . [the] princes' death'. Adopting the 'crime and punishment cycle' the balladeer stresses God's vengeance on the duke, who having quickly fallen out with Richard is 'forced to lose his head' and who, without moral redemption, is wicked to the last.[32] Conversely, in 'Buckingham Betrayd by Banaster' the duke's revolt and betrayal are used to highlight Richard's tyranny and Bannaster's perfidy, the implicit message being that betrayal of one's lord is a heinous crime. Though they must be treated with caution, both ballads reflect the extremes of popular opinion through the generations. They also demonstrate, despite the work of Richard's early apologists, the endurance of the Tudor tradition which remained almost unchallenged until the mid-seventeenth century.

Richard's first serious apologist was Sir George Buck whose work was completed in 1619 but not published until 1646. Less constrained by the political climate than earlier writers, he could eulogize Richard in a way that would have been difficult a century earlier. While ascribing the duke's rebellion to greed and ambition and his easy seduction by Richard's real enemy, John Morton, Buck puts his own stamp on the rising. He says the duke rather than Lady Beaufort's servant, Reginald Bray, made contact with Henry Tudor, and he is the first to mention a rendezvous site near Gloucester where forces led by the duke in Wales, the Marquess of Dorset from the north, and the leading gentry in the various sectors were to march 'in all haste'. In terms of the revolt his account is well grounded in fact: Richard was well placed for success, having 'good intelligence', 'a good army' and 'being an excellent captain'. As for Buckingham, an 'inundation' prevented his men from crossing the Severn; later, they 'forsook the duke and came away'; after his capture he was brought to the king by his 'false servant', Ralph Bannaster. Yet the duke's 'unhappy end' was the result of Bishop Morton, who 'brought [the duke] to destructi[on]'. As for the rebels, they 'fled. . . . And all were glad to hide themselves.'[33]

Buck's defence of Richard III inspired a number of eighteenth-century apologist works as well as traditional histories, none of which add much to our knowledge of the 1483 rebellion. None the less new developments were reflected in the historical literature as the Age of Reason with its contempt for the Middle Ages gave way to the Age of Romantic Revival with its admiration for the period. The new approach to history was based on an increased desire for industrious investigation and a new emphasis on government records and private correspondence as valuable sources of historical information. Caroline Halsted, *Richard III as Duke of Gloucester and King of England* (1844), reflects these developments with her use of state papers and private material including the Bodley, Cotton, Harley, Paston and Plumpton papers and the publications of the Camden, Selden and Antiquarian associations.[34] Halsted views the rebellion afresh. Though hinted at in the Crowland chronicle from which she has drawn heavily, Halsted is the first to stress that the duke most probably spread the news of the princes' deaths for his own gain. Yet his hope of promoting his Lancastrian claim was soon dashed because of the sympathy of the country 'for the offspring of King Edward IV'. She is also the first apologist to accent the independent role of the gentry and the scale of the revolt. Indeed by 21 October 'the greater part of the kingdom was in open rebellion'.[35]

While Halsted's work presaged the start of modern political analysis, J. Gairdner, *The History of King Richard the Third* (1898), provides the most systematic discussion of the rebellion. From the Crowland chronicle he notes that a rising on behalf of the princes was mounted in southern England involving 'cabals' organized from Kent through to Devon, and that Buckingham was appointed leader directly the rumour of the boys' deaths became known. Stressing its organization, the sectors of revolt, its official date and Kent's premature activity, he rounds out the bare facts with reference to Richard's shock at the duke's defection; his urgent request for the great seal from his chancellor, John Russell; his call for assistance from York; his proclamations against the duke and his instructions for the royal muster. Following Holinshed, Gairdner cites Lord Scope's indictment of the rebels at Torrington; and later details the commissions issued to claim the rebels' lands, the names of the rebels from the act of attainder and the names of some who received pardons over the following months. Most importantly, he is the first to stress the significance of Buckingham's rebellion in terms of Richard's reign. Though Richard had an easy victory, Gairdner stresses its role in Richard's downfall: the king's unease after the rebellion, his trouble in managing the south, the growing colony of refugees abroad and much more. In broadening the terms of reference Gairdner's work marks the first significant break from the traditional preoccupation with personalities. The rebellion itself becomes a critical event through his interpretation with its emphases and sustained political analysis based on records of state, the Crowland chronicle, York Records, Richard's own correspondence and the work of numerous antiquarians. Somewhat paradoxically, and in order to highlight its new status, Gairdner is the first to refer specifically to the rising as 'Buckingham's Rebellion'.

It is surprising that the revolt did not figure more significantly in most early accounts of the period, given its element of drama and its role in Richard's reign. Of course it is only with the benefit of hindsight that its impact can fully be understood. While the rising doubtless produced a wealth of anecdotal material, the fact that so little hard evidence is extant has made life difficult for scholars of the period. In the process of selection and interpretation the narrative sources, vernacular chronicles and the early sixteenth-century histories clearly have their place; but historians need first to scour the limited range of official and private material and, with reference to the later primary works, evaluate the conflicting evidence over key issues concerning Buckingham's disaffection and his alleged leadership of, and role in, the rising. In this context one of the earliest sources, the

Crowland Abbey chronicle, is most instructive. It is significant that latter-day historians who have paid close attention both to the official material and the chronicle have come to see the revolt as much more than Buckingham's rebellion, rather a powerful movement in which the gentry took the lead at a huge cost to the crown. Given most earlier historians' preoccupation with personalities as a result of prevailing attitudes and academic fashion, it is noteworthy that the actual detail on the gentry in the various sectors, gathered from official and court sources, remains substantially unaltered from Vergil's time; and that the additions made by his successors are indeed plausible in view of those sources.

For the general public in 1483 there were few hard facts to inform their judgement of the episode but there was a wealth of gossip and rumour to entertain and excite the imagination. For those in educated and informed circles, the first fragments they obtained from official documents were later amplified by the chronicles and the early histories. While manuscripts were hard to obtain, it is noteworthy that this was the age of the printer-publisher, William Caxton, who had operated his printing press at Westminster since 1476. Patronized by Margaret Beaufort in 1483, Caxton's greatest patron at court until his execution by Richard just days before his coronation, was Earl Rivers, Edward IV's brother-in-law and governor to the young prince. Caxton seems to have been in eclipse

The coat of arms of Anthony, Earl Rivers.

during Richard's reign but found favour once more at the court of Lady Margaret's son, Henry VII and his young queen, Elizabeth. Indeed his association with Lady Margaret had been rekindled by 1489 when she returned to him a copy of the French romance *Blanchardin and Eglantine*, which she had first sought in 1483, with a request that he translate and print it. Interestingly the storyline of the romance paralleled in some respects the events of 1483 in regard to Margaret Beaufort's intrigue with Elizabeth Woodville at Westminster, close to Caxton's quarters, and almost certainly Buckingham and Morton at Brecon. Like the characters in the plot, the young Elizabeth in sanctuary at Westminster feared her enemies while her future husband in exile, Henry Tudor, who had promised her his hand, risked his life to fulfil his pledge.

In view of the real-life drama it is instructive that some of Caxton's other works from the period reflect the same milieu and emphasize intrigue, corruption and the politics of disaffection, so that life seems almost to have mirrored art. For example, Caxton's dedication to Elizabeth Woodville in *Knight of the Tower* draws attention to the sequence of events set in train by Richard and has clear parallels with the dynastic manoeuvre that united the Houses of York and Lancaster. *Curial*, translated by Caxton at the request of Rivers and published after Richard III's accession, also appears to offer commentary on the politics of the period. From the late fourteenth century its theme deals with court and country, courtier and gentleman; the one debased and superficial, the other depicting the 'true and rightful life'. Significantly it left the press when the household was in disarray with many of Edward's own courtiers and servants in exile abroad or at home. Dedicated to Richard III and commissioned by a squire, *Order of Chivalry*, a declamatory work calling for the restoration of knightly duties and virtues, is perhaps an interesting choice in the context of the times.

Like many others Caxton sued for pardon early in 1484, and while there is no evidence to suggest that he was actively involved in sedition, nevertheless his patronage during the period focuses attention on the nature of his publications. Despite the political climate, though, Caxton was above all a businessman, guided by, and responsive to, the demands of the market. Personal preference played little part in his choice of publications; he perceived a ready market for certain works and published accordingly. For the historian attempting to gauge the interest of contemporaries in the politics of the day, the titles provide valuable insights into the nature of the topics under discussion in cultivated homes. Of course it was the market that held the key to the rapid dissemination of information, and it is in this context that Caxton's works are most significant. They satisfied public demand and reflected not simply the interests of the late Earl Rivers, Margaret Beaufort and other prominent public figures, but some of the concerns of educated society during an unprecedented period in English political history.[36]

CHAPTER 2

Kings, Lords and Landlords

At Lincoln when he heard the news of Buckingham's rebellion, Richard III made quickly for Leicester, well placed for the royal muster. The city held many memories for the new king, and only recently it had enabled him to showcase his splendour; yet most of his memories of Leicester were associated with conflict rather than celebration. Twelve years earlier it had acted as a base from which Edward IV and the nineteen-year-old Richard, as Duke of Gloucester, had planned their strategy against their traitorous cousin the Earl of Warwick, blockaded behind the walls of Warwick castle. In fact Richard had spent considerable time there and at other bases during Edward's period of crisis from 1469 to 1471. He had also increased his knowledge of the south during that time. Following the king's success at the great battles of Barnet and Tewkesbury, Gloucester had captured and tried dissidents on behalf of his brother and had led commissions of array in the south. He had stayed at Westminster during the victory celebrations and on other occasions for official duties. During his visits he made excursions into London's trading world where he had numerous connections.[1] Nevertheless it is hard to gauge just how well Richard knew the south before his coronation. While he spent much of his short reign on the road, the records allow just the briefest glimpse into his affairs in the south prior to 1483. Despite having substantial estates from Kent to Cornwall, from the early 1470s his main interests were in the north where he spent most of his time.[2] Though he made an attempt to redress the situation during the first leg of his royal progress after his coronation, clearly he had the task before him.

Edward, on the other hand, knew both the south and his servants well. For their part, the records show that his subjects were well acquainted with their late king and his lieutenants. This is significant, as one of the most critical issues of 1483 concerns not only the gentry's ability to stage a rebellion against the crown, but also the power structure of the south and the social and political connections within the ruling classes that created the framework for their revolt. Without some insight into, for example, the important estates held by crown, nobility and gentry, the degree to which each was a presence in the south and the nature of the links between them, only superficial conclusions can be reached about the political independence of the gentry or about what the rebellion actually says about the polity, and of course its significance for Richard III's reign.[3]

Given their proximity to court the king's southern subjects had a huge advantage over their more distant cousins. Being close to court meant royal visits and the chance of patronage for those who caught the king's eye; and with an abundance of crown lands in the south, opportunities existed for members of the aristocracy and the yeomanry alike. Visits from Edward had been especially welcome, for his enviable powers of recall meant he rarely forgot a face.[4] The crown, in fact, generated substantial employment at its castles such as Greenwich, Windsor, Woodstock, Rochester, Guildford and Winchester, which were among the various palaces favoured by Edward for both business and pleasure, and through its duchy of Cornwall and duchy of Lancaster estates. The former were mainly in Cornwall, while duchy of Lancaster manors were more widely scattered. Needless to say, Cornwall benefited most directly from its duchy status, and able servants were treated to an array of offices from the highest ranking receiverships to those of bailiff and reeve, plus custodies, leases and direct grants to favourite sons. In Cornwall the Prince of Wales as Duke of Cornwall chose the sheriff and nominated a steward; he controlled the mines and reaped the profits of excise on a number of goods. For the king's subjects, especially the gentry, the importance of

Greenwich Castle, one of Edward IV's favourite royal palaces.

this royal connection was vital. Cornwall's duchy status meant both court in county and its corollary, county at court. Gaining the favour of a leading official close to the prince often meant rewards in the form of duchy appointments, and sometimes an entrée to court.[5]

As the Earl of March and the Yorkist heir, Edward had also inherited vast territory in the south. In addition a number of estates passed firmly into his hands following the acts of attainder and resumption in the early years of his reign, many of which were granted to the Duke of Clarence in the 1460s. Clarence gained more lands in the south through his match with the Earl of Warwick's daughter and in the early 1470s he shared with his younger brother Richard the newly forfeited Warwick and Spenser lands. The scission of these estates marked the beginning of Gloucester's power in the north, which increased over the years with further royal grants. Conversely, Clarence became one of the leading landowners in the south-west where he led a formidable retinue and dominated political life through the early 1470s.[6]

After Clarence's death in 1478, the Woodvilles, Edward's relatives by marriage, collected many of his estates, especially in the west where they were already a force. The queen's brother Anthony Woodville, Earl Rivers, had become receiver-general of the duchy of Cornwall in 1473; in the following year her son Thomas Grey, who became Marquess of Dorset in 1475, acquired a slab of Somerset and Devon through his marriage with Cecily Bonville, step-daughter of the lord chamberlain, William, Lord Hastings. Clarence's attainder delivered to Dorset the wardship and marriage of the young Earl of Warwick, Clarence's son, and a number of his manors; while the proposed match between his own son and Anne Holland, daughter of the Duchess of Exeter and Sir Thomas St Leger, the king's brother-in-law, promised further rewards when in 1483 she was declared heiress to all the Exeter estates. Dorset's burgeoning wealth was reflected in his appointments as administrator both of the queen's lands and of the duchy of Cornwall.[7]

Garter stall plate of George, Duke of Clarence (d. 1478).

Clarence's fee'd men, a number of whom had also known Woodville lordship in the early 1470s, came more directly within their orbit after his death and profited handsomely.

Of course there were many other less well-connected nobles with significant purchase in the south. Yet by the early 1470s a number of old aristocratic families including both resident and non-resident magnates had become casualties of extinction and forfeiture. Among those attainted in 1461 were the Duke of Exeter, the Earls of Devon and Wiltshire, Lord Clifford and Robert, 3rd Lord Hungerford, while the baronies of Botreaux and Bonville had died out through both attainder and extinction. Of the northern and midland nobles attainted in the early 1470s, Richard Neville, Earl of Warwick (d. 1471), had the most significant lands in the south. Of the resident nobles, the Mowbray Duke of Norfolk died in 1476, and with him the title until 1483, while the titular 13th Earl of Oxford, John de Vere, was attainted in 1475, and his title along with the earldom of Wiltshire (revived briefly in 1470 for John, Lord Stafford, d. 1473) lay dormant until 1485. Relatively speaking, nobles came to be thin on the ground and some of those who survived, such as Henry, Viscount Bourchier and 1st Earl of Essex, and William Fitzalan, 15th Earl of Arundel, were aged and ineffectual in regional affairs. Two points are significant. By 1483 power at the top and in the regions had changed hands. The Woodvilles were pre-eminent in the east as well as the west, while John, Lord Howard, had become a major force in East Anglia and the south-east.[8] Simultaneously, the depletion of the aristocracy sharpened a process which was not a new development, but was clearly stimulated by events of the period. As power changed at the top, so too, within the counties, a number of rich local landowners of comparatively modest standing were able to challenge the supremacy of many of the entrenched nobles. Thus a sizeable group of barons and leading gentry whose fortunes had increased through the century began to establish their own territorial power. Skilful marriages, purchase and royal patronage had enabled the lesser aristocracy to build up large bodies of estates that formed the basis of their position.

Of the great northern and midland powers with influence in the south Thomas, Lord Stanley, Henry Percy, 4th Earl of Northumberland, William Herbert, Earl of Pembroke, Francis, Lord Lovell, Viscount Lisle, and Lords Bergavenny, Zouche, Audley, Dudley, Ferrers, Mountjoy and Hastings held between them a sizeable block of estates. Yet none surpassed the oldest and wealthiest non-resident noble, Henry, Duke of Buckingham, the direct descendant of Thomas of Woodstock, youngest son of Edward III. With eight widespread receiverships his southern estates were extensive. Though he favoured Brecon in south-east Wales, his manors of Thornbury (Gloucestershire) and Tonbridge and Penshurst (Kent) were also favourite residences. By early 1483 the most powerful nobles in the south were connected with Buckingham; they included the Duke of Suffolk and the Earl of Arundel, as well as prominent courtiers such as the upwardly mobile Lord Howard, whose assets rivalled some of the great magnates.[9] This category also included the Sussex power Richard Fiennes, Lord Dacre and John, 5th Lord Cobham, whose family had transferred its interests from the south-west to the south-east, as well as the young West Country nobles, Lords Stourton, Lawarre and Dinham, from families of great wealth and antiquity.

Given their regional standing and obvious options in the marriage market it is instructive that many of the barons married into the gentry rather than the nobility, indicating resources that belie the accepted notions of gentry wealth. In an age in which society turned increasingly on connection, the gentry had made marrying money almost into an art form. West Country powers William Berkeley, Giles Daubenay and Thomas Arundel had forged amazingly lucrative ties with Lords Stourton and Dinham either through their own or their fathers' matches. Wiltshire's Sir Roger Tocotes had married into the baronetcy of St Amand; Sir Thomas Lewkenor of Sussex was connected through old alliances with the Wests, Lords Lawarre and the noble House of Neville, while his own match linked him with the barons of Audley. From Oxfordshire and Berkshire Sir William Stonor and Sir William Norris had both made brilliant matches with noblewomen: the former with Anne Neville, daughter of John, Marquess Montagu, brother of the late Earl of Warwick and Richard's cousin; the latter firstly with Jane de Vere, heiress of the deceased Earl of Oxford, and then to Isobel, widow of Marquess Montagu. From the south-east, Richard Guildford had taken as his second bride Jane, sister of Lord Vaux of Harrowden; and though John Gaynesford and Kent's Sir John Fogge married within their own class, Fogge's judicious union with Alice Haute linked him with Queen Elizabeth Woodville, no less, while Gaynesford's match with the asset-rich heiress Margaret Sydney won him a place among the wealthiest gentry in Sussex.[10]

While they had feathered their nests and furthered their interests through marriage, they were viewed by the aristocracy as attractive catches in their own right. Of course there was often little to distinguish leading gentry from the families into which they had married. All were of old stock though Roger Tocotes and William Norris were relative newcomers to the south: the former was from Yorkshire, while the latter's father was from Lancashire where the family had lived since Norman times. The Arundels of Lanherne had been in Cornwall since the mid-twelfth century, while the families of Daubenay, Stonor, Lewkenor and Fogge had been established in their principal seat from at least the reign of Edward I. The Guildfords had prospered in Kent for nine generations, and the Gaynesfords, whose main seat had been acquired in 1338, had long been a family of substance in the region. Again, all could boast great landed wealth and while it is impossible to be precise about their net worth, their assets by contemporary standards were impressive: Tocotes's main seat of Bromholm and his other estates in Wiltshire were valued at £100 in 1484, while some other southern lordships plus his Cheshire lands were assessed at an annual value of 1,000 marks. Norris's wealth was widespread and his Middlesex lands alone amounted annually to 500 marks. An inquisition taken after Stonor's death put his landed wealth at £400, clearly far short of the mark as most of his lands are not listed. Guildford's main holding of Rolvenden with lesser lands was valued at 200 marks in 1484; Lewkenor held twenty-nine manors in Sussex and Fogge at least twenty manors in Kent; Gaynesford held upwards of twelve Surrey estates with a vast acreage in adjacent counties. In the south-west Berkeley possessed at least twenty-three manors in Somerset and Wiltshire and a large slice of Hampshire, though his principal seat was in Gloucestershire. With his main sphere of influence in Somerset, much of Daubenay's wealth in the west was the legacy of his Stourton mother, and with lands in the midlands and elsewhere he was on a par with the wealthiest gentry in the country. His brother-in-law, Sir Thomas Arundel, was possibly even more affluent. Solid wealth in seven counties amounted to well over £2,000 after his father's death in 1476.[11]

Given their longevity, wealth and connections, it is not surprising to find that the principal knights and squires represented an élite bound by both their blood-affinity and common interests. Recent work on gentry societies in fifteenth-century England has shown that whether lineage-based or free from resident lordship, the gentry's social and political ties were largely shaped by the pattern of landholding and the kinship network; this, in turn, promoted social cohesion and gave rise to shared landed interests and activity. The leading families thus bound usually played a role in administration for the crown which reinforced their local status.[12] While the evidence has been drawn in the main from midland and northern studies, it was especially the case in southern England where old gentry families had interacted successfully on a number of levels for generations. As leaders of society they drew men from their own ranks to conduct business and compose quarrels, usually with great success. At the local level a knightly family was often at the centre of a circle of influence acting on behalf of subordinates as executors, supervisors and trustees, or pulling strings through personal contacts. They also employed the best legal minds in their vicinity to deal with the complexities of the business world. In the west-Wiltshire borderland, for example, lesser gentry from Corsham to Mere were part of a network dominated

Corsham House, a Wiltshire seat held by Walter Hungerford from 1464.

by the Hungerfords of Heytesbury, including Thomas Tropenell of Hindon, about eight miles south of Heytesbury, John Wittocksmead, Henry Long, Michael Skilling and the prosperous John Mompesson who interacted with Walter Hungerford in numerous ways. In central Somerset Sir Giles Daubenay led a group which included John Huggins, Thomas Tremayle, John Stowell, William Case, William Hody, John Biconell and John Heron, most of whom were eminent lawyers in the service of Lady Beaufort.[13] As one of the most successful and well-connected gentry families, the Stonors were much in demand as witnesses and trustees with the Hampdens, Crofts, Harcourts and Norrises and others in their region. Further east such circles revolved around leading gentry including the Guildfords and Hautes.[14]

While some had married into the nobility by 1483, many had chosen brides from their own ranks resulting in a tangle of blood-ties. In the south-west, for example, Thomas Arundel, Edward Courtenay, Giles Daubenay, John St Lo and Robert Willoughby, from Cornwall, Somerset and Devon were affines, while John

Cheyne of Wiltshire was a kinsman both of Willoughby and Gloucestershire's William Berkeley, and was distantly connected with St Lo. The pattern prevailed elsewhere. Sir Thomas St Leger, originally from the west but most often to be found in the east, was linked with both Richard Guildford of Surrey and John Cheyne. Surrey's Sir George Brown was stepfather of the Sussex knight Edward Poynings, which also meant affinity with the Wiltshire Delamares. To complicate matters further, Sir John Fogge and Richard Guildford were loosely tied, thus connecting the former with the St Leger and Cheyne circle.[15] Such affinities across the south and the interaction they entailed saw the gentry often on the road, conducting business, renewing links and oiling the wheels of kinship and service. In the space of one month, John Cheyne, say, or Sir Thomas St Leger, might have been found collaborating in Devon, Oxfordshire and Kent (royal duties permitting). Their aristocratic ties were as numerous, and powerful kinsmen made useful partners; for example, in the south-east, Fogge, Richard Guildford and Richard Haute, who boasted kinship with the Woodvilles, cooperated with them in all manner of business. In the central-south the Norrises had long acted with, and for, some of the most powerful nobles in England such as Marquess Montagu, the Dukes of Norfolk and Suffolk, John, Lord Howard, Thomas, Lord Stanley, and Margaret Beaufort.[16] This activity, in turn, augured well for their interests at court and with the greatest powers in the land.[17]

Sir William Stonor epitomizes the links forged by well-connected gentry. The Exeter merchant Richard Germyn, wanting satisfaction in a business matter in 1481, urged his part as he was considered 'the greatest man with my lord [Dorset] and in his conceit: his servants report of you that ye be the most courteous knight that ever was'. Stonor also took Lord Lovell's part in his dispute with the crown over the latter's Oxfordshire lands obtained from Richard, Duke of York.[18] Evidence of intimacy between gentry and lords is found in extant wills, and aristocrats often died indebted to friends. Earl Rivers, for example, before his execution in June 1483, appealed to Sir John Guildford to satisfy his debts, including 200 marks owed to Sir Thomas Vaughan; and Sir Robert Willoughby's cousin, Robert, died owing money to Elizabeth Woodville, John, Lord Dinham and Lady de Vere. Then again, the well-connected often gave or received gifts including plate or jewelry, such as John Howard's gift of a gold cup to Gloucester in May 1483, and Richard's own gift of a ring with a diamond to his servant William Mauleverer. Such gifts might also include furniture, such as the bed adorned with the Buckingham arms in silver which Sir Robert Willoughby acquired from his cousin, Robert, Lord Willoughby.[19] Importantly, their connections ensured further credit at court where they mixed with the king and his family, prominent courtiers and pre-eminent guests: just rewards for keeping such distinguished company.

Moat House, Kent, held by Anthony, Earl Rivers, in the later fifteenth century.

Not all, though, was smooth sailing. In a society where land was the greatest source of wealth, it was also the greatest source of conflict. Wrangles were usually settled by the gentry themselves, obviating the need to go to law, and records indicate that John Trevelyan, Giles Daubenay, the Harcourts, Stonors and others were successful as final arbiters in local disputes.[20] Indeed, tact and diplomacy seem to have been the guiding principles in conflict resolution and the gentry often showed good sense when equilibrium at the local level was threatened. The crown, moreover, was happy to take a passive role in what it considered to be essentially private matters.[21] It was active, however, in crimes which threatened its own equilibrium, often using its knights and squires as investigative agents. In the West Country from the early 1460s Henry Bodrugan established something of a reputation as a pirate whose exploits were the subject of a number of commissions of inquiry and arrest in Cornwall. In 1474 St Leger and Willoughby, together with Arundel and Courtenay, were members of at least two commissions aimed at Bodrugan's arrest. Most involved had served on earlier commissions with Bodrugan, and continued thus. In 1483 Oxfordshire's Sir

Richard Harcourt was commissioned to round up the rebels after Buckingham's rebellion, one of whom was his nephew, John Harcourt. Yet this he did, and with no sign of friction judging by later records of family transactions. Similarly, in the south-east Richard Lewkenor was ordered in November 1483 to besiege Bodiam Castle, Sussex, where his nephew Thomas was entrenched with a number of rebels. James Haute, brother of Sir William and uncle of Richard esquire, both of whom rebelled in 1483, received a grant of William's lordship of Ightham Mote, Kent, for his service against the rebels, yet the Lewkenors and Hautes like the Harcourts continued to co-operate after Henry Tudor's accession in 1485.[22]

Some disputes involved principal knights and the king's own kin, and the litigious and wayward Stonor was often at the centre of the discord. In 1480 the queen, well aware of his previous offences, scolded him for trespassing within the forest and chase of Barnwood, while for the offence of deer hunting out of season he incurred her 'great . . . displeasure'. Yet despite her reprimand he remained Elizabeth's 'trusty and well-beloved' knight, receiving from her a gift of a doe in 1481. Only weeks later Stonor was again in trouble, this time with Gloucester no less, necessitating a bond for himself and his guarantors including John Harcourt and William Norris. Anxious for a resolution, Stonor's cousin and factor, Walter Elmes, advised him to meet the demands of the recognizance and, moreover, that 'if you have any certainty of your men . . . come show it, for my lord of Gloucester and my lord chamberlain be gone, and now be here your friends'. Whatever the nature of the dispute Stonor continued to prosper at court during the early 1480s, and under Gloucester both as protector and as king.[23] Indeed the crown exploited the gentry's ability at a corporate level in a number of its own cases. For example, Thomas Arundel's father, Sir John, having actively supported the readeption of 1470–71, was fined 6000 marks by Edward IV as a penalty for treason. After Arundel had raised 2000 marks, Edward nominated as his guarantors John Fogge, Richard Harcourt and Stonor's father, Thomas, among others. Arundel's own trustees were engaged, in turn, by Harcourt after Sir John's death to satisfy the remainder of the debt. Like some sort of late-medieval quango the men involved represented every region of southern England, and met directly or through their agents for the crown over a period of close on twenty years until the matter was concluded in the late 1480s.[24]

By 1483 it was really a case of 'chicken and egg' for the principal gentry: court contacts influenced the type of royal patronage they received, which in turn reinforced their local status. Or was it the other way round? Whatever the case, the skills acquired from years of landholding – a potent mix of wealth, power, local nous, and of course the king's confidence – determined the scale of royal favour that they enjoyed. Repeatedly chosen for key positions on crown lands as stewards, constables, keepers and custodians, they clearly met the criteria for the top jobs in a hierarchy of service ranging from the highest ranking receivers-general to the bailiffs and reeves; from aristocrats who became titular heads or who received hereditary positions in land management, to the lesser gentry for whom an office was more a social coup and a lucrative sideline. While it is simplistic to assume that wealth always determined the type of patronage the gentry received, in the main the lesser officials who served as revenue collectors in the ports and on the land were men of moderate means, like the vast majority of gentry families with two or three manors, whose power was localized within their county. A second category can be identified as a select group of talented careerists who specialized in estate management; often men of solid wealth, diverse interests and knowledge of the law, they represented families who had served the crown for generations as receivers and auditors. Both John Harcourt, receiver of Clarence's forfeited Warwick and Spenser estates, and Nicholas Gaynesford, receiver of Elizabeth Woodville's duchy lands in the south, fit into this category.[25]

Edward IV from a window in Canterbury Cathedral.

Elizabeth Woodville from a window in Canterbury Cathedral.

Yet both can also be included in the first category, those who repeatedly obtained the choice royal pickings in their region of influence. In fact a pattern of patronage existed in which leading families, some of whom, such as the Courtenays, Hungerfords and Bourchiers, had been ennobled, held hereditary positions in crown and duchy administration.[26] Indeed over the years old wealth had served the crown well and by 1483 leading knights and squires were well schooled in such service: Daubenay, Berkeley, Gaynesford, Fogge, Tocotes, St Leger, Lewkenor, Stonor and Norris, for example, held between them an impressive array of stewardships, keeperships and constableships; the latter, in fact, was keeper of Windsor Forest and of Wychwood in Oxfordshire, the meeting-place, as legend has it, of Edward IV and Elizabeth Woodville, his future bride.[27] Other spoils derived from the forfeitures and escheats which came to the crown after 1461 and allowed key gentry to further consolidate their power.[28] There were also appointments by the crown of officials during the minority of nobles: Norris did well with the custody of the Marchioness Montagu's lands during the minority of her son, while Daubenay and Berkeley also acquired useful perks. In addition, meed for service included direct grants to gifted servants and duchy patronage in the form of profitable leases such as Fogge's grant in 1471 (renewed in 1480) of the gold and silver mines in Devon and Cornwall, or the gift of 10 marks yearly to Thomas Treffry from the issues of the duchy. Others such as Sir Roger Tocotes received rewards such as a portion of the crown's rent from customs at Bristol, amounting to a tidy annual sum of £74.[29]

Royal patronage created further opportunities for gentry leaders through job-sharing or as deputies on royal lands with the likes of Hastings, Howard, Rivers, Dorset and others.[30] In turn great lords tended to favour them with offices on their own estates, and the Earls of Devon, Arundel, Kent and Oxford and the Dukes of Norfolk and Suffolk had long dispensed patronage to the local leading families.[31] For their part, offices for absentee lords were most highly prized by the gentry, for both their cash rewards and the influence and patronage which derived from them, and many knights and squires had served the Houses of Neville, Percy and York.[32] Yet it was the Dukes of Buckingham who had forged more connections than most with the gentry; and by 1483 those on their books included the Uvedales, Delamares, Twynyhos, Trevelyans, Arundels, Poyntzes and Berkeleys in the south-west, and further east, the St Legers, Gaynesfords, Guildfords, Pympes, Cheynes and Harcourts.[33]

In addition to their business acumen, their knowledge and experience of the law and bureaucracy were also marketable skills which prompted great men to offer the gentry worship and 'to pay for the privilege'.[34] A number of Stafford retainers had a history of service in both administration and the family's affinity. The 1st Duke of Buckingham's council, for example, included the kinsmen of Sir

William Berkeley, Sir Robert Willoughby and Robert Poyntz. They had also provided the core of the 2nd duke's council, with among others, Sir Richard Darrell, Buckingham's stepfather, Sir William Knyvet, Henry's uncle by marriage, Sir Nicholas Latimer, chamberlain of the household, and John Twynyho, Buckingham's attorney at the Exchequer.[35] Most were not exclusively Stafford annuitants but served members of the aristocracy in various ways from Cornwall to Cambridgeshire, Sussex through to Berkshire. Daubenay used his legal training on behalf of his colleagues William Berkeley, Thomas Arundel and Lord Stourton. Others, like the solicitors Nicholas and John Gaynesford, were high fliers who had acted with the doyens of the legal world including Edward IV's attorneys, Richard Fowler, John Catesby, Humphrey Starkey and John Fineux, and were associated in a professional capacity with the Marquess of Dorset and Earl Rivers.[36]

Few of the above could be construed as political appointments. The gentry were retained by the nobles for their legal or administrative skills, and profited in terms of cash and contacts. Yet their service to the crown was invaluable to them in terms of local reputation and standing. While royal favour was a beacon for noble and ecclesiastic patrons, it also made the 'good lordship' of the local leaders eminently attractive to lesser kinsmen and neighbours. Further, royal office ensured that key gentry were not just recipients of patronage but dealers themselves in the localities who could offer gifts and influence appointments and, on occasion, elections. Royal office required assistants, while demanding schedules with enforced absences meant a good deal of networking, of organizing clients in caretaker roles who could be paid in cash or kind. In such a way the most pre-eminent knights could hold great sway within their region.[37] The principal rebels of 1483 could thus be categorized. Stonor, for instance, counted among his agents his relatives Walter Elmes and Thomas Mulle, along with Richard Germyn and Richard Page. In 1479 he paid a stipend to the king's secretary, Mr Hatcliff, no less. Sir John Fogge, however, was in a league of his own. A man who enjoyed the confidence of royals and nobles alike, his sphere of influence incorporated the southern counties as well as the Marches. As a councillor and tutor to the Prince of Wales from 1473, he was empowered to administer duchy of Cornwall lands during the minority, with, in theory at least, the power to 'hire and fire' all manner of duchy officials, to grant pardons and offer rich patronage. He was a leader in Kent, yet his weight in the south-west enabled him to influence parliamentary elections and to ensure that in 1478 his associates John Fineux, John Bamme and Henry Frowick were returned for Cornwall, while his own son John was returned in the same year for Launceston.[38]

Such reputation and favour provided regional leaders with an entrée into the king's own circle. Both Nicholas Gaynesford and Fogge were young hunting companions of Edward IV in the mid-1460s and received Christmas presents of

This illustration, depicting a group of courtiers on a boating expedition, featured in one of Edward IV's books.

wine for good service and also to have on hand for the next royal visit 'that we in our hunting for the hare may have it for our drinking'. That Edward was both accessible to his servants and a confidant of some is evident in a deposition of 1496 made by Sir John Risley who recalled hunting with the king in Waltham Forest and 'being able to consult him about business there'.[39] Clearly they had the king's ear when he visited his favourite haunts for the hunt: Windsor Forest and Wychwood in Oxfordshire, for example, Norris's territory. In fact Sir William probably attended Edward at Windsor when he welcomed Louis de Bruges,

Governor of Holland (who had entertained him in exile in 1470). Likewise St Leger attended the king at Guildford in 1479 when he concluded a treaty with Maximilian and Mary of Burgundy for the marriage of his daughter, Anne, to their son Philip. It is hardly surprising that these men mixed with the higher aristocracy and had access to the king. For 'the man who got wealth would get status, especially if he invested in its supreme demonstration, land'.[40] And the gentry did just that. By the second half of the fifteenth century, they had consolidated through patrimony, purchase and patronage and were courted by kings and nobles alike. As part of an élite, an aristocracy of wealth, they had been bred and schooled in a tradition of service within the counties and beyond and had proved their worth over many years. In 1483 when the south was relatively free from intrusive magnate presence, and the crown was the principal force within the shire, the gentry were indeed well placed to dominate local society.

Like their fathers and grandfathers before them they were also the men of 'means, worship and wisdom . . . by whom it may be known the disposition of the counties', chosen by the advice of the king's council to serve in the household, attending the monarch and ministering to his needs as knights and squires of the body, knights carvers and sewers, cupbearers, gentlemen and yeomen ushers, grooms and pages of the chamber.[41] Each designation had rigidly prescribed functions with attendance on a quarter-yearly basis, regulated by an ordinance of 1478 and checked by Edward himself. His closest attendants were king's knights such as John Fogge and knights of the body, the latter 'which wait most upon the king and lie nightly in his chamber . . .' including Norris, St Leger, Daubenay, Stonor, George Brown and Thomas Bourchier;[42] William Twynyho was a king's squire and John Harcourt a king's usher, while Walter Hungerford, John Cheyne, William Berkeley, William Uvedale, John Wingfield, John Norris, Thomas Fiennes, Thomas Arundel and Nicholas Gaynesford were squires of the body; the latter distinguishing himself both as king's servitor and usher of the chamber. A number of the gentry, whose designation is unclear, appear in official records loosely termed 'king's servant', including Edward Courtenay and Roger Tocotes. Yet others benefited through the household positions of close kinsmen including William Brandon the younger, whose father Sir William was a servant of the household in January 1460 and king's servitor in January 1462, Edward Poynings, Thomas Lewkenor, John Gaynesford and Richard Guildford.

Aside from chamber service some were 'busy about the king' in other areas: St Leger and Cheyne had positions in the stable, the former as master of the harthounds, the latter as master both of the henchmen and of the horse; these offices were consistently held by the king's closest chamber servants and required frequent attendance on Edward with his fondness for the hunt. Others held senior administrative positions: Fogge was treasurer of the household and keeper of the wardrobe; St Leger, controller of the mint; John Guildford, controller of the household; and George Brown, clerk of the hanaper. They served as king's councillors: Berkeley's father, Sir Maurice, a knight of the body, had mixed with Sir William Brandon and Fogge who was also a councillor to the young prince. Edward's knights and squires of the body represented him in diplomacy abroad and were prominent in Anglo-French affairs and in Anglo-Burgundian trade delegations both before and after the king's exile in Bruges in 1470. Thus Fogge served the king, mixing with notables including the royal servant and Calais stapler William Caxton, while he also served his own trading interests. A number were courtier-knights whose military élan and leadership qualities had greatly assisted Edward during periods of political upheaval; men who responded to the chivalrous culture of the court, and who embodied some of the medieval traditions of the chivalric ideal as guardians of the realm. Though the period was relatively free from large overseas campaigns, none the less Edward's French expedition of 1475 allowed men such as St Leger, Norris, Brandon (the elder), Daubenay, John Cheyne, Walter Hungerford and Willoughby to indulge their military artistry. In the event, each was well prepared for warfare with the knights of the body having contracted to provide more than one hundred men. However, it was in recognition of their role in negotiating a settlement between England and France that some in the household, including Cheyne and St Leger, received gifts from the French king, Louis XI.

The squires of the body and the gentlemen ushers were also able to display their prowess in horsemanship at jousts and tournaments: great spectacles of grace and skill which sometimes included Edward and the lord chamberlain as participants, though more often as spectators. Chamber staff could also exercise their social skills as hosts for the monarch at glittering events for distinguished visitors, as in 1480 when Berkeley attended the king's sister, the Duchess of Burgundy, during her visit to court.[43] In many ways the queen's household complemented her husband's with many of the same names and a number of the same duties pertaining to it. In fact the wives of Fogge, Norris, William Uvedale, Richard Haute, Nicholas Gaynesford (who incidentally transferred from Edward's service to Elizabeth's as an usher of the chamber) and Thomas Vaughan served Elizabeth as courtiers, quite possibly with Stonor's mother Jane, who certainly enjoyed the queen's confidence. This was a pattern of generations' standing, and provides another insight into gentry service for the crown. It also provided some couples with a solution to the long separations which many were forced to endure.[44]

Edward IV (1442–83).

In the main the household was financed by Edward's scheme of 'land and lordship', which also provided much of his income. Indeed from 1471 he set about redefining the boundaries of regional authority and increasing the royal demesne, a policy conditioned both by the need to 'live of his own' and to broaden his power-base through a scheme that would absorb the established patterns of local lordship and also strengthen the Yorkist régime. In the south leading gentry benefited because, as regional powers and king's servants, they were the natural conduits of royal authority to the regions. Thus it was the household men who acquired both patronage and influence through their service on crown lands. In turn as stewards, constables, keepers and custodians they directed land revenues to the household treasurer and the cofferer, reaping their own rewards as well as financing the king, who channelled the profits into huge public works programmes at Windsor and elsewhere, and upgrading hunting facilities in Kent.[45]

While they performed prescribed functions in the household, it is difficult to slot the gentry into particular roles and to give sharp definition to the different levels of service. Though Edward redefined the court in a political and cultural context most markedly in the 1470s, to provide both clarity and substance to the household in terms of personnel, structure and duties, there was some overlap between the roles, so that while the administrators often had legal training, a number were courtiers who in turn were often councillors and diplomats.[46] Thus their offices at court, as in the regions, were testimony to their talents. What is also clear is the way in which members of the household responded to the courtly culture. Indeed, inspired by the upheavals of the mid-decades of the fifteenth century, there was a self-conscious revival under Edward of the chivalric traditions of an earlier age which glorified courtly culture and knightly values, and found expression in ceremonial and lavish courtly entertainment. It is of course of great significance that the men who provided the substance of Buckingham's rebellion were king's courtiers, and among those who responded most strongly to the literature of the period; to works such as *Curial*, originally sponsored by Earl Rivers and published in the latter part of 1483, and other themes that dealt with the morality of courtly culture, disaffection and intrigue. These were themes which, for many, doubtless had an appealing resonance, particularly during Richard III's short reign.[47]

CHAPTER 3
Politics and 'The Powers that Be'

Following the chronicle sources it was long fashionable to highlight the colourful aspects of the Wars of the Roses: dynastic rivalries, aristocratic blood-feuds, fractious court favourites and aggressive warlords. Against this backdrop civil strife was rampant, vicious and disruptive, involving most regions for sustained periods. Revisionists have largely debunked these views and have shown that the fighting was less pervasive and destructive than was often depicted. Campaigns could not be sustained for long periods and victorious armies, by and large, did not obtain the keys to the city. Still, when Edward, Earl of March, took the crown in 1461 the country was at a low ebb, crushed and chaotic following the civil war that had erupted in 1459. In some areas few men between sixteen and sixty had been unaffected by the fighting, as local conscripts through commissions of array, as servants or tenants of dissident lords, or indeed as men with their own axes to grind. Even East Anglia, the area least affected by the conflict, saw ugly episodes in 1464 requiring a royal visit; several years later, there was a Lancastrian conspiracy involving Master James Mackerell, probably in league with the Earl of Oxford, who remained a thorn in Edward's side. In the Home Counties, Oxfordshire and Berkshire, royal shires with their great honours long since absorbed by the crown, mostly kept the peace, though royal arms were disfigured at Oxford University, incurring for the criminals savage punishment from Oxford's Chancellor in 1461. In neighbouring Berkshire acts of cruelty in 1461 required a commission which found that men were harrying the region and worrying the locals. Bloody riots erupted in the aftermath of the Battle of Tewkesbury in 1471, and Oxford's proctors were given cash rewards to help quell revolt.[1]

The south-east witnessed great activity during the 1460s. Close to London, Kent was traditionally volatile and with its many townspeople and independent freeholders it had often been politically active. The region had been a stamping ground of Richard of York in the late 1450s and, after his death at Wakefield in 1460, it remained thus for Edward, the Earl of Warwick and their supporters who used the English garrison at Calais, Warwick's stronghold, as a base from which they could cross into England either to Sandwich or Dover in Kent, or to one of the Cinque

Ports. In 1469 Warwick, then in league with Clarence against Edward, again used parts of the south-east as a launching-pad for invasion and in his recruitment drives. Edward, however, was most vulnerable in the south-west; so accessible to invasion from France and Brittany, the area remained of major concern with its reputation for revolt. Led by disaffected nobles and often with French backing, sedition had flourished in its ports and towns including Dartmouth, Poole and Plymouth, and in its sacred houses such as the Benedictine Abbey of Cerne or the Franciscan House of Beaulieu, whose franchises and lay holdings often provided rebels with temporary respite. In 1485 Richard was to proclaim that 'Henry Tudor had plotted to allow foreign invaders to despoil the crown and realm',[2] a sentiment that would have been shared by Edward who was well aware of France's interest in supporting those at odds with the crown. On a number of occasions Exeter had mustered forces for Lancastrian dissidents who had secured support first from Charles VII of France and then from his son, Louis XI, both of whom at strategic times sought to embarrass Edward IV.[3]

Despite Edward's victory in the gruesome battle on the snowy slopes at Towton in 1461 and the slaughter of a number of his greatest enemies, his power was brittle, especially in the north, Wales and the west, and his achievements against the Lancastrians piecemeal. The lack of strong central authority was reflected in the nature of court politics; always a competitive and mercurial environment in which magnates could exploit conflict for favour and gain, with some of their followers, also royal retainers, unable to avoid their power-play: Sir Thomas Brown, for instance, John Trevelyan and Piers Edgecombe, who were servants of the Duke of Exeter; Sir John Arundel and Hugh Courtenay, the Earl of Devon's men; and John Nanfan, who had followed Warwick's father, yet supported Henry VI's queen Margaret of Anjou along with Edmund Hampden, William Norris, John Willoughby and Nicholas Latimer. Among those indicted in Edward's first act of attainder were men most closely associated with the Lancastrian régime: Courtenay, Lord Hungerford, Nicholas Latimer and John Morton among them.[4] Undeterred by defeat and the loss of great nobles including the Earls of Devon, Wiltshire and Northumberland, Queen Margaret actively campaigned for French support. Edward in turn urged the men of the west to resist the French and raise a fleet at their own expense. Yet not all complied. John Nanfan as Governor of Jersey was in a position to help the French take the island on behalf of the queen, while John Arundel and John Trevelyan were charged with inciting rebellion against the crown.[5] Ironically, Sir Hugh Courtenay, whose piracy from 1461 antagonized Edward and encouraged the French, was on a commission with

William Treffry and others to array the men of Cornwall in response to the French threat. Edward's fear diminished when he managed to put his seal to a truce with Louis XI against the queen; and in 1464, when the northern garrisons finally fell, the crown could enjoy a brief respite from rebellion.[6]

The traditional focus on high politics and 'over-mighty' subjects also obscured a polity that was much more inclusive than the narrow band of nobles who circled the crown and, for that matter, was far more resilient. By the 1460s the English polity was highly evolved, clearly defined and well integrated with royal influence percolating far down the social order, reaching men of independent mind and wealth, country knights and squires, educated men of local influence, the secular and saintly, lawyers, merchants and every kind of official, all of them royal subjects with a vested interest in strong central government. Of course many from the knightly class were themselves king's retainers, representing ruling élites who were tired of the graft and collusion spawned by feckless kingship, and had welcomed Warwick and Edward in 1460. Allegedly Fogge and other royal captains joyously opened the gates at Canterbury for the Yorkists, and within months were using their talents in the royal chamber and their influence in the counties: John Cheyne, Roger Tocotes, Nicholas Gaynesford, John Guildford, Thomas Bourchier, Robert Poynings, Robert Fiennes, John Stourton and John Dinham were among their ranks. Others who may not have encouraged York ensured continuity between reigns, such as Sir William Brandon and, less enthusiastically, Sir William Norris. Of course in the 1450s Richard of York had fee'd numerous knights and squires of the ilk of the Treffrys, Twynyhos, Harcourts, Stonors and Wingfields.[7] For other families the issues at stake were less clear cut. John Wingfield's own nephew, Sir Henry, for instance, fought for Queen Margaret, was knighted at Northampton in 1460 and attainted after Towton. Then again, West Country knights William Courtenay and his father Philip (d. 1463), cousins of the Lancastrian stalwart, Sir Hugh Courtenay, assisted the Yorkist régime.

Through the 1460s Edward depended on Warwick, the power behind the throne, and on his brother Clarence, who was fast becoming pre-eminent in the west. The other major political affinities centred round the 4th Mowbray Duke of Norfolk and to a lesser degree round John, Duke of Suffolk, and Warwick's brother-in-law, John de Vere, 13th Earl of Oxford, in East Anglia. The latter, imprisoned in 1468 and pardoned in 1469, joined Margaret of Anjou in 1470 and was the main force in the region through the readeption, supported by men such as Sir William Knyvet and John Paston. Conversely, Norfolk, Norfolk's father and Suffolk, though a minor, had all joined Edward by October 1460 and fought for him at Towton. Norfolk died in November 1461, his son John obtaining livery in 1465, and the young Suffolk two years later. Through the 1460s Mowbray influence permeated the Home Counties as well as East Anglia, and Norfolk exploited his alliance with Edward. For his part the king was sure of the duke's support on the national stage and exploited his powerful gentry networks, the only hiccup occurring in 1468 when John Poynings, servant to the Duchess of Norfolk, was executed for his alleged treason at the time of Margaret of York's wedding to the Duke of Burgundy. Leading gentry including Sir William Knyvet, Sir William Brandon, John Howard, John Wingfield and rising star John Risley were retained by Norfolk, and in some cases also by Suffolk. The pattern prevailed in the Home Counties with the names of Lewkenor, Gaynesford, Stonor, Norris, Harcourt and Brown on their books. Surrey's Sir George Brown was also connected with the Earl of Oxford in East Anglia and the Duke of Clarence along with Knyvet.[8]

Yet Clarence's support in the 1460s came mainly from the west where the bulk of his estates lay and where his heft was most strongly felt, and from some whose fathers had followed the Earl of Devon, fought for Margaret of Anjou and been patronized by the House of Neville. Many featured in Clarence's household or on his estates; with five large receiverships in Kent and Norfolk as well as his estates in the west, his patronage networks were impressive.[9] Of course there were others in the region, such as Humphrey Stafford, Lord Southwick, who jostled with him for influence and favour. Yet as king's lieutenant Clarence was supreme and shone in his new role, as the Bohemian diplomat Leo of Rozmital observed when he was dazzled by a lavish banquet hosted by Clarence at Salisbury in 1466, having just come of age at sixteen.[10] His position – largely built on the attainders of Exeter, Devon, Wiltshire and Hungerford, and the extinction of the baronies of Botreaux and Bonville in the early 1460s, and buttressed by Neville support – was indeed formidable. It was maintained, needless to say, by the rich preferment bestowed by the king.

Edward enjoyed only brief periods of tranquility though the treason of 1469 came with a double sting, committed as it was by Warwick the Kingmaker and Clarence, his minion; both were trusted kinsmen from within his own camp. The plot to unseat Edward IV and reinstate Henry VI followed years of civil unrest in which local violence, blood-feuds and treasonable activity were commonplace. Rioting took place as far afield as York and Wales, with the most serious incident involving Henry Tudor's uncle, Jasper Tudor, in league with Louis XI, who was defeated in August 1468 by Lord Herbert. Fear engendered fear and a spy network in the counties controlled by the sheriffs uncovered more dissidents. Household yeomen went into the country to arrest the rebels. Two men committed to trial at Salisbury before Gloucester were Henry Courtenay, the brother of the deceased Earl of Devon (d. 1461), and Thomas, the son of Lord Hungerford, executed after the Battle of Hexham in 1464. Around this time the Earl of Oxford was arrested and sent to the Tower, presumably because his father and brother had both been executed for treason, while others were beheaded for alleged dealings with Lancastrians. How much it was a matter of real threat or simply alarmist behaviour by the crown is open to question. What is clear, however, is the level of popular discontent with Edward's government. Aside from Warwick's self-indulgent gripes, others could see little change in the years since his accession and felt that the king's in-laws, the Woodvilles, had simply replaced the despised courtiers of a decade before (those

Margaret of Anjou (d. 1482), drawing of a stained-glass portrait in the Church of the Cordeliers, Angiers.

whom, ironically, Richard of York had maligned in 1460); targeted for hostility, they were widely perceived as greedy upstarts who flaunted their connections, which Warwick and his Neville kinsmen were quick to exploit.[11] What is equally clear is that disaffection could only flourish if the royal house were divided. Indignant over his status, jealous of the king's courtiers and piqued over Edward's refusal to support a match between Clarence and his elder daughter Isabel, Warwick began to plan his coup having won over the king's brother and a number of key Lancastrians. In 1469 the rebels produced a manifesto, ghosted by Warwick, which set out their grievances and indicted king's councillors, including Earl Rivers and Sir John Fogge, as having undue influence with the king.[12] Skilful in manipulating popular opinion (like York before him, and strategists to come), Warwick crafted a message that resonated with the populace. He appealed to them directly, presenting himself as a champion of English liberties, and creating an ideological framework for his cause to legitimize his action. There was great mileage for malcontents in maligning court favourites, in blaming society's ills on evil counsel, and in promising reformation of government; it was powerful rhetoric which masked of course the rebels' true agenda.[13] Warwick's reasons for courting the duke are clear; moreover his timing was perfect, and his subject most willing. As an immensely engaging figure, Clarence was also capricious and covetous and, according to the Italian Dominic Mancini, driven by jealousy. No longer Edward's heir apparent and unsure of his place at court, he despised the queen's ability to garner for her family the best of Edward's patronage and the pick of the available matches. Added to this was the tantalizing possibility that he might just become king. The Warkworth chronicle alleges that central to the rebels' agreement was the issue of the succession which was to pass after Henry VI's death to his son and his progeny, and then to Clarence.[14] Thus ripe for intrigue, the duke supported Warwick's plan for a match with his daughter, whom he married in Calais.

As in the early 1460s, some followers of great lords were again compromised. Clarence's revolt in 1470 drew in a number of his clients, some of whom had been active or implicated in the Lincolnshire revolt earlier in the year, including his chief councillor Roger Tocotes, Sir Hugh Courtenay, William Twynyho, Richard Edgecombe and Nicholas Latimer, whose arrest was ordered on 8 February 1470. Courtenay defied commissioners sent down to the country to bring him to book and continued to harry the region, laying siege to the city of Exeter. In the south-east George Brown, steward of Clarence's Kent estates, was arrested in April 1470, while John Guildford, lieutenant of the Cinque Ports under Warwick, and William Knyvet also rebelled with the duke.[15]

With Edward's flight to the Low Countries in September 1470 and Henry VI's readeption, there was no radical shift in the trajectory of gentry politics, with some no doubt driven by sedition or self-interest, though many more were concerned to maintain stable government. Of course active supporters of the rebels received the pick of local offices; rather alarmingly Hugh Courtenay, who only months earlier had sallied forth against Exeter, received the city's bounty, was admitted to its freedom, and ranked next on the bench to Clarence and Warwick. None the less the duke lacked widespread support from his clients in 1470 and many including the Treffrys and Robert Willoughby were deemed too unreliable for service. Willoughby personalized the conflict, attacking his neighbour across the Tamar, Richard Edgecombe, Clarence's follower. Clients of the East Anglian grandees including Brandon, Wingfield and Norris were in eclipse with the dukes; others like Thomas Stonor, despite his strong ties with the House of York, along with Sir Thomas Delamare, served the crown.[16]

Warwick and Clarence found least support from royal retainers in the south-east, Brown and Guildford being two important exceptions. Most of those who had made their mark in Edward's household, including St Leger, Hungerford, Fogge, the Hautes, Thomas Vaughan, John Gaynesford, Thomas Lewkenor and Thomas Bourchier, went into sanctuary in England or exile abroad. Fogge had infuriated Warwick in 1465 when he had challenged his jurisdiction as constable of Dover. Altogether he wielded too much power for the earl's liking. No doubt his talks with Edward's ally Philip of Burgundy in Flanders in 1467, at a delicate stage in affairs between England, France and Burgundy, had raised Warwick's ire, as the duke had been negotiating simultaneously with Louis XI. Moreover as treasurer of the household Fogge assumed the rank of an earl when the steward was absent from court with a twenty shilling per day allowance when touring himself![17] Not surprisingly Fogge and St Leger spearheaded household resistance to the rebels and joined Edward in exile. Some who remained in England were placed under arrest including Bourchier, while others, disconsolate, retired to their estates.[18]

Within six months a gloomy exile had given way to a spirited return by Edward which had an electrifying effect on the household, binding men with a singular commitment to his régime and others who had remained neutral in the conflict. The energy and passion which Edward's return kindled was reflected in his support at the battles of Barnet and Tewkesbury by nobles and gentry alike, who recorded two awesome victories for the crown. With Clarence back in the fold, having defected from Warwick in early April, the deaths of Warwick at Barnet, the Prince of Wales at Tewkesbury and Henry VI mysteriously in the Tower, the Lancastrians' hopes were dashed, and the decade of two crowned kings was over; the disruptive forces at work through the 1460s were laid to rest. And if there were private recriminations, in public the royal family displayed a united front.

Edward's strength was reflected in his rewards both to the victors and the vanquished in the form of knighthood, grants and offices. Well known for his generosity, perhaps with Machiavellian insight he decided to keep his 'friends close' and his 'enemies closer', as Clarence's men were most richly rewarded. Tocotes, Brown and Latimer had already been created bannerets; the Powderham Courtenays quickly resumed local political life as did Sir John Guildford, who once again attended Edward at court. In East Anglia Knyvet, the Pastons and others were pardoned late in 1471.[19] Even the staunch Lancastrian Sir John Arundel, who had fought for the Prince of Wales at Tewkesbury in May, was given the royal nod in July and restored to local office despite his debt of 6000 marks to the crown. In the west Sir Hugh Courtenay, one of the few not to accompany Clarence at Tewkesbury, kept officials busy by stirring rebellion in Devonshire. In the south-east Fogge and others were active in subduing the last pockets of resistance from Warwick's cousin, the Bastard of Fauconberg, and having arrayed the men of Kent, they ably defended London against his onslaught. In late May and early June Edward deployed his most reliable captains in Kent at Rochester, Sandwich and Dover; St Leger was among them, though it was Fogge who carried out most of the investigation into Fauconberg's revolt.[20] Yet it was Gloucester who took the prize, finally capturing the Bastard at Southampton after weeks of piracy and sedition.

The king's desire to reward his supporters and win over former dissidents was not new, and Edward could afford to be generous. Sure of his power in the south-east since his accession, the men who controlled the regions were, in the main, loyal servants without conflicting interests. Certain also of the east, the Mowbray interest displayed the depth of its support. Importantly the West Country, long a hotbed of sedition and the region that had proved most difficult to subdue, had given encouraging signs at Tewkesbury that faction might now have given way to solid support for the crown. Yet the crisis marked a turning point for the king in a number of ways. Edward returned from exile with a spirit of optimism and a clarity of focus not present in the 1460s. He had seized the initiative in 1461 when he had captivated London and taken the crown. Ten years on he displayed the same qualities, though reinforced with a more aggressive political leadership. Restless for change and with limitless energy he stepped up his campaign to restructure both the household and the regions, to shore up his power. At the heart of the polity the household was the perfect instrument for political change, vital as he knew for more effective control. Admittedly he was in a position to alter course. Assisted by Clarence's return to the fold, he knew that Warwick's government with the feeble Henry VI as figurehead had had many powerful critics. Certain nuances had escaped the earl who had patronized his kin to the exclusion of others, thereby creating a Neville pre-eminence comparable with their position in the early 1460s, and in aligning with Louis XI against the king's brother-in-law, Charles of Burgundy.[21] The deaths of the conspirators and the Lancastrian movement gave Edward a free hand to reorganize the kingdom; the crises were over and the business of consolidation about to begin.

While the king could relish his position he could not be complacent. Only too aware of the problems that could arise from a narrow power base and land-hungry nobles, his campaign to redefine his authority underscores his talent for kingship and his flair with his servants. Driven by the need for stability and economy, Edward's policies had been under scrutiny since the early 1460s, when suitable agents were promoted in the regions: the Nevilles in the north; the Herberts in Wales and the Marches; Hastings in the midlands; Lord Stafford of Southwick with Clarence and Warwick in the west; the Duke of Norfolk and local leaders such as John Howard, Fogge, Scott and others in East Anglia and the south-east. The process gained pace from October 1469 when, in response to the deepening political crisis, Edward began to bind the household into a more effective political unit by lifting the profile of his men and investing them with greater responsibility in the face of revolt. Seen also as arbiter of their disputes, Edward began to tighten the bonds between himself and his affinity. On his return from exile in 1471 the fruits of his labour were apparent in battle.

From the early 1470s the royal family, especially Clarence and the clannish Woodvilles, were central to the new scheme. The power of Gloucester as Warwick's political heir was affirmed in the north where the Percies, lately restored to the earldom of Northumberland, were also accommodated. In the north-central midlands, Edward's chamberlain Lord Hastings became steward of the honour of Tutbury, part of the duchy of Lancaster estates, while Lord Stanley, the new steward of the royal household, became supreme in Lancashire, and his brother Sir William in Cheshire and north Wales. The centrepiece of royal policy took shape in the form of a huge unit of regional government based on the council of the Prince of Wales at Ludlow, Shropshire. Designed to combat Marcher lawlessness, from 1472 it was assimilated into Edward's scheme of land-based lordship; as the king steadily increased the nominal power of the prince, it was the Woodvilles, particularly Earl Rivers as head of his council, who acquired enormous power in Wales and the Marches. Already receiver-general of the duchy of Cornwall and governor of the prince's household, Rivers became the boy's steward in 1476.[22] By February 1483 Woodville members (as well as their clients) dominated the council and held unprecedented influence in the prince's affairs. What had been created at Ludlow was in fact a second court with servants whose

Ludlow Castle, Shropshire.

allegiance was to the prince. It was not a rival court vying for power with Westminster, but a separate royal household in which Prince Edward became the object of his servants' ambition and loyalty, and to whom they looked for advancement.[23] The powers which devolved on the council were great. Rivers was able to place men on a number of the boy's estates and both he and his colleagues such as Fogge influenced local political offices. Their strength was further realized at the muster, and by 1482 Rivers could potentially raise three thousand men in Wales, and Lord Stanley four thousand more: an enormous power base had been created. The prince's household is crucial in understanding men's loyalty and allegiance to the boy-king, Edward V, on his father's death. For Edward had created not simply a royal household, but a framework for effective rule for use in the event of a crisis.

There was little room for Buckingham in the new structure. While often at court for festivities and formalities, and a royal follower when the occasion demanded, from the time that he was granted livery in 1473 he had been refused most honours that a Plantagenet prince of the blood royal might have expected. Though appointed steward during Clarence's trial in 1477 and allowed to assume the arms of his forebear, Thomas of Woodstock, in a political context he was largely untried. Excluded from the bench in all counties except Stafford, the duke, having contracted to go to France in 1475 was mysteriously absent from the king's army. Moreover Edward had refused to grant him his full share of the Bohun inheritance which snaked across the Welsh Marches, the south-east and the midlands, for which he had often petitioned in the 1470s. Much has been made of Henry's exclusion from power. Perhaps Edward saw him as a potential royal rival manoeuvring for political gain. Then again his attitude may well have been influenced by financial considerations as the Bohun estates realized well over £1000 a year for the crown. Still he was not the only casualty in the king's restructuring. The 2nd Earl of Pembroke was virtually dispossessed, and it would be rash to assume that the duke had been singled out for ostracism. None the less Buckingham's was a rather hollow title without the dignities that were his due, and thus he had good reason to feel disgruntled.[24]

The political changes of the 1470s altered patterns of patronage as the king's rule strengthened and royal retainers became more powerful. In the south-west the gap left by Henry Stafford (d. 1469) was soon filled by Lords Dinham and Stourton, St Leger and others who picked up confiscated estates and offices within the duchy of Cornwall. Clarence remained pre-eminent, though there was a shift away from him from around 1473 as clients broadened their horizons through the lordship of others.[25] In East Anglia the Duke of Norfolk and John, Lord Howard, and his son Thomas were king's agents, while across the south the household managed the regions supervised by the king, much as their fathers and grandfathers had done before them. Yet at a time when the aristocracy was greatly reduced by attrition and attainder, it was the Woodvilles who came to dominate political life. Well connected among the nobility mostly through their matches in the 1460s, they counted among their affines the Greys of Ruthin and the Ferrers of Groby. The Duchess of Buckingham, the Countess of Pembroke and Lady Strange were all sisters of the queen, while two other sisters married the heirs of the Earls of Kent and Arundel. Leading gentry including the Hautes, Fogges and Vaughans were part of this kinship network.[26]

By 1478 the Woodvilles supported younger men who had entered the household after Tewkesbury: William and Robert Brandon, Fogge's son John, Richard Guildford, Edward Poynings, William Stonor, William Berkeley, John Cheyne, Giles Daubenay, William Uvedale, Edward Courtenay and Thomas Arundel, all of whom greatly profited through their lordship.[27] Woodville influence is best reflected in the parliament of 1478 when Daubenay, Stonor, Vaughan, Fogge and his son, Richard Haute, Nicholas Gaynesford and John Fiennes represented their counties. Admission to their charmed circle meant ties with their satellites such as John, Lord Strange (whose title Sir George Stanley inherited in 1479), from whom Stonor sought a retainer in 1478, and with major powers such as Lord Stanley, his son George and his brother Sir William.[28] By 1483 the family's influence had permeated every region in the south, stretching north as far as the palatinate of Chester and across the country to East Anglia. Indeed the powerful subsidy commission of 27 April 1483, following Edward's death, reads like a calling-card of Woodville clients.[29]

Widely known as parvenus, the Woodvilles have long been reproved for their exploitative tactics, ambition and greed. Their critics have noted that their council at Ludlow and offices in the Marches created a victim rather than a beneficiary of Lord Herbert in the early 1470s, while through their actions Buckingham remained in political isolation. They jealously guarded the prince's patronage, excluding established lords such as Grey of Ruthin, Maltravers and Lord Strange. Others suffered at their expense through the resettlement of the Mowbray and Holland inheritances including Ralph, Lord Neville. Not content with their power it is said that in 1477 they orchestrated a movement with the king's affinity to destroy the Duke of Clarence, their common enemy.[30] They allegedly created division among courtiers, were reviled for their gains and resented for their marriages. It remains, however, a fact that they caused no irredeemable rifts in political society after 1471, despite their apparent friction with Hastings. Even Clarence's death in 1478 did not threaten the period of calm. Indeed the unity at court and commitment to stability betokened a new and positive era for which the Woodvilles, with others, were largely responsible.[31]

With Edward ably assisted by his lieutenants, flexibility had been the hallmark of his rule, particularly evident after Clarence's treason in 1471. Yet the flexibility displayed after Tewkesbury was not new: after periods of conflict men were most often guided by the crown's policy towards recalcitrants; relationships were malleable and local differences seldom interfered with royal service. Certainly by the mid-1470s the appearance of a younger set of gentry faces injected new life into the regions. Flexibility had also encouraged less a sense of sharply defined counties as regions in the south, whose borders were fluid and whose concerns were entwined. Again, this was not new, though it was enhanced by a unique set of circumstances. Undeniably, though, the polity was vibrant, eclectic and broadly supportive of Edward's rule. It would be foolish to argue that the periods of conflict from 1461 were simply brief interludes in an otherwise tranquil society. The lists of proscribed undermine this thesis. Yet the stability after Tewkesbury vindicates the king's rule and underlines the maturity of the Yorkist polity, a maturity that bound the gentry in common action in 1483.[32] Never before had political society made such an unequivocal statement against the crown. Buckingham's rebellion in itself is the biggest tribute to Edward's kingship, and to his policies both at court and in the country.

What is most apparent from the period is that the actions of the king's affinity were determined not so much by their inability to avoid the troubles, but in the interests of good government and in the collective as well as the individual's interest. Of course it was easier for key gentry to exercise choice if their networks remained free from faction, but a pattern is evident from the late 1460s in which men's behaviour was shaped more by their desire for good government than by their attachment to a particular lord. As a powerful knight could usually exercise choice in the matter of his patrons, so indeed he exercised his informed judgement in matters of the greatest political weight. For royal retainers and ruling élites the critical issues that most often informed political choice were the calibre of the king and the quality of his kingship; thus in the battles for the crown in 1471 Edward commanded a broad affinity. Even in this age of bastard feudalism the royal affinity was, of course, bound by ties of fidelity, honour and service. However, in the increasingly king-centred politics of court and country,

Edward IV's tomb. St George's Chapel, Windsor.

evidence suggests that such duties and obligations sat well with naked ambition because of 'freedom of choice'. This is not to underrate the importance of the ties between a servant and his sovereign. None the less, in a world where court and country, private and public were so entwined, ambition was clearly a factor in political decision-making. In his influential essay 'Bastard Feudalism' (1945), K.B. McFarlane explored the role of the system in the lives of fifteenth-century gentry, its impact on the growth of political society, as a catalyst in lawlessness and as an agent for magnate rebellion and social unrest. His contention was that the system sought to preserve not undermine the ideals of 'responsibility, loyalty and good faith'; it did not exacerbate aristocratic rivalry, nor was it the root cause of the Wars of the Roses. To see it thus would be to misunderstand and misrepresent the position of the gentry both at court and in the country.[33] Thus for McFarlane, service and ambition were not mutually exclusive. Moreover, the effective king pretty much enjoyed the fidelity of his followers.

CHAPTER 4
Allies and Enemies

Edward IV's death on 9 April 1483, following what appears to have been a stroke, left his twelve-year-old son, Prince Edward, as his heir. Too young to rule outright, it seemed likely that some sort of caretaker régime would govern until the young king came of age, though its form was unclear. Whether Edward would have favoured a fully-fledged minority for his son or his direct accession and power-sharing through a council is unknown. Though historically both were problematic, there was no immediate reason to assume that the young king's closest family might not be able to co-operate in the nation's interests, and certainly the signs were promising. During Edward's second reign the royal succession was more stable than it had been since 1422 and with two healthy princes close in age, the only Lancastrian claimant languished in exile without help, or it seems hope, of transforming his position. Edward's brother, the thirty-year-old Richard of Gloucester had proved his worth in peace and war, and the king's allies, Earl Rivers, Lords Hastings, Howard and Stanley, had stood firmly about the throne. Even with Edward gone it was unthinkable that the succession might become unstable. While there was probably little love lost between Earl Rivers and Richard, nor is there direct evidence of political friction. Few, of course, would have doubted that such co-operation could easily be achieved. With their heightened status and inflated ambition the Woodvilles would not relish sharing their charge with Gloucester, losing their overriding influence over the young Edward and possibly their acquisitions in the process. Richard in turn had shown himself to be almost as acquisitive and self-serving as they, but now, of course, there was much more at stake than office and interest. As Edward's lieutenant in the north, chief steward of the duchy of Lancaster and leader of the immensely powerful Neville affinity, he had virtually become an independent power in the region. As the king's brother, constable of England, admiral and great chamberlain he was also the mightiest and most respected subject in the realm. He had assiduously cultivated his interests during Edward's second rule, and he was not about to see his fortunes slide under a Woodville-dominated régime. While each party was aware that its immediate response to the imbroglio was crucial, the Woodvilles could not expect support from courtiers such as their chief rival Lord Hastings, or the disenchanted young Duke of Buckingham who felt diminished by his marriage into their family; like the majority of the political nation they looked to Gloucester for leadership in the crisis. On his deathbed Edward had exhorted his affinity to bury their differences and co-operate in the interests of the realm, yet in those early days after his brother's death Richard became convinced that he had both devoted friends and deadly enemies; and with an adroit series of manoeuvres he was soon to show a most independent cast of mind.[1]

Richard was in the north, probably at Middleham Castle, when false news of his brother's death arrived at York around 1 April. Edward V was then in the care of his maternal kinsmen, his uncle Earl Rivers and his half-brother Sir Richard Grey, at Ludlow Castle, while Buckingham was at Brecon in south-east Wales. When the king's death was confirmed in York around 15 April, Gloucester led the city's notables in paying homage to Edward V; vouchsafing his fealty to the sovereign in a dispatch to the council at Westminster, he nevertheless pressed his claim to the protectorate. Thus far Gloucester had been a model of loyalty. By month's end, however, he had crushed the Woodvilles and seized back the initiative which clearly he believed had been theirs. They had held, after all, the person of the king along with the late king's treasure, split three ways between the queen, Dorset and Sir Edward Woodville. The latter's behaviour, moreover, gave the council cause for concern. As admiral of the fleet he had been sent against Philippe de Crèvecoeur at the end of April with a force some two thousand strong, and within days appeared to be menacing the south-east coast; as Dorset may also have had up to a thousand men in his charge doubtless the council came quickly to rue its commission. The queen's party had successfully pushed for an early coronation on 4 May, much to the consternation of Lord Hastings. After a council meeting towards the end of April he implored the queen to scale down her retinue to accompany Edward V from Ludlow to London, and promptly wrote to Richard in York urging that he 'hasten to the capital with a strong force'. According to Mancini, if Gloucester in the north feared some sort of a Woodville putsch there were those in London of like mind; and though an unlikely event, their early tactics were sufficiently self-serving to be worrying in the extreme.

A meeting was planned at Northampton between Richard, en route for London from the north, and the royal party, also proceeding to the capital, to allow both parties to accompany Edward V to Westminster. The plans took a twist when Rivers missed the rendezvous; leaving the king at Stony Stratford, he retraced his steps to Northampton ostensibly to welcome Gloucester. This may have been a ruse to buy

Seal of William, Lord Hastings.

time for his kinsmen to prepare for a showdown with the protector at their manor of Grafton Regis which bisected the towns, but most probably Rivers simply wanted the tactical advantage of reaching London with Edward V before Gloucester. None the less Richard read more into the gesture and having bid farewell to Rivers after a pleasant meal, by night's end he had decided to rout the young king's minders at Stony Stratford the next morning, 30 April. Earl Rivers, Sir Richard Grey, Sir Thomas Vaughan and Sir Richard Haute, Edward V's most respected councillors, were arrested on a charge of treason and spirited to prison in the north, and in little over a week Gloucester was styling himself protector. It is significant that Buckingham had joined Richard at Northampton that day, had supped with Gloucester and Rivers and after the latter's departure sat talking with Richard well into the night, probably confirming, perhaps encouraging, Richard's worst fears of a Woodville takeover, and pledging his loyalty and support in the event.[2]

After the events at Stony Stratford, however, the Woodvilles' future looked bleak with the queen and her family in sanctuary, Rivers under lock and key, and Sir Edward having fled to Brittany, after a confrontation off Southampton Water. Gloucester surely had little to fear. Yet his notion of a conspiracy persisted and on 10 June he sent an urgent message to York, asking for help against Queen Elizabeth whom he claimed was plotting his murder and that of his cousin, the Duke of Buckingham.[3] Next, in an extraordinary turn of events, Hastings was accused of treason at a council meeting on 13 June, and after a fiery exchange with Richard he was dragged ignominiously from the chamber by Thomas Howard and beheaded without trial on Tower Hill. Present at the same meeting and also accused of plotting against him were Bishop John Morton, Thomas Rotherham, Archbishop of York, and Thomas, Lord Stanley; they were imprisoned. Events then moved with alarming speed: on the 16th Richard recruited a reluctant Thomas Bourchier, Archbishop of Canterbury, and John Russell to persuade the queen to release the Duke of York from sanctuary to allow him, as it was said, to attend his brother's coronation on 22 June. Nevertheless with York safely under his wing, Richard postponed the coronation until 9 November; he had Rivers, Grey, Haute and Vaughan beheaded on 25 June and on the next day called himself king. Thus matters stood. While some among the

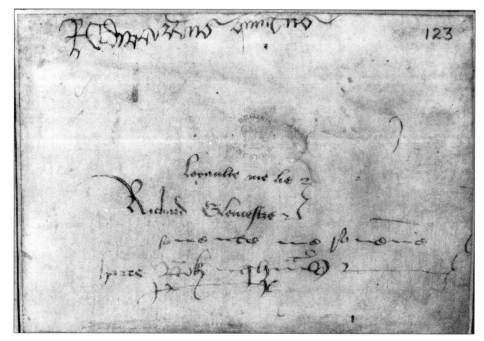

Signatures of Edward V, Gloucester and Buckingham on a document dating from the Protectorate.

council had probably suspected his motives since the end of May, Gloucester had finally declared his hand.[4]

Hard evidence for a Woodville plot to murder the protector is scarce, though the family obviously sought to maintain their position with the king and scrambled to secure their financial and military assets. According to Mancini, Richard had found caches of arms which he alleged were theirs and later displayed in London as evidence against them; the Crowland chronicler observed that he knew of men 'close to the king' who had sworn to 'destroy' his 'honour and his life'.[5] The Woodvilles, of course, were already unpopular, and Mancini depicts Hastings and Dorset as rivals in love and office, and suggests ill-feeling between Gloucester and the queen's kin. Yet by 1483 the conflict and jealousy aroused by their position had long since diminished, and such tensions that existed among the royal affinity had clearly not affected good government for over a decade. Indeed until Richard's pre-emptive strike against them, family members served the council's wishes despite their anxiety over their influence with the king. Though the Crowland chronicler has it that Edward's most loyal councillors did not want the Woodvilles to be 'great about the king' during his minority, nor would they countenance Gloucester's intentions. Thus senior councillors intrigued with the Woodvilles through the agency of Elizabeth ('Jane') Shore, a former mistress of Dorset and Hastings, and John Forster, a servant of both the latter and the queen and formerly steward of St Albans, who carried news between Dorset, in sanctuary there, and the lord chamberlain. Richard had fostered stable government for over four weeks. None the less the mood had changed markedly by 10 June with his urgent plea for aid against the queen, the murder of Hastings and the imprisonment of his cohorts.[6] According to *The Great Chronicle* and Vergil, Stanley survived only because Richard feared repercussions from Lord Strange, his son, at large in Lancashire. Whatever else, Gloucester's moves in June were not a knee-jerk reaction to his increasing insecurity, but more likely formed part of a considered strategy from April when he may well have faked his own ambush and then alleged a sinister plot to rid himself of Hastings and frighten his enemies. What is clear is the provocative nature of Richard's own actions and the ruthless manner in which he cleared all obstacles between himself and the throne. It is tempting to believe that the execution of Hastings was a retaliatory measure for scuttling his plans, as he and senior councillors had refused to arraign Rivers and Grey on a murder charge. It demonstrated to Richard that their support for him was conditional on his role as protector, not as king; while Hastings's death in mid-June illustrated to the council that Gloucester's quest for the crown was non-negotiable.

As Richard's great ally and partner in power, the Duke of Buckingham's loyalty was never in doubt. Almost before Edward was cold the two were in contact, with the duke pledging his firm support to Richard in his bid for power. During the summer of 1483 he attained a spectacular position in the affairs of English politics. His reward for assisting in Richard's usurpation was an unprecedented array of offices in Wales and the West Country, where for a short time his influence was supreme. In May 1483 he was appointed justiciar and chamberlain of north and south Wales, constable of all royal castles in the principality and in the counties of Shropshire, Herefordshire, Somerset, Dorset and Wiltshire. In all the Marcher lordships belonging to the crown he was given the offices of constable, steward and receiver. He was empowered to levy troops at his discretion in the principality of Wales, to issue commissions of array in the English counties where he was castellan, and to appoint the sheriffs, escheators and all other officers in the counties of the principality; in addition he was given the supervision of the king's subjects in Wales and the Marches, Somerset, Dorset and Wiltshire.[7] In July Buckingham's position was further strengthened with the receiver-generalship of the duchy of Cornwall, formerly held by Rivers. Thus Woodville control of the Prince of Wales's affairs and the power they had wielded through exploitation of duchy of Cornwall patronage came at a stroke

Edward Stafford, 3rd Duke of Buckingham (d. 1521), from the portrait at Magdalene College, Cambridge.

within Buckingham's orbit. He also received the contentious Bohun lands which enabled him to consolidate his already vast holdings in the south, and he replaced Rivers as constable of England. Held briefly by Gloucester, the constableship was an office of hereditary significance for the Staffords. Buckingham's grandfather, the 1st Duke, was constable in 1442 while Duke Henry's son Edward was to wrangle with Henry VIII over his claim to the position in 1514. The office was not conferred lightly and in terms of actual and potential power the constable was among the most important officers in the entire realm.

Authorized to act summarily against those suspected of treason, he was able to pronounce sentence without appeal. The position carried with it not just formal obligations but in the event of a crisis such as the king being killed in battle, or if his power were deemed to be tyrannical, the constable was empowered to take over the reins of government.[8]

It was not unreasonable to expect that Henry might receive such a prestigious office at an early age. As great officers of state the Staffords had held impressive credentials as key figures in national affairs for more than 100 years. Created a duke in 1444, Henry's grandfather, Humphrey, had been at the centre of national politics in a military and political context since the 1420s. He had tasted service in France by 1420 and was a royal councillor in 1424. By 1432 he had held office as constable of France, governor of Paris and lieutenant-general of Normandy. Acquiring the captaincy of Belleme Castle, he became constable both of Calais and of England in 1442. Politically, the first duke had steered a middle course through the decades, serving the crown through the vicissitudes of government. And he had continued to prosper, receiving the constableship of Dover in 1448 and the office of warden of the Cinque Ports in 1450. His great military power had made him a valuable asset to the crown; for example, in February 1454 he mobilized support for Henry VI to the tune of two thousand liveried followers. Playing a decisive role in the Duke of York's defeat at Ludford in 1459, Buckingham as warden of the Cinque Ports was able to mobilize the south-east coast against attack from supporters of York and the Earl of Warwick.[9]

His death at Northampton in 1460 had been preceded by the death of his eldest son Humphrey in 1457, making his grandson Henry his heir at the age of five. The young duke came of age in 1473 at just eighteen, having already acquired some prominence at the court of Edward IV. A member of the king's household after his wardship was purchased by Edward in 1464, Henry was quickly betrothed to Elizabeth Woodville's younger sister Katherine, whom he married around May 1465. Entering the queen's household three months later, Buckingham was created a Knight of the Bath at Elizabeth's coronation, together with his brother Humphrey, Viscount Lisle, and the new Earl of Oxford. Taking part in the festivities and formalities of courtly life, in 1468 he attended Lord Scales when he contested the Bastard of Burgundy in a grand tournament, along with the Duke of Clarence, the Earls of Arundel and Kent, and Lords Herbert and Stafford. Attending most official banquets, he was present at the Christmas celebrations at Westminster Palace in 1471 where he sat on Edward's left. He attended a banquet in honour of the Burgundian envoy, Seigneur de la Gruthuyse, in 1473 where he danced with the Princess Elizabeth, and he was prominent at the Duke of York's wedding in 1477. In 1478 he paid homage to the young duke, with Gloucester, Dorset and others, on the occasion of a feast for

Prince Edward. That same year the king became godfather to his first son, Edward, giving the infant a gold cup as a christening present. Prominent also in Edward's period of crisis between 1469 and 1471, Buckingham was among those who rode through London to greet the king on his return from York after his captivity, with the Dukes of Gloucester and Suffolk, the Earls of Arundel, Northumberland and Essex, Lords Hastings, Dacre, Mountjoy and an array of knights, squires and London officials. After the Battle of Tewkesbury in 1471 and the Bastard of Fauconberg's abortive rising in the south-east, the duke was a member of Edward's entourage when he triumphantly entered London on 21 May, together with the Dukes of Clarence and Gloucester, Norfolk and Suffolk.[10] Nevertheless his high public profile fooled none, least of all Duke Henry whose exclusion from serious political activity must have rankled deeply with him. Thus his newly found fortune must have seemed almost too good to be true, and in return his support for Richard was rock solid.

Throughout the turbulent weeks that followed Buckingham was at hand to display his great military strength as the most powerful subject in the land. Before Edward V left for London on 24 April, Buckingham reportedly promised Gloucester 'a 1000 good fellows if need were' though it seems that no more that 300 Stafford retainers accompanied the duke to Northampton where he met Gloucester five days later. Over the next few days, however, his men were among the armed retainers who flocked south 'in numero terribili et inaudito', during the flurry of military activity. According to John Rous, the duke himself boasted that not since the time of Warwick the Kingmaker had so many men worn a single badge; and both he and Gloucester must have made an impressive sight as they rode into London with Edward V on Sunday 4 May.[11] As well as military support Buckingham put his skills to work, shaping strategy and making appearances on Gloucester's behalf. Crowland notes his suggestion to house Edward V in the Tower of London. After the alleged plot against the protector's life he supervised the investigations into the activities of Rotherham, Morton and Hastings. When Richard finally made clear his intention to seize the crown, Buckingham approved and encouraged the protector's claim and in seductive tones fudged reality to suit his rhetoric, arguing on 24 June for the illegitimacy of Edward's sons through their father's invalid marriage to Elizabeth Woodville; this speech he 'so well and eloquently uttered and with so angelic a countenance'. Flying high with the constableship recently conferred on him, according to Edward Hall he looked very much the part as the mightiest prince royal, making a splendid progress through London at the head of a large entourage. When the protector had himself crowned King Richard III on 6 July, Buckingham as the great chamberlain played a central role in helping him to dress at various times before and during the ceremony; taking responsibility for the offerings made by

Richard during the service and bearing the king's train with 'a white staff in his hand'.[12]

The duke also commanded brief but great power within the household during the early weeks of Richard's reign. Though Hastings was replaced by Lovell as lord chamberlain, Buckingham was better placed to lead the household party as mediator and regulator of patronage, replacing Rivers and Dorset as the dominant figure in the competition for royal bounty. He was also poised to take command of the north midland power-base of Lord Hastings, even though the wardship of his son went to his widow Katherine. There is little evidence that Hastings had controlled the flow of patronage to the West Country knights in the 1470s and early 1480s. There were others there whose influence was much stronger despite his duchy position and his prominence in the household. However, after his death and the eclipse of the Woodvilles, it was Buckingham's lordship that regional leaders would have sought. As well as vast control in the south-west and Wales, he probably also expected the midlands to fall into his hands. Indeed a letter to Sir William Stonor, written soon after Hastings's death, by Simon Stallworth, in John Russell's employ, with its ambiguous comment 'my lord chamberlain's men become my lord of Buckingham's men' could allude to the duke's probable patronage of the household party. More likely, however, it refers to Buckingham's proposed take-over of Hastings's retinue in the midlands, whose support he had hoped to galvanize in October along with the Marcher lords.[13]

Aside from Buckingham, Richard appeared to have solid support from the other super-powers. Indeed his coronation was attended by most of the nobility including the Percy Earl of Northumberland, the Earls of Lincoln and Kent and Lords Howard, Stanley, Lovell, Fitzhugh and Scrope. As Richard's strong man in the north, Henry Percy must have been delighted that Richard's kingly duties would fully occupy him in the south, allowing him greater control of the region. As for Stanley, who had almost lost his life under Richard, his relations with the king must have been tense. Nevertheless as a military colossus in the north-west, Richard could not afford to bully him and chose instead to win him over with promises and rewards. Already the greatest powers were jostling for the spotlight, among them John Howard, whose acquiescence in Richard's coup was secured with the dukedom of Norfolk and the office of earl marshal of England. On 26 June he had been prominent at Richard's acclamation, positioned on the right of the marble chair that bore the king at Westminster, and was steward of England at Richard's coronation. Not to be outshone, Buckingham ensured his pre-eminence as high steward at the celebration with 'the chief rule and devising' of the same, though his duchess, Katherine Woodville, was absent from the glittering spectacle.

In view of the exceptional circumstances, the occasion must have seemed to Richard an outstanding success, with the vast majority of the polity conspicuous by their presence rather than their absence, the notable exception being Richard's former chancellor, Thomas Rotherham. Over one hundred knights, the majority of whom had served in Edward's household, attended the gala occasion, including his knights and squires of the body. Edward's intimates who had officiated at his funeral on 16 April, among them George Brown, Walter Hungerford, Thomas St Leger, Robert Poyntz, Nicholas Gaynesford, William Berkeley, John Cheyne, Thomas Bourchier, Giles Daubenay, William Stonor and William Norris, were involved in Richard's ceremony, with Cheyne and St Leger receiving gifts of cloth of silver (the latter also velvet for use in the vigil procession) and Stonor, among others, carrying the carpet. In a timely display of largesse Richard lavished gifts on proven friends and those he had yet to win over. Among those knighted on the vigil of the coronation were Thomas Arundel, William Berkeley and Thomas Lewkenor.[14] Some of the more prominent knights omitted from the celebrations include Robert Willoughby, Roger Tocotes, William Haute and John Fogge. The omission of the last two is no surprise. Fogge had scuttled to sanctuary at Westminster with the Woodvilles in early May, and though allegedly reconciled with the king on the first day of his reign, he was either not invited or absented himself from the coronation. Likewise Haute, brother of the recently deceased Sir Richard, who was replaced as sheriff of Kent by Sir Henry Ferrers, was either excluded or refused the invitation.[15]

Richard assumed leadership of his brother's affinity with grace and aplomb, and continuity of service was a feature of his rule from May until October 1483. Most who had served the prince at Ludlow moved on to Westminster despite their Woodville connections, and Edward V rode into London on 4 May with a circle of royal retainers including John Norris and Walter Hungerford. There is no reason to assume other than that continuity prevailed in the chamber, and of the six southern knights of the body who later rebelled Richard almost certainly retained Stonor, William Norris, Daubenay and Bourchier, and probably St Leger and Brown, though the latter soon lost offices at court.[16] Of the eleven southern squires of the body who were to rebel in October, all apart from Poyntz, a kinsman of Earl Rivers, served Richard, though Cheyne soon fell from grace. Lesser men who maintained their royal status are known to us through to their subsequent revolt: the yeomen of the crown William Knight, Richard Cruse,

Garter stall plate of William, Lord Hastings.

William Frost, Richard Potter, Richard Fisher, John Boutayne, Roger Kelsale (also usher of the chamber) and William Strode.[17]

Gloucester's confidence in the royal affinity when others in high places were under suspicion is evident in his use of them for sensitive tasks: on 10 May he ordered Sir Thomas Fulford and John Halwell to investigate Woodville's tactics off Southampton, with the fleet in tow and over £10,000 in gold coin; four days later he directed William Berkeley, William Uvedale and Roger Kelsale to victual a fleet, and John Welles, Thomas Greyson and Edward Brampton to move against Sir Edward, who still managed to slip away to Brittany with two ships.[18] Clearly Richard saw no reason to dismiss the vast majority of Edward's household officials though the treasurer, Sir Thomas Vaughan, was not replaced; John Cheyne, who was heavily involved in intrigue, lost his position in June as master of the henchmen and master of the horse; he was followed by St Leger in July as controller of the mint and master of the harthounds. In September Peter Curtis was temporarily removed from the wardrobe, while George Lovekyn, the king's tailor (an associate of Cheyne), forfeited the serjeanty of the great wardrobe to Henry Davy.[19] Other posts had been vacated around the end of July with the alleged plot and execution of John Smith, a groom of the stirrup under Edward (whose superior had also been Cheyne), Stephen Ireland, a wardrober in the Tower, Robert Rushe, serjeant of London, and William Davy, pardoner of Hounslow. Some administrators also went, including, not surprisingly, Fogge, who lost the keepership of the writs of the common bench, and Robert Morton, who had been master of the rolls, on 22 September. Some others, however, prospered, such as Dorset's client, Thomas Lovell, in chancery.[20]

Nor was there a grand design by Richard to replace members of Edward's affinity with his own servants on crown estates, as the duchy of Cornwall posts vacated by the Woodvilles and used by him to sweeten the household indicate.

Edward's squire, John Sapcote, replaced Rivers as receiver; his brother-in-law, Lord Dinham, obtained the stewardship; while Avery Cornburgh, formerly steward of the duchy, won Vaughan's position as controller of the coinage of tin. Others gained lesser offices such as William Cheyne, bailiff of the stannaries of Penwith and Kerye, Cornwall.[21] Though Edmund Haute lost an annuity to Walter Hungerford and Robert Poyntz lost prime royal office in Gloucestershire and Hampshire, the vast majority of servants scored offices, grants and confirmations; and in view of his scarce resources, Richard's generosity to his brother's affinity must have been reassuring to those who had feared wholesale changes among royal servants.[22]

A number of changes in county administration, however, indicate Richard's edginess as he strove for the right balance among ruling élites: St Leger, John and Alexander Cheyne, Richard Morton, the Brandons, Sir William Haute, John Wingfield, George Brown and Thomas Lewkenor were replaced on the bench; some no doubt as a result of competing interests rather than political eclipse. St Leger, omitted in Southampton and Surrey, kept his Devon commissions until after 28 August. Others were perhaps overlooked in the uncertainty following Edward's death. Many, though, were promoted, like John Norris, Thomas Cheyne, Edward Courtenay, Thomas Arundel, John Halwell, Sir Nicholas Latimer, John Guildford, Sir Giles Daubenay and Nicholas Gaynesford. Surprisingly Fogge also kept his place in Kent, probably as a ploy by Richard to win over the Kentish gentry, and to be seen as conciliatory and not hell-bent on reprisals. Indeed the king's treatment of Sir John underscores his dilemma. Unhappy with his own influence in Kent, he was forced to compromise with several men, including the former king's knight. Outwardly though, his promotion of the royal affinity at court reflects their perceived reliability as much as his need to cultivate them as adjuncts to his rule in the country. The powerful August subsidy commission presumably indicates his mind on the matter and except for Fogge, the Hautes, George Brown and John Cheyne, he used his brother's affinity exclusively.[23] Patently, the Woodvilles' downfall did not interrrupt the flow of patronage to the gentry. In fact many who were to lead Buckingham's rebellion received their best rewards from the new king and through the good offices of the Duke of Norfolk, Viscount Lovell and briefly the Duke of Buckingham.

It is hardly surprising that the household was courted for its expertise. Continuity of government between reigns was a standard practice, and like kings before him Richard relied heavily on the royal affinity as local governors and spokesmen on gentry affairs and prospective servants. As his success or failure depended on winning over the ruling élites, he determined on a smooth transition in government, and the changes that did occur were insufficient to create a climate of uncertainty among the gentry, in terms, that is, of their livelihood. While some Woodville colleagues and protégés were excluded from office, other omissions may have been the result of conflicting interests or simply of personal preference. Beneath the surface, however, rumour and intrigue at court and in the counties were rife, and while this did not translate into wholesale changes in government, a steady trickle of disaffection fed Richard's fears and found expression in commissions of enquiry and executions. None the less, of all the former king's servants the future rebels had the least reason to rebel, and there is little to suggest the approaching tide of disaffection. Yet in little over three months more than one-third of the southern gentry present at the coronation were in open rebellion.

When the new king and his ally parted company after the coronation, both in high spirits, the scenario about to unfold would have been unimaginable to Richard; indeed within weeks of his plea to York for aid for himself and Buckingham against the Woodvilles, the duke became involved in a second inter-connected plot intended unequivocally to destroy the king. No stranger to intrigue, according to the Crowland chronicler, as soon as the king left London on his post-coronation progress, a plot was hatched in the south to deliver the princes from the Tower of London, while those in sanctuary proposed to rescue the princesses from Westminster and send them to safety abroad. Richard reacted by ordering a guard under John Nesfield to vet all activity at Westminster. John Stow divulged the plot centred on Smith, Ireland, Rushe and Davy to rescue the princes by diverting attention from the Tower of London to fires in another part of the city. This intrigue foreshadowed what Richard could expect from the household, as it was led by John Cheyne and almost certainly involved Margaret Beaufort. Allegedly those who were executed had written both to Henry Tudor and his uncle Jasper inviting an invasion, and if any credibility can be attributed to Dominic Mancini's report of a rumour that the princes were widely believed in the capital to be dead by early to mid-July, then it indicates Henry Tudor's status as a credible candidate for the throne before July was out. At the very least he was a focus for the disaffected within weeks of Richard's coronation.[24]

The king's disquiet is reflected in a letter written to his chancellor on 29 July from Minster Lovell, having heard of an enterprise towards the end of the month, most probably connected with the Cheyne-Beaufort plot. Whatever its nature, the king 'doubts not' that Russell has heard of the affair, and cautions his chancellor to take matters in hand, 'fail ye not hereof'.[25] Another plot in early August focused on Margaret Beaufort's half-brother, John Welles, who organized a conspiracy at the Beaufort manor of Maxey in Northamptonshire. On discovery, he forfeited his lands on 13 August and joined Henry Tudor in Brittany. Suspecting further trouble Richard ordered two thousand Welsh bills from Nicholas Spicer on 17 August at Leicester, and instructed Buckingham to head commissions into treason in London, Surrey, Sussex, Kent and the other Home Counties. On 22 September Richard foresaw trouble in other quarters and Robert Morton was dismissed from office. On the same day the king's directive to the sheriff of Southampton outlawing retaining and the use of liveries highlights royal concern behind the general attack on the practice which caused 'great division and jeopardy'. On the following day the queen's brother Bishop Woodville had his 'worldly' goods seized.[26] Most significantly, however, on 24 September Buckingham, now fully committed to the rebellion, wrote to Henry Tudor informing him of the rising and asking for his cooperation.[27]

Edward Hall's suggestion that Buckingham was informed of the Beaufort-Woodville plot during a chance encounter with Lady Margaret on the road between Worcester and Bridgnorth invites speculation. Related by marriage, Margaret had used the duke as a go-between in talks with Richard in June and July 1483 concerning her son's return from exile and marriage with a princess of York. Lady Beaufort had long held powerful contacts with the Woodville circle through her marriage with Lord Stanley and at the court of Edward IV generally. Since the early 1470s she had canvassed Yorkist support for her son, and won favour for her political acumen. Her efforts culminated in a document written in Edward's presence on 3 June 1482, whose main thrust was that Henry might return to England 'to be in the grace and favour of the king's highness'. Her relations with Richard were less cordial, and though she accompanied Stanley at the coronation, the king mistrusted them. Already involved in intrigue, Margaret for her part gave direction to Richard's opposition in the south as he journeyed north, and perhaps involved Buckingham. Once at Brecon, Buckingham held further discussions with Morton who cogently argued in favour of a match between Henry Tudor and Elizabeth of York.[28]

The duke presumably reached south-east Wales in early August. He was certainly at his castle by the 23rd when an order passed under his signet to the keeper of the park at Chilton Foliat to deliver a buck to John Isbury. Richard, meanwhile, was still blind to Buckingham's intrigue, for as late as 16 September he had issued writs to the receivers in north and south Wales directing them to pay their accounts to the duke.[29] Not until towards the end the month did he hear of the conspiracy involving Bishop Woodville and Robert Morton, and began to suspect Buckingham. The bishop was involved in diocesan business concerning the appropriation to Magdalen College of the chapel of St Katherine in the church at Wanborough, Wiltshire. On 22 September Woodville issued letters to

Thornbury Castle, Gloucestershire, held by the Duke of Buckingham.

the Abbot of Hyde who was conducting the appropriation. Of great interest is their place of issue: 'in domo habitacionis nostre in Thornbury Wigorn' dioc'. In other words, Woodville was in Gloucestershire at Buckingham's principal seat. The evidence, or lack of it, concerning Woodville's whereabouts in all the contemporary records suggests that he was at Thornbury on a voluntary basis and was involved in intrigue with the duke. Thus it seems scarcely coincidental that

Buckingham contacted Henry Tudor on 24 September. According to both the Crowland chronicler and Vergil, Richard had already put a close watch on Buckingham; he in turn, feeling the noose tightening, wrote to Henry Tudor.[30] Richard's suspicions were confirmed by the beginning of the second week in October, as his letter to Russell requesting the great seal on 12 October indicates that the chancellor already knew of the duke's defection: 'as lately by our other letters we certified you our mind more at large'.[31] Thus on the 11th at Lincoln, the king began to call men to his authority.

It is difficult to reconcile the position Buckingham attained in the affairs of national politics in the summer of 1483, the actual and potential power made available to him through his role in Richard's coup, with his defection and downfall in October. Indeed from May until September the duke could do no wrong. The recipient of the most lavish patronage at court, he was Richard's closest ally and confidant. The intrigue that began in April with the Woodvilles was fed initially by a desire to curb Gloucester's power. Later it aimed at reinstating Edward V and by early June had embraced Hastings, Morton, Rotherham, Stanley and others. Still later, a second, inter-connected plot sought to overthrow Richard III and place Henry Tudor on the throne, uniting the Houses of Lancaster and York with a marriage to suit both parties. Margaret Beaufort may well have been an early conspirator; she had certainly entered the picture by July. While the rationale of most of the key players seems relatively straightforward, the duke's revolt, in view of all he had gained and all he stood to lose, is far more challenging. The only given is that his agenda was self-serving; yet any attempt to second-guess his motivation begs more questions than it answers. That he risked his power in support of a political unknown, when Henry Tudor's accession would presumably have restored Woodville supremacy in Wales to his own detriment, is perplexing. Perhaps his great rewards led to an insatiable appetite that led him to covet the throne. Certainly in his letter to Henry Tudor on 24 September, he made no reference to the latter claiming the crown. This, though, presupposes his eventual overthrow of Henry Tudor, having obtained the support of the broad Yorkist affinity. Even with his shortcomings, Buckingham surely would have realized the folly of the plan. Thus it is worth speculating on the crime which alienated the household and led to a revolt whose success, if he had not defected, would have destroyed him.[32]

Following traditional sources the duke was the pawn of John Morton at Brecon, and if their alleged conversations in August and September are grounded in fact then Buckingham must have known of the boys' murders.[33] There is indeed primary evidence of Buckingham's direct involvement in the crime, the earliest of which is the College of Arms Ms 2M6, which posits that the boys 'were put to death in the Tower of London by the "vise" [meaning either advice or device] of the duke of Buckingham'. *The Divisie Chronicle* is fairly dismissive of the view that the duke had the boys killed to further his own claim to the throne, though 'some others will say' as much. Jean Molinet also mentions Buckingham in this context, but is sceptical of the story, while Philippe de Commynes first has Richard committing the act before taking the crown, then vice versa, before asserting that it was in fact the duke who worked the dastardly deed. Altogether the charge seems unconvincing. If Buckingham had first enthroned Gloucester in order to seize the crown, then credence could be given to his direct responsibility for the princes' murders. However, it is unlikely that a man of his stature would thus have wasted his talents. With his double descent from Edward III through his Beaufort mother from John of Gaunt, and as the unchallenged heir of Thomas of Woodstock, why wait for Richard's coronation to depose him? Yet again, it is naive to assume that if intent on taking the crown for himself he would have succumbed to Morton's argument that Henry Tudor had the better claim and would have led the rebellion, shelving for the time being his own aspirations. It is difficult to countenance that any subject of the realm, whatever his standing with the ruler, would take it upon himself to murder a deposed king, and there is a weight of evidence in contemporary English and foreign sources that suggests Richard III was the man directly responsible for the princes' fate. He stood to gain most from their deaths and had the power to conceal the crime, which, in an age devoid of the modern notions of accountability and transparency of government, was subsumed in a culture of cover-up and silence. None the less, taking into account Buckingham's role in Richard's coup and the favour he enjoyed with the king, it is indeed possible that he effected a plan which he had discussed with Richard before they both left London. In fact, according to a contemporary English source among the Ashmolean manuscripts in the Bodleian Library, Richard sounded out the duke before the murders. It could be that Buckingham was acting directly on Richard's orders, or at least with his knowledge and consent, or that he took rather too much upon himself and brought about a result which until then had simply been discussed. Whatever else, it is likely that Buckingham played a prominent role in the murders, in encouraging and abetting the crime. In view of the vitriolic response touched off in Richard against his ally, the one 'who had best cause to be true', such activity seems entirely plausible.[34]

It is in this context that the duke's defection can best be explained. Before he left London for Brecon at the end of July, he would have become aware of the growing hostility in many quarters against the king over his usurpation and the disappearance of the princes. Frightened by the reaction to these occurrences and aware both of his own complicity and Richard's ebbing political power, Buckingham was apprised by Morton of the full momentum of the scheme to overthrow Richard, which doubtless he felt would succeed and which would destroy him as the king's closest ally, if he did not defect. Over the next few weeks he decided to lead the rebellion and embarked on a campaign to denigrate the king in an attempt to cover his own tracks and lend authenticity to his about-face. Indeed the Crowland chronicler mentions almost in the same breath the public proclamation asserting Buckingham's leadership in the enterprise and relates that 'a rumour arose that king Edward's sons . . . had met their fate'.[35] To this effect it is quite possible that he used his office as constable of England with its attendant powers both to legitimize his action and to whip up public sentiment against a king widely believed to have killed his nephews and whose rule was viewed by many as tyrannical. Fully committed to the plan by September, Buckingham had 'so many men' at Brecon on 18 October that he was able 'to go where he will'.[36] In truth, of course, he was unable to organize sufficient support in south-east Wales, and was ultimately defeated by Richard's captains and the atrocious weather conditions; the plunder of Brecon Castle by Thomas Vaughan of Tretower Court compounded his problems. Just ten days after the campaign began the hapless duke was betrayed to the sheriff of Shropshire by his childhood servant, Ralph Bannaster, who had been 'loved, favoured, and trusted' by the 1st Duke 'above all his servants'. Retribution was swift. Escorted to Salisbury by Sir James Tyrell and Giles Wellesbourne, Buckingham was summarily executed on Sunday 2 November, having been denied an audience with the king.[37] As tradition has it, Henry was beheaded in the Market Place at Salisbury, in the courtyard of the Blue Boar Inn. A nineteenth-century journeyman excavating the kitchen of the Saracen's Head, adjacent to the inn, found the mutilated skeleton of a man of above average height, perhaps the Duke of Buckingham, which, when disturbed, crumbled to dust. As both the Church of St Thomas and Greyfriars in Salisbury also lay claim to his remains, the punch is somewhat removed from the story. Yet the headless skeleton, also missing its right arm which was sawn off below the shoulder, is stuff for the imagination. Perhaps Richard was able to take out his frustration on the corpse of the man he had come to loathe.[38]

It is tempting to believe that Buckingham, driven by arrogance and optimism, had decided to play both sides for fools; indeed that the rebellion had provided him with rich opportunities and, having betrayed Richard III in his quest for the crown, he would also have betrayed Henry Tudor. As a man whose ambition

The tomb of Thomas Stanley, Earl of Derby (d. 1504), and his wife. Ormskirk Church, Lancashire.

exceeded his ability, it is difficult to believe that he would have acquiesced in the new régime. In view of all the circumstances, however, Buckingham betrayed Richard because he had no choice, and his defection is testimony to the weight of the rebellion. The great irony is that his own revolt probably sealed the rebels' fate. Buckingham's new position confronted the authority of the Stanleys, as well as Marcher and north midland powers. It is unlikely that they would easily have accepted this challenge on their own doorstep, and though Stanley was involved as Lady Beaufort's husband, he along with others possibly withdrew his support when the duke's leadership was announced. In this context Richard's promotion of his lieutenant almost certainly enabled him to prolong his rule. Such a concentration of power in Buckingham's hands, however, had also upset the fine balance that Edward had cultivated for over a decade. While the late king had greatly favoured the Woodvilles with office and interest, power was diffused through a number of royal servants.[39] Conversely, Richard had created a situation which his brother had wisely avoided.

CHAPTER 5

Buckingham's Rebellion

Despite his own poor showing, Buckingham's rebellion had almost all the right ingredients for Richard's overthrow in 1483: Henry, of course, the usurper's underling as figure-head; a defeated family eager to claw its way back into power; a mother long dedicated to her exiled son's interests and wholly committed to securing his crown; and it was driven by a dead king's affinity, anxious for Richard's overthrow and the union of the Houses of York and Lancaster. It was never the duke's rebellion and it is ironic that he had such a small part in the revolt that bears his name. While it is certain that his projected role was much larger, the act of attainder gave him a spurious importance when it charged him with inciting rebellion in each of the sectors. Though his family's estates had facilitated the intrigue, the duke was a lightweight in the revolt: he was John Morton's coadjutor at Brecon, valued for his status and his potential military strength, but after his downfall scorned for his weakness as a politician and a lord. Following Tudor sources historians have made much of his failure at the muster and his perceived cowardice, his disloyal servants and tenants, and his inability to harness noble support for the cause. In fairness to Henry, it was never going to be easy. Buckingham's extraordinary power in Wales and the Marches had angered powerful gentry such as Rhys ap Thomas, while on-going feuds in the region also helped to shape local reaction to him in 1483. The conflict between the duke's tenants, the Vaughans of Tretower Court, and Jasper Tudor, Henry's uncle, who had executed Thomas Vaughan's father in 1471, provides a case in point, and helps to explain Vaughan's attitude towards the rebellion and his destruction of Brecon after the duke left his castle for Weobley around 18 October. Of course Buckingham's failure to suborn the Stanleys and the Talbots – the major powers in north Wales and Cheshire, and the Marches and the north midlands respectively – and also the powerful Hastings affinity was of critical importance to the revolt. The key to the rebels' success lay in raising south-east Wales and the midlands, which would have formed one prong of a forked movement that could have skewered Richard en route for the west. While the major powers were challenged by Buckingham's political ascendancy, Lord Stanley at least, already compromised as Margaret Beaufort's husband, may already have pulled back or

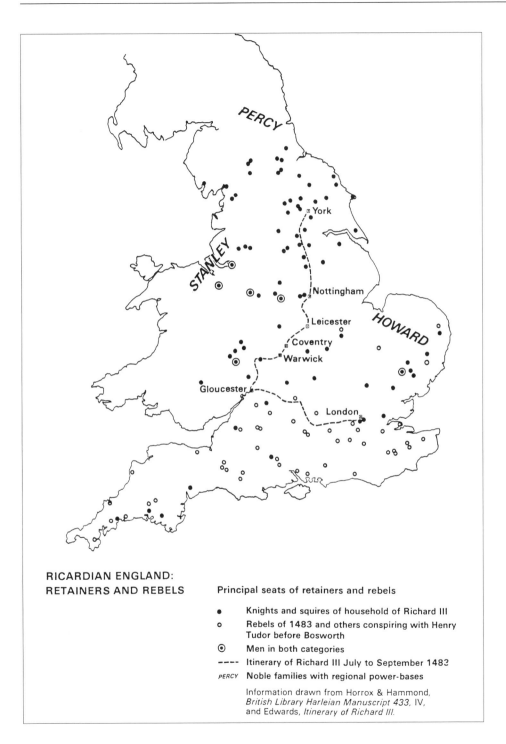

RICARDIAN ENGLAND: RETAINERS AND REBELS

Principal seats of retainers and rebels

- •   Knights and squires of household of Richard III
- ○   Rebels of 1483 and others conspiring with Henry Tudor before Bosworth
- ◉   Men in both categories
- ---- Itinerary of Richard III July to September 1483
- PERCY Noble families with regional power-bases

Information drawn from Horrox & Hammond, *British Library Harleian Manuscript 433*, IV, and Edwards, *Itinerary of Richard III*.

have been poised to join the rebels and dissembled until he saw that the rising was doomed.[1]

Paradoxically Stanley was among the king's following at Lincoln when news of the rebellion broke, and where Richard remained for five or six days gathering intelligence and preparing for the royal muster before beginning his journey south. An urgent call to arms went out to York and Lancashire on 11 October, while royal followers including Lovell appealed to powerful kinsmen such as William Stonor to array for the king. The Duke of Norfolk was busy fortifying the capital and advising the council at Westminster, having delegated authority to Lord Cobham, John Middleton and John Norbury, whose force of around 100 men occupied Gravesend in Kent and held the passage across the Thames. In the north-west both Buckingham and Richard canvassed support from Lord Strange, Stanley's son, who left Lathom for an unknown destination around 20 October, allegedly with ten thousand men. The contingents were to meet at Leicester, while a body of horse dispatched from distant Southampton was to join the royal host which arrived at Coventry on 24 October. Pausing at Grantham on the 19th, the royal party proceeded to Leicester where Richard was met by his northern levies including three hundred York men under the command of Thomas Wrangwysh. With mobilization under way, Richard, a seasoned campaigner and a wily tactician, doubtless took military counsel from members of his retinue such as Stanley, experienced in the campaigns of his youth that had threatened Yorkist rule, and Viscount Lovell and Lord Zouche whose knowledge of the south was perhaps greater than his own.[2]

Deliberating in the midlands, he planned to drive a wedge between Buckingham, Morton and the rebels in the west, and the other insurgents in the south before turning his full strength on the duke and Henry Tudor. He might have struck at Buckingham in Gloucestershire by way of the road which joined Coventry and the Severn Valley, or via the old highway known as Watling Street which would have taken him into the west by way of Cirencester. Another possibility would have been to take Watling Street directly through to London and on to the south-east. He was just out of Coventry when firm news of Buckingham's failure to cross the Severn into Gloucestershire enabled him to make his move. Buoyed by Norfolk's defence of the capital and Cobham's success in the south-east, Richard could concentrate his strength on the south-west; thus he altered his route and headed due south from Coventry, probably along the Oxford–Salisbury road. Pausing at Oxford on 28 October, he pressed on through North Tidworth and Hungerford reaching Salisbury, which conveniently bisected the main centres of revolt, on 2 November. Leaving around the 4th, Richard rode deep into the west through Dorchester and Bridport, reaching Exeter by the 8th 'where all his enemies had made a stand'.

Richard III's itinerary: 11 October–25 November.

The series of risings was protracted, widespread and well supported even though the rebels were surprised by Richard's agents who kept him informed of developments throughout the south. Men were in arms well before 18 October, the day stipulated by the act of attainder as the official date of the risings. Kent, of course, had risen prematurely by at least 10 October; at Salisbury men were grouped ready for action by the 17th, while at Brecon Buckingham was prepared well before the day. The duke's standard was raised on the 18th at Exeter, though just when Henry Tudor was expected to invade England is problematic. While Henry's preparations had been under way from at least mid-September, Polydore Vergil gives 6 Ides October, or the 10th, as the possible date of his departure from Brittany, though this seems far too early. Even if Henry had determined to make the south-west coast of England by the 18th, his flotilla would have been delayed by the appalling conditions in the Channel from around the 15th to the 25th. Whatever the case he was still moored in Breton waters on 30 October, and did not drop anchor outside Plymouth Harbour until the first week of November.

The conditions would also have prevented aspiring rebels from remote areas of Cornwall from reaching Exeter. Others from Truro, Fowey and Bodmin managed to join forces, negotiating quagmires before reaching the main road through the rich stannary districts of Callington and Liskeard, crossing into Devon over the flooded Tamar and on through Tavistock eastwards to Exeter. Men from Plymouth took the main road through Tavistock, battling the Walkham and Tavy rivers at Horrabridge and Harford Bridge, which opened out on to the central corridor of Devon, until the nineteenth century one of the main routes to Exeter from Plymouth. Perhaps some from the coastal areas of Dorset and Somerset picked their way through the flooded saltways and on to Exeter as best they could. In the central-southern shires men from south-east Oxfordshire made for Newbury along the Icknield Way, passing seats of prominent rebels such as Stonor, while others from Banbury, Deddington and Chipping Norton crossed Akeman Street, running east–west through the county, before taking one of the many roads across the border, negotiating the River Witney at Stanton Harcourt or Minster Lovell. The Hampshire rebels reached Salisbury by the Winchester to Old Salisbury road, or came from Southampton and Southwick along good pack-horse routes designed to cope with the heavy traffic from the textile industry. Still others from eastern Somerset and Dorset took a section of the ancient road, Fosse Way, between Bath and Cirencester which cut across into north-west Wiltshire, joining up with the Oxford–Salisbury route. In the south-east the road from the capital linking the centres of rebellion at Dartford, Gravesend, Rochester and Maidstone must have been hard going as both the rebels and their pursuers were forced to negotiate isolated areas of the Weald, little more than tracks for moving cattle to and from the upland manors to the Wealdon pastures. 'Sad, deep unpassable road[s] when much rain has fallen', they could well have been sodden in the unseasonable conditions.

Standards were raised in Buckingham's rebellion but it was a conflict without pitched battles and with few clashes of arms, only minor skirmishes and messy affrays. Though the act of attainder and the extant accounts stress the leaders' fiery rhetoric and grisly intent, very little blood was spilt in the struggle (apart from the odd murder and around ten executions). Yet for the knights, squires and gentlemen committed to Richard's overthrow the situation must have been tense as anticipation mounted in the days surrounding the 18th. In the far west the leaders, having deployed men to scan the horizon from Plymouth to Poole for signs of Henry Tudor's flotilla, also watched and waited, fearing the worst with the passage of time, and initially encouraging, later placating, their friends and allies and keeping in check both retainers and tenants. Further east numerous riders were abroad both for crown and country before the 18th; but as time wore on flight characterized the rebels' activity as news of the king's formidable host assembling in the midlands filtered down through the Home Counties. In Kent the bravado of captains whose fearsome orations were designed to invoke an electric atmosphere gave way to exhortations to hold fast, and later still, to contingencies to be adopted by the rebels either for escape or for pleading for their case to an appropriate lord. None the less the leaders showed great resolve in the circumstances. The Exeter rebels under Thomas St Leger, Thomas Arundel, Edward Courtenay, his cousin Piers, Bishop of Exeter, and the Marquess of Dorset and his son waited until the end of the month for the duke's appearance or for Henry Tudor to make land-fall with his Breton army, allegedly 5000 strong. Despite staring defeat in the face, many held out long after reason dictated otherwise, falling back first on Torrington, St Leger's patch, and then on Cornwall before again unfurling their banner at Bodmin on 3 November, the day after Buckingham's execution. A general muster was issued by the Courtenays and John Treffry; local gentry Remfry Densell, Geoffrey Beauchamp and John Rosogan answered to Arundel's authority with men-at-arms, while Ralph Arundel, the latter's cousin, had been pressed by Buckingham himself. The leaders incited the crowd, furnished with swords, clubs, bows and arrows, to 'murder, slay and utterly overthrow the king himself, and . . . to set up another king in his place'. With great endurance, the rebels held Bodmin Castle until mid-November.[3] Eventually, though, even the die-hards were forced to capitulate in the shadow of the royal host. At some point in the conflict the valiant St Leger was captured with two others and beheaded at Exeter Castle on 13 November, almost a week after Richard reached the city.

Little is known of the rebels' activity in the central-south except for their rallying points at Newbury under the leadership of William Norris, William Stonor, Richard Woodville, William Berkeley and others, and at Salisbury under Walter Hungerford, Giles Daubenay, John Cheyne and Lionel Woodville, where their forces gathered before the plan to converge with the rebels from the other sectors. The risings here were abortive as Richard was aware of the Newbury and

Sir Thomas St Leger (d. 1483), and his wife, Anne Plantagenet, Duchess of Exeter (d. 1476). St George's Chapel, Windsor.

Salisbury sectors by 23 October. For the insurgents, his speedy journey through the midlands indicated both Buckingham's failure in Wales and the Marches and Norfolk's success in the capital and Kent, and when the royal host passed through Oxford on 28 October and entered Salisbury on 2 November, the rebels had long since flown.[4] In Kent, however, the men who had earlier risen in the Weald were not so easily dispatched. Numerous rebels caused a riot at Gravesend fair on 13 October where one 'Bonting slew Master Mowbray with diverse others'; perhaps this was John Boutayn, the yeoman of the crown who was sent by Norfolk to quash the rebels but who joined their ranks and was attainted at

Bodiam Castle from the air.

Maidstone. At least one of their number, the yeoman of the crown William Clifford of Iwade, had been arrested by 15 October and was later executed.[5] And though their original plan to hold London before joining the other contingents in a huge show of strength was doomed, they none the less managed to assemble at Maidstone on 18 October under Fogge, Brown, the Gaynesford, Guildfords, Thomas Lewkenor, Richard Haute and more. With the king's men scouring the area they were forced to disperse before regrouping on Penenden Heath; pressing on, they reached Gravesend by way of Rochester on 22 October. Shadowed by the Earl of Surrey and Lord Cobham, they shifted south-west for forty miles reaching Guildford in Surrey by the 25th. Gathering support and provisions, they could well have stopped at Buckingham's estate of Tonbridge and a number of gentry manors in south Kent before crossing into Surrey. Still hounded by the earl at Guildford, a number of rebels led by Thomas Lewkenor retreated to Bodiam castle in the Sussex Weald, where they held out against the king's forces until the second week in November. During the incursion one of Kent's most able captains, Sir George Brown, along with four royal yeomen, was captured and beheaded in London on 4 December.

The collapse of the sectors cited in the attainder did not end the rebellion and it continued well into the new year. Richard's veiled threat in an open letter to the mayors, inhabitants and officers of Plymouth and Saltash on 13 November looms large behind his caution that they 'assist' Thomas Mauleverer, originally sent to watch at Plymouth for signs of Henry Tudor, for 'as long as he shall continue there'. On 6 December he read the riot act at Gloucester for dissent and retaining, only one of the 'divisions' which had 'risen . . . in diverse places within . . . [the] realm', and imposed an oath of loyalty on Southampton. The situation in Kent was critical, however, and for several months royal agents were widely deployed to counter sedition. By mid-January the king was driven to exact an oath of loyalty from all men between the ages of sixteen and sixty at Rochester, Aylesford and Ashford, in numerous towns and hundreds including Rolvendon, Sandwich, Maidstone and Tonbridge, all rebel strongholds, and in all ports in the county except Faversham. Canterbury, a stamping-ground of its hereditary alderman, the late George Brown, and of John Fogge, had already been warned against retaining earlier in the month, and with the rest of the county its people were urged not to 'succour, harbour, nor favour' the rebels and traitors. Tenants and servants from the Kent manors of Brown and Fogge, the Guildfords and other rebels were advised to assist the newcomers, 'not failing hereof as you . . . will eschew our grievous displeasure at your peril'. None the less, according to the Crowland

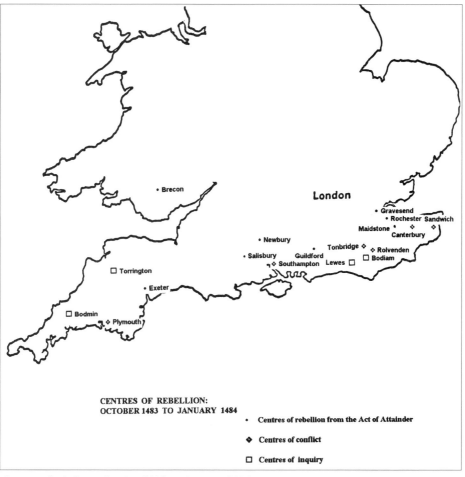

CENTRES OF REBELLION:
OCTOBER 1483 TO JANUARY 1484

•   Centres of rebellion from the Act of Attainder

◆   Centres of conflict

□   Centres of inquiry

Centres of rebellion: October 1483 to January 1484

chronicler, the south reacted violently against Richard's policy of planting northerners on southern estates, supplanting a tradition of generations' standing. The south-west also remained disaffected and, in order to prevent West Country merchants assisting the rebels into exile, in March 1484 the king ordered the Earl of Arundel's son John and Lord Scrope to patrol the Channel. With only limited success, Arundel was charged in August to ensure that all who took to sea pledged their commitment to the régime.[6]

While falsely implying that the rebellion was confined to the period around 18 October, the attainder also deals very broadly with the main centres of revolt.[7] Apart from outbreaks of rebellion at Brecon, Exeter, Newbury, Salisbury,

Maidstone, Rochester, Gravesend and Guildford, there were many ancillary centres entirely omitted as evidenced by the two surviving indictments at Bodmin and Torrington. As these provide the names of only nine of the eighteen men attainted under the Exeter sector, clearly there were other centres of rebellion and other inquisitions, perhaps at Exeter itself or Plymouth, or other trouble spots.[8] East Anglia was completely ignored by the act yet it was represented by leading household gentry, the Brandons, Wingfields and Brewes, who rose in Kent. Rebellion and disorder in Sussex resulted in numerous commissions including one issued by Richard at Exeter on 8 November to deal with the two-week Bodiam siege; while an inquest was held at Lewes into a riot and a murder attempt on Thomas Combe, an associate of Buckingham, who narrowly avoided being stabbed to death with pitchforks by a large crowd on 28 October. Canterbury was volatile and required a royal visit, while Southampton's mayor, Walter Mitchell, was later attainted for colluding with the rebel William Berkeley, its constable, who was in residence on 8 and 21 October, and his kinsman Edward, a key official in the town.[9]

While the act represents a large number of attainders, it does not provide a realistic assessment of those involved in the rebellion; conversely, an attempt to gauge raw numbers must remain purely speculative despite indications of considerable popular support. At Bodmin, for instance, the rebels allegedly raised 'multitudes of people'; while at Torrington the Exeter antiquarian John Hooker cites five hundred indictments. John Stow, responsible for the only surviving account of the Kent rising, wrote that when 'Buckingham was up in the West Country there were many up in Kent; to wit Sir George Brown, Sir John Guildford and his son, Fogge, Scott and Hautes . . . with many other to the number of five thousand'. While Stow's estimate cannot safely be taken literally, nor, given the stature of the rebels, can it altogether be dismissed.[10] The majority, of course, were the rank and file of the rising, lesser men recruited by the leaders who fielded companies of friends, retainers and servants. Most of the royal retainers were from families with a strong soldiering tradition: men whose forbears had been called on to defend the realm for past warrior kings, and whose own military experience included both civil and continental service. Hungerford, Bourchier, St Lo, Norris, Brown, St Leger, Cheyne and others had already won their spurs in battle, and were among the élite band of courtier-soldiers whom Edward had called to France in 1475; others were the scions of families renowned for active service such as Courtenay, Arundel, Guildford, Poynings and Daubenay, who was attainted in 1483 with six of his yeomen.[11]

Many other notables who were caught and lost their lands but avoided attainder would also have commanded solid retinues; according to Harley Manuscript 433 the royal servants Thomas Bourchier, Thomas Audley, William Twynyho, Sir John Donne, Sir William Brandon, Sir William Haute, William Cheyne, John

Wingfield, Anthony Brown, William Tyler and Richard Latimer were among them. The Torrington and Bodmin inquisitions also boast some powerful recruits such as St Leger's brother Bartholomew and Sir William Norris's brother John.[12] While few names are known of the several hundred rebels with Henry Tudor in Brittany, *Materials for a History of the Reign of Henry VII* provides evidence of the depth of Henry's support both in exile and in England, with men of the calibre of John Halwell, William Knight and Robert Skerne, Peter Curtis's kinsman, among the recipients of Henry's bounty. Some were connected with both Tudor and Buckingham; these included John Harper, a Stafford retainer whose brother Richard remained with Lady Beaufort from 1484 until Tudor's accession. Many were from the midlands, including Lincolnshire merchant William Brown, whose brother Edward was also involved, along with the wealthy John Brown, a merchant, alderman and under-sheriff of London. Others were in service to John Welles, Daubenay, Poynings and John Cheyne. Mostly, though, they were men not generally recognized as having lived in exile, such as attainted Newbury rebel Edmund Hampden and from the west Walter Courtenay, William Froste, James Bonython, Stephen Calmady, William Willoughby and Anthony Brown. While the knights and squires had a pool of recruits at their disposal, most of the above would have arrayed men for the cause, while the lesser gentry might also have contributed four or six 'stout fellows'.[13]

Limited though the attainder is, it does offer up some clues which, with a little digging, provide insights into the various links between the centres of revolt. The Woodvilles were well represented in each sector either directly or through their kinsmen.[14] Margaret Beaufort, whose half-brother John Welles was attainted in January, avoided the sentence and was placed in her husband's custody for financing the rebels; Stanley was given her lands for life which were to revert to the crown on her death, and in the short-term he was to ensure that she dismissed her servants and cut all ties with her son. Though mortifying for Margaret, the terms were relatively light, indicating the importance to Richard of Stanley's support. The household component is reinforced with the attainder of eight yeomen of the crown, while the cathedral clergy are represented by the Bishops of Ely, Salisbury and Exeter. Apart from John Morton, Bishop of Ely, at first glance Buckingham's sector seems to have little to connect it with the rebellion. Though the duke heads the official list of rebels, only four men named in the act were with him at Brecon, and while he had assorted ties with most of the principals, he was apparently represented by only one member of his own affinity in another sector, Nicholas Latimer of Dorset, his chamberlain, proscribed at Salisbury. In fact his

Margaret Beaufort at prayer.

cohorts at Brecon represent an odd quartet: his prisoner, the crafty and persuasive Morton; William Knyvet, a chief councillor who managed to avoid attainder; Cambridge master of arts, Thomas Nandyke, termed a necromancer but whose disciplines more accurately embraced medicine and astrology; and John Rushe, a merchant, quite possibly the father of Robert Rushe, executed for his alleged role in the July plot to free the princes from the Tower.[15] Yet Rushe and Knyvet are interesting East Anglian figures who give the rebellion a certain cohesion. A deputy of customs at Yarmouth in Norfolk for the late Earl Rivers, Rushe was also a client of Margaret Beaufort, Lord Stanley and William Stonor. Knyvet had ties with the East Anglian grandees and the Earl of Oxford whose interests he may well have represented at Brecon. Both men had been indicted in Richard's proclamation of 24 October with Dorset, Bishops Morton and Woodville, William and John Norris, George Brown, John Cheyne, Walter Hungerford and other leaders around the south and were crucial as couriers linking Morton and Buckingham with the other centres of revolt.

The attainders provide hard evidence of the rebels' aristocratic connections and include the heir to the earldom of Devon, Edward Courtenay, and members of a number of baronial families such as Hungerford, Willoughby, Poynings, Fiennes and St Amand. Thus it is hardly surprising that suspicion fell on a number of the nobles, apart from Stanley, whose relatives were involved. After years of service to the crown, John Touchet, Lord Audley, whose brother Thomas was among the Dorset rebels, lost his peace commissions in the south and the midlands. On 29 December he was issued with a general pardon, while both he and his son James were pardoned in February 1484 along with Thomas.[16] Robert, Lord Poynings, whose relative Edward was attainted in Kent, was indicted soon after the rising; Sir Richard Fiennes, Lord Dacre, father of the rebel Thomas, was off the bench in the south and the midlands, as was Thomas West, Lord Lawarre, in Southampton and Sussex, and John Bourchier, Lord Berners, in Essex. Indeed, most worrying for Richard was the disaffection of the Bourchiers, a staunch Yorkist family whose scion, Thomas, rebelled in Kent. Again, while the king seemed to have the solid support of his new lieutenants who had been assiduous in their service against the rebels, both the Duke of Norfolk and Viscount Lovell may well have been sympathetic to the revolt which touched a number of their own clients and kinsmen.[17]

The gentry account for around eighty attainders: twenty knights, twenty-five squires, the yeomen of the crown, twenty-four gentlemen, two merchants and one unstyled (though of gentry status), the vast majority of whom had been among Edward's closest servants.[18] In fact each sector was represented by its royal retainers, members of ruling élites who could draw on established networks forged through kinship and service, patronage and profit, providing the rebellion with unity and cohesion. Thus the social and geographical organization of the revolt reflects the pattern of royal office-holding, itself dictated by landed interests, and from Kent to Devon the stewards, constables and keepers were prime agents of conspiracy: Fogge, Lewkenor, Berkeley, Cheyne, St Leger, Halwell and more within a broad band stretching from Rochester, Guildford and Bodiam in the east to Poole, Torrington and Exeter in the west.[19] Prominent families had also managed to spread themselves widely, providing a uniform chain of command best exemplified by the Cheynes: John and two of his brothers were attainted at Salisbury, William, another brother, was indicted in Kent and two more were pardoned at Newbury, one of whom, Alexander, was later attainted. Thomas St Leger had been especially active at Torrington with his brother Bartholomew, while another brother, James, rose in Kent. The Brandons, Browns and Norrises followed suit.

Other patterns of organization are discernible with the aid of grants of pardon issued from February to June 1484, which provide the addresses of men either proscribed or under suspicion. Before the rising rebels had grouped at strategic centres with their relatives or colleagues: Alexander Cheyne was at West Shifford, William Norris's Berkshire manor, with John Norris senior; his brother Roger was at the family's seat, Enburne, with John Kentwood; and William Bampton and Michael Skilling were at another Cheyne manor, Falleston, in Wiltshire. Anthony Brown was found at his brother's Surrey manor, Betchworth, with his sister-in-law Elizabeth. In Somerset William Case was at Daubenay's main holding, South Petherton; John Heron gathered with his co-conspirator and fellow Bridgwater customer, John Baker, at his manor of Lamport Estoner, a principal seat of his patron Margaret Beaufort; while Reginald Bray was at another Beaufort seat, Woking, in Surrey. Many others provided the addresses of the leaders from Kent to Cornwall.[20]

After the main sectors collapsed contingencies went into effect: as Newbury crumbled William Berkeley

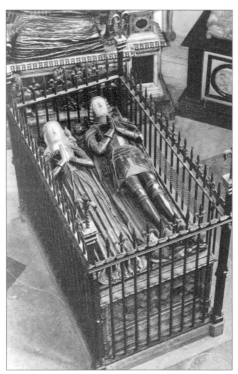

The tomb of Giles, Lord Daubenay KG (d. 1508), and his wife, Elizabeth Arundel. Westminster Abbey.

fled south to alert John Cheyne at Salisbury and to conspire at Southampton. William Norris also headed south with other rebels 'in large number', meeting up with Cheyne and Buckingham's agent and customer at Poole and Bristol, John Kymer, called to account at the exchequer. Initially it would seem that Kymer, realizing that Cheyne and Norris blocked his way to the exchequer, sent his servant instead who was allegedly robbed by Norris. It is more likely though, especially in view of his later activity, that Kymer was in cahoots with the leaders and faked for effect the robbery of his servant. Perhaps he joined the rebels in Brittany, for on 4 February 1484 his goods in Poole were seized; Kymer, 'late customer within our port' having 'departed and gone away with certain duties amounting to a great sum of money . . . by reason of our customs there'. In fact like the constables and stewards, the customers were very much in evidence at flashpoints, including Thomas Brandon at Plymouth; the late Earl Rivers's deputy, Thomas Croft, Kymer's colleague at Bristol; and Reginald Hassall and John Flasby, Buckingham's deputies with Kymer at Poole. Richard Morton, the bishop's brother, listed among the Dorset rebels, was a controller of customs at Poole while Berkeley, who held the same office at Southampton, was joined in rebellion at Newbury by the customer there, Roger Kelsale. Further east Robert Brent, a yeoman of the crown, who was indicted in Kent, was a controller at Sandwich. The customers were well placed to abscond to Brittany with the crown's money to aid the colony in exile, and many were under suspicion as their pardons early in 1484 indicate. Kymer and Cheyne were certainly warmly thanked by Henry VII in 1485 with the toll and petty custom of Poole, and the custody of Dorset lands during the minority of Edward, Earl of Warwick; while Hassall, who fought for Henry at Bosworth, retrieved a post in Staffordshire for 'good and trusty service' beyond the sea and 'on this side', and by Christmas 1485 he was in service to the king's mother.[21]

In the aftermath of the rebellion men had to fend for themselves as best they could. Cheyne made for the west where he was ferried to Brittany with his companion Giles Daubenay, and John Halwell from the Exeter sector, by Devon merchant Stephen Calmady. Other locals assisted the fugitives into exile. Initially at least, some may have found safety and solace in numbers. The Brandons, Thomas and his father, seem to have fled first to Henham in Suffolk with the rebel William Loveday before going into sanctuary. With Richard's men scouring the area, however, home would have been only a temporary haven, and for some a trap as by 2 November Richard had begun to seize the rebels' estates. Thus it was for the headstrong William Brandon the younger, whose Essex manor became the focus of a large-scale riot in mid-December because he refused to relinquish it to Richard's squire, Thomas Tyrell. What followed was a messy affair involving some three hundred armed 'malefactors', who threatened to burn him out.

Eventually Brandon's own kinsman and sworn enemy, Thomas Bruin, ejected him with a large armed posse and held the manor 'against the peace' until 22 January.[22] Kent rebels sought help from family and friends. Walter Roberd of Maidstone, who had sheltered both John Guildford and George Brown, was exposed and later attainted, while Brown was taken and executed. Guildford was captured, tried, attainted and imprisoned in Newgate, but managed at least to escape with his life. Richard Haute was also taken after the revolt and handed over to Lord Cobham in Kent. Some threw themselves on the mercy of the Duke of Norfolk and Viscount Lovell who proved to be sympathetic to their plight. Others sought the assistance of the church which played a role if not in abetting, then certainly in aiding, the outlaws. In Hampshire, Beaulieu Abbey with its franchise 'as it is said . . . as large as the franchise of Westminster', harboured Robert Poyntz and Lionel Woodville. As it was situated on an inlet to the sea, doubtless the abbey facilitated speedy access to an escape route for the rebels. Its significance did not escape Richard, who believed it might also have sheltered the Marquess of Dorset and visited the abbey in November on his way to London following his success in the west. It remained a thorn in his side, however, and on 15 December Richard ordered the abbot, Thomas Nende, to Westminster to provide him with proof of the abbey's sanctuary rights. Clearly Nende was able to plead for his case successfully as Woodville remained there for some time.[23]

Buckingham's rebellion vastly altered the political landscape in the south. While the crown had long maintained networks of servants to manage its interests, the changes in regional policy and patterns of local lordship from 1471, which increased the responsibility of royal retainers, also saw an increase in the crown's reliance on gentry networks. As direct servants of the crown, of course, the gentry had the pick of positions in royal administration, serving their own as well as the king's interest. They also channelled royal authority to the shires through their role as sheriffs, justices of the peace and as commissioners for a range of projects dealing with anything from maintaining the king's canals to levying his taxes and raising his troops. Their role in local government was conducted on a voluntary basis, the only criterion being local pre-eminence. The sheriffs and justices were in fact selected from 'the most sufficient' residents of the shire. Unpaid and onerous though such duties were, principal gentry could hardly avoid such royal service, while for those of more middling status, selection meant at least that they had 'arrived'. In a very real sense, though, the king had to maintain the goodwill of the leading gentry in order to govern effectively, since apart from their role as local governors and administrators, they were his eyes and ears in the country, providing him with vital information on local concerns and prospective servants. During Edward's second reign the system worked well: his knights and squires worked hard in the counties, and under the king the country prospered.[24]

In the absence of rival aristocratic powers and with leadership spread among a number of families in the south, it is possible to make a fairly accurate assessment of the political impact of the revolt against the crown. An analysis of a sample of fifty-five rebels in relation to their household status and local appointments as sheriffs and justices during Edward's last years provides some striking results. Of the forty or so squires of the body under Edward, twenty-four were from the south, eleven of whom rebelled: Thomas Arundel, William Berkeley, William Uvedale, John Cheyne, Thomas Fiennes, Nicholas Gaynesford, Walter Hungerford, Thomas Audley, John Norris, Robert Poyntz and John Wingfield. Of the remaining thirteen from the south, five had already lost peace commissions after Richard's usurpation, while two more rose in 1484. Ten of the twenty-four knights of the body known to have been alive at the time were southerners; six of these rose in 1483: Thomas St Leger, William Stonor, William Norris, George Brown, Giles Daubenay and Thomas Bourchier. Thus, 50 per cent of Edward's southern knights and squires (seventeen of thirty-four royal retainers) led the rising: a striking percentage, based as it is on the known rebels.[25]

Not surprisingly, 48 per cent of the late king's sheriffs in fourteen counties from Cornwall to East Anglia for the years 1478 to 1482 drew their swords in 1483, while 35 per cent of his peace commissioners also took the offensive against the crown. The survey of southern justices and sheriffs averages out at 40 per cent, and provides a useful benchmark of household gentry who reacted against the new régime.[26] It also reaffirms the notion of a pattern of royal service in which the local law enforcers, like the royal administrators, raised the southern counties from the Thames estuary to Land's End. They were, however, Edward's men, selected by the council and approved by him. It may be instructive to see how Richard fared with his own selections for local office and whether or not he found them reliable. While Edward's sheriffs were still in office in October 1483, the peace commissioners had been appointed by the advice of Richard's chancellor and council and approved by him after his accession. Based on the sample, 35 per cent of Richard's own bench selections rebelled, while the percentage soars to 61 with the inclusion of the men stood down directly after the rising.[27]

The great difficulty for the new king was that the rebels far outdistanced their loyal colleagues in terms of wealth, power and position. The sheriffs appointed in 1482 help to illustrate the point. Of the ten officials selected in November 1482, four rebelled: John Treffry (Cornwall), Robert Poyntz (Hampshire), Sir William Haute (Kent), and John Wingfield (Norfolk-Suffolk). (Poyntz was replaced in May 1483 by William Berkeley who also rebelled.) Collectively they held an impressive array of local offices and impeccable connections with the House of York as squires of the body. Of the non-rebels, Sir William Courtenay had the best credentials, but at Edward's death his court connections were enjoyed vicariously, while his local offices fell far short of the workload shouldered by many of the rebels. An intermittent peace commissioner, he was on assorted commissions in Devon in Edward's last years, with his career highlight being his selection as sheriff in 1482. Of the rest, none had solid court connections, and though men of local note they had comparatively little substance.[28] The same applies to the rebel justices. On the August 1483 peace commission in Somerset, for example, Sir Giles Daubenay was the only commissioner, excluding the high-flying legal careerists (most of whom, with their more junior colleagues, side-stepped the rising) with both local and household appointments. While the non-rebel lawyers Thomas Tremayle, John Fitzjames and John Chokke were active in their shires, the only non-legal officers who continued to serve the crown were locals Robert Stowell and William Colowe, Daubenay's clients. Though promoted by Richard in a number of southern counties, neither man approached the others in terms of office-holding, and stalled in comparison with Daubenay.[29] From a family long active in local government, Sir Giles had been sheriff and under-sheriff in the west on four occasions from the mid-1470s, a justice from 1475, a member of parliament for Somerset in 1478, and a royal steward, constable and keeper. Tellingly, none came close to Daubenay's court status as a knight of the body; in short, he was virtually irreplaceable. This is attested by the local additions to the bench after the revolt, of whom, apart from Morgan Kidwelly, Richard's attorney-general, Edmund Gorges, son-in-law of the Duke of Norfolk, and Sir Reginald Stourton were the most eminent, and though the others were men of some local note, Daubenay had regional status.[30]

In Berkshire the situation was more critical still: having already lost the expertise of Sir Thomas Vaughan, Sir Richard Woodville, Richard Grey and Alexander Cheyne by June, three of the remaining gentry commissioners rebelled in October; the three were knight and squire of the body William and John Norris and Sir Thomas Delamare. The others were lawyers. Unrivalled in terms of local office, their revolt left a chasm that Richard could not fill with local men. In fact two of the three added to the December commission were known outsiders: the Northamptonshire lawyer William Catesby, a knight of the body under Richard, and Edward Franke of Knighton, Richmondshire, an associate of Francis, Viscount Lovell. Even in Kent with its high percentage of household knights, Richard was over-stretched. Already without the experience of the Hautes, two of the fifteen members on the 30 July commission were later attainted (John Fogge and John Guildford), while Thomas Bourchier rose but avoided attainder, and John Scott and Roger Brent were under suspicion. Thus the crown lost the rich expertise of a knight of the body, a keeper of the wardrobe, two king's councillors, a treasurer and controller of the household and a marshal of the marshalsea: royal retainers who were viewed by Richard in July as those best qualified to serve the crown. Given that Kent was the traditional training-ground for household servants, their rebellion should not have created the same problems for him as in Somerset or Berkshire, yet the remaining royal servants on whom he depended were lesser gentry.[31] Of the locals, grocer Richard Lee, one of Fogge's satellites in Kent, was a yeoman of the crown, alderman of London and former sheriff; Roger Appleton of Dartford, possibly a Cobham retainer, was a customer with Robert Brent at Sandwich and a purveyor to the household; John Alfegh was a royal receiver along with Richard Page, one of William Stonor's agents in Kent; Robert Reed of Chiddington was termed 'king's servant', and Reginald Sande had served the crown at Dover. None the less, along with the replacements they lacked the solidity of the attainted rebels.[32]

The changes to the traditional patterns of gentry service in the south set in train by the rebellion were immense and their consequences for Richard only too clear. As regional powers with a tradition of service, the rebels' exodus from public life deprived the crown of local knowledge and expertise acquired not simply in a lifetime but over the generations and impossible to replace. To add insult to injury, most were men whom Richard had aggressively cultivated after his brother's death: the royal affinity that was absolutely vital for effective rule. Their revolt forced him to replace over 40 per cent of principal officials in the south including sheriffs and peace commissioners, keepers, constables, stewards and collectors; men who had also served royal needs and offered counsel on local concerns, maintaining the link between king and country. The nexus was ruined by the rebellion. The nature of the upheaval is reflected in Richard's use of his northern retainers after the rising. Twenty-eight of his knights of the body came from north of the Humber/Mersey compared with six during Edward's entire reign. Moreover, his promotion and patronage of a large number of parvenus within the household after the rising highlights the shortfall of eminent gentry available to him because they were either disaffected or under suspicion.[33]

Accepted wisdom discredits the notion of Buckingham's rebellion as a faction-riven movement in which old Lancastrians, many former Clarence associates, or indeed the Woodvilles took the lead. Though it is tempting to cast Margaret Beaufort in a Lancastrian mould for promoting her son's interests in 1483, after twenty-two years of Yorkist rule most disaffected families had long since made their peace with the régime. None the less a group of rebels from breakaway

'Lancastrian' families can easily be identified, such as the Devon earl apparent, Edward Courtenay, disappointed under Edward who favoured first Clarence with the Devon estates and then numerous royal servants after the duke's death. If this rankled with Courtenay, he may well have used the instability in 1483 as a vehicle to achieve his territorial ambitions which were, in fact, realized under Henry VII in October 1485. Like Courtenay, the Lutterells, who had forfeited their lands through Sir James's treason in 1461, failed to secure a reversal. James's son Hugh rebelled in 1483, and in Henry VII's first parliament Sir James's attainder was reversed. The father of John Welles (Lady Beaufort's half-brother), Lionel, Lord Welles, had been attainted in 1461 and John was prevented by Edward from inheriting the barony which was his due by the mid-1470s. Walter Hungerford also may have had an axe to grind because both Yorkist kings had failed to reverse the attainders of his father and brother.[34] Most cases, however, tend to lose their currency against the facts. Courtenay, for instance, not much in evidence at court under Edward, was favoured by Richard. Nominated for knighthood at Edward V's coronation in May, he attended the July coronation, was appointed to the bench in Cornwall and, with other gentry leaders, to the powerful August subsidy commission. Conversely, Hungerford and Welles had prospered under Yorkist administration, becoming two of Edward's most valued squires, and were courted by Richard with gifts from May. Welles provides another dimension to the debate by his early rebellion in August 1483 to restore Edward's son, putting paid to any hint of self-service. Then there were so-called Lancastrians who had a number of incarnations, including Sir Nicholas Latimer. First attainted in 1461 he was reconciled with York in 1463, drawn into Clarence's rebellion in 1471, then came back into favour at Tewkesbury. Having entered Buckingham's service in the mid-1470s he again suffered attainder in 1483, though he spent the rest of Richard's reign trying to dig himself out of trouble. While Latimer turned to Buckingham in 1475, others of Clarence's followers, such as the Courtenays, Edward Hungerford, the Arundels and Berkeleys, John Guildford, George Brown and William Knyvet, became clients of the Woodvilles.

As men who were close to the throne the gentry's patrons reflect their status, and most attempts to identify patterns in the treason of 1483 are as frustrating and ultimately as fruitless as searching for an individual's motivation. In a society tightly bound by kinship, custom and interest, in which views were widely held and deeply felt, it is not surprising that the rebels had solid support from family and friends, exemplified by the Cheynes, Browns, St Legers, Norrises, Brandons, Arundels, Courtenays, Daubenays, St Los and Willoughbys, most of whom were blood-affinity. It could, perhaps, be argued that Cheyne's ties with his kinsman, William Berkeley, encouraged the latter's revolt, or that the links between John Fogge and Richard Guildford, which connected the former with the St Leger and

Cheyne circle, perhaps influenced Fogge. Or that Sir John was unable to avoid the rebellion, like the Hautes, Guildfords and the East Anglian Wingfields because of his connections with the Woodvilles. Or indeed that Cheyne, Fogge and St Leger had lost ground under Richard and like the Woodvilles had a common bond in sedition. Again, some may have been influenced by their service to the queen, such as Nicholas Gaynesford, or to the princes, like Fogge and the Hautes. Assumptions could also be drawn from the family ties between Roger Tocotes and his rebel stepson Richard Beauchamp, Lord St Amand, or between Edward Poynings and Baron Poynings, in trouble with Richard after the revolt, or indeed between Thomas Lewkenor and either Lord Lawarre or Audley, both of whom were implicated in sedition. Clearly such assumptions are problematic and it would be rash to overplay family connection in men's motives, both in view of the complexity of gentry networks in the south and also because of families' apparently divided allegiance, as in the case of the Hautes, the Powderham Courtenays, the Treffrys, Hampdens, Lewkenors, and Harcourts. On the other hand, though some families doubtless hedged their bets in 1483, perhaps others who appeared loyal to the régime were the lucky ones who escaped detection. It may be significant, for instance, that Bartholomew St Leger, indicted at Torrington, provided the Devon address of the Powderham Courtenay, Sir William of Yelston, who apparently did not rebel (though in view of the revolt of two of his brothers, Piers and Walter, it is not exactly a revelation); or that the Sandwich customer Roger Appleton, who helped to crush the rising and was promoted in Kent by Richard, was found to be at Sir William Stonor's Kent manor, Horton, prior to the revolt.[35]

Kinship and friendship certainly played a role in the rebellion, while opportunism, divisions in local politics and wrangles with non-rebels over estates may also have had some influence. Yet if self-interest were a key factor, then petty political point-scoring or disputed patrimony seem unlikely reasons for revolt. Thomas Arundel's quarrel with Sir James Tyrell, his step-sister's husband and one of Richard's favourites, over the Arundel inheritance is a case in point. Under Richard, Arundel received a number of important commissions in the south-west, became a Knight of the Bath and was granted a lucrative custody and marriage. He was unlikely to play fast and loose with his position and indeed his heritage for £200 and a block of manors which were in contention. An inveterate Lancastrian, his father Sir John had come to terms with York after Tewkesbury, and had lived long enough to see his son consolidate in the far west under Edward as a squire of the body. Career-wise, Edward's death had been a boon for Sir Thomas, and much the same may be said for most of the rebels who, in terms of securing local office, fees and annuities held under Edward and in view of the patronage they enjoyed of Richard's gift, had no reason to rebel and every

indication of a bright future under the new king. None the less, research has
produced some interesting reasons for an individual's action. Sir William Stonor's
rebellion, for instance, has been viewed both as the outcome of his hostility to
Gloucester which sent him into the Woodville camp and also as the result of his
links with the Nevilles through his marriage to Anne, daughter of Marquess
Montagu, and thus the world of the higher aristocracy. Whatever else, Stonor was
not compelled to act through self-interest, because as Viscount Lovell's kinsman
he stood to gain handsomely through service to Richard. Nor did his other court
connections dictate his role. To cast him thus would be to underplay his own
position and his appreciation of the political situation.[36] Most probably Stonor
would fit into C. Ross's group of household servants loyal to Edward, who were
appalled at Richard's behaviour towards his nephews and thus demonstrated their
distress in October 1483.[37] Of course if Sir William had been lured into political
intrigue through his connection with the likes of Montagu, he would have had
little time for loyalty to a dead king with whom the Marquess had had an on-
going feud over the Neville inheritance!

Needless to say, Ross's contention makes most sense. It was primarily a Yorkist
rebellion led by the late king's servants who were prepared to accept Gloucester
as protector, but not as king, and whose revolt was the outcome of Richard's coup

Window commemorating the Yorkist royal family. Canterbury Cathedral.

and the presumed murders of the princes. It was not a Woodville revolt. While they had hatched the original plot, it received little household support in May or June. In fact the rebels' original plan to place Edward V on the throne became a bid to replace Richard with Henry Tudor (when it became clear that the princes were dead) through Henry's promise to marry Princess Elizabeth to appease Yorkist opinion, a plan that gained substance through Buckingham's offer of leadership. While loyalty was a key dynamic in the actions of men like Stonor, their impetus in 1483 derived in the main from their desire for effective rule. With strong personal and popular support, the rebels were able to exercise choice in the interests of good government and in the collective as well as the individual's interest. Thus in the king-centred politics of court and country, both royal retainers and ruling élites were reacting against the calibre of the king and the quality of his kingship.

CHAPTER 6

Richard's Response

Richard's failure to master his brother's affinity forced him to re-invent himself in the south. Unhappily for the king his urgent concerns to legitimate his rule, restore stability and counter the Tudor threat, while not insurmountable, created policies that were met with increasing hostility. The revolt of the household had dealt him a hard blow and may account for the severity of the rebels' punishment, and perhaps why they and not others were attainted. Yet the king's response to Buckingham's rebellion was ambivalent and reflects his predicament. Forced to limit the number of attainders to one hundred and three, an unusually high figure passed at a single session of parliament, only the top layer of gentry society was involved. His leniency, however, in waiving the act for many more was not born of high-mindedness or altruism but of necessity, as credible replacements for the royal retainers would be difficult to find. Always insecure and by now deeply unpopular, he was also mindful not to antagonize, more than was humanly possible, powerful gentry circles in the regions. While the number of attainders was necessarily restricted, his treatment of the rebels was unprecedented and again reflects his bind. Though twenty-two attainted rebels and scores more who evaded the sentence received pardons, few obtained even partial restoration of their estates, none received peace commissions within their respective counties, or remained in the household. After the blood-letting surrounding Edward's accession, and again in 1469 to 1471, attainders had been served, men had died and forfeited estates and offices. Yet political society was disciplined and flexible and even some of the most recalcitrant subjects were encouraged back into public life by the crown, sometimes within months of their disaffection. This was not the case with the 1483 rebels. While a number were abroad, the crown made little effort with most of those who remained in England until late 1484, despite growing tension within the regions over Richard's plantations and in the household as opposition to him grew. For their part, though a number of rebels or their proxies took steps to regain favour with the crown, the flight to Brittany of men who might successfully have thrown themselves on the king's mercy, and indeed of others who had not been implicated in 1483, reflects the crown's impossible position.

Richard hit the rebels hard. While the attainders were not formalized until parliament sat in January 1484, he promptly confiscated all offices and seized the land of those under sentence and others who were implicated. While this in itself was not unusual, Richard's haste in redistributing his booty was highly irregular. Forced to replace the top echelons of political society, within weeks he began to reconstruct the south to the advantage of outsiders: his northern imports, servants from the west midlands and East Anglia, as well as reliable southerners, often under the proviso 'as long as the king pleases'. Loyalty, or perceived loyalty, was the price, and withdrawal of office was in Richard's power. Yet royal office in itself could not guarantee status and local acceptance. As the basis of the gentry's power was vested in the land, it was thus the source of their status, and while the grant of office and estate provided an entrée into a county, it meant little else. Moreover, in his desperation to confer status on his new servants, the king bypassed the legal conventions of formally identifying the owner of the forfeited estates, thereby failing to give the forfeiture legal sanction.[1] Just how successful his policy was is a point for later discussion. Yet it is doubtful that Richard enjoyed even a short period of 'unchallenged authority', and likely that he came quickly to realize that status and political acceptance could not be thus conferred. Like the land itself they were not obtained in a lifetime, but won over the generations.

Richard's treatment of the rebels and the patterns both of pardon and punishment are instructive and shed light not only on his response to the crisis but its serious, long-term ramifications. The king imposed five types of penalty in the aftermath of the revolt: attainders, pardons, fines, bonds and imprisonment. The form of punishment meted out to individuals owed as much to topography, timing and connection as to the perceived scale or degree of the treason. John Wingfield and William Knyvet escaped attainder, even though they were included in the act, while many others were proscribed in the various centres but avoided the sentence, such as Sir William Brandon, who was obviously in the right place at the right time. As men were rounded up in Kent some were able to throw themselves on the mercy of the Duke of Norfolk, Lord Cobham and others whose lordship they had known, and who themselves had a vested interest in the outcome of the advocacy. In fact the dealings with the rebels were tinged with corruption, with fines as well as forfeits often being a condition of mercy. Wingfield, for example, avoided attainder by conveying to Richard his claim to the Mowbray inheritance, to the advantage of Norfolk and Sir William Stanley. Brandon no doubt also did the same, forfeiting his manors to Sir James Tyrell,

Edward Redmane (d. 1519) and his wife, Alice Walleys. Harewood, Yorks.

though his son William was attainted. Similarly Knyvet avoided attainder by relinquishing four of his Norfolk manors to Tyrell, for which he was to have recouped several hundred pounds from Richard, but apparently did not collect. In his petition to Henry VII's parliament for restitution, Knyvet claimed he had been pinched by the crown for the sum of 800 marks as well as the estates, and that if he had 'not agreed . . . he should have lost his life, livelihood and goods'.[2] In exchange for their pardons, John Forster and Richard Edgecombe forfeited lands to the northerners Sir Robert Brackenbury and Edward Redmane. Genuflection also met with success in the south-west, where prominent gentry who avoided attainder had either pulled back from revolt before the royal captains arrived, or else submitted to Scrope at Exeter, Torrington and other hot spots; Hugh Lutterell, William Hody, Thomas Brandon, Richard Morton and Bartholomew St Leger were among them. Conversely, the majority of the exiles also came from the south-west including many of the Bodmin rebels, who either chose flight or were forced out to sea owing to the harsh terrain and the king's proximity; these rebels included Dorset, Sir Robert Willoughby, John Halwell, Arundel, Edward and Walter Courtenay, the latter's brother Piers, Bishop of Exeter, William Froste and more who were assisted by good harbours and sympathetic merchants. Curiously, the number of attainders resulting from the Newbury and Salisbury sectors contrasts sharply with those in Exeter and Maidstone, in that almost all the leaders rounded up in the central-south were attainted.[3] There was obviously no plea-bargaining owing to the speed of the royal host and uncertainty among the leaders, Daubenay and the Cheynes, Edmund Hampden and John Harcourt, who preferred to go into exile rather than remain to test the water with Richard. Though in Kent men were better placed to bargain for their lives through powerful sponsors in the absence of the king, leaders including Richard Guildford, Edward Poynings, John Darrell and later, William Brandon junior, also took to sea.

While the attainders reflect circumstance and contacts as well as choice on the part of the rebels, the procedure for pardons varied accordingly and underlines the significance of the revolt. The grant of a pardon was generally the outcome of a consensual procedure between the recipient and the crown, and though the king seldom granted a pardon under the great seal without some initiative first shown by the rebel, he might publicize the fact that he would be sympathetic to their petitions.[4] Rebels who immediately petitioned the king received an informal pardon within days of their treason, and Richard himself drew up lists of men who might approach him, at Beaulieu Abbey in November and at Nottingham in the spring of 1484. Sir Thomas Lewkenor's petition refers to pardons of 'most sorrowful and repentant subjects whose names be marked with the king's own gracious hand in the book of exception', a procedure which, though lacking the authority of an official reprieve, provided a basis for later action. Rebels then approached the crown for a pardon in chancery, and many of these were formally recorded in the first six months of 1484. Speed was clearly a factor and those who wavered paid a price. John Norris, who may well have been sponsored by his kinsman Viscount Lovell, secured a pardon and avoided attainder, having been summoned to appear before Richard in February, 'in all goodly haste'.[5]

For those under attainder, like Sir William Norris, the process became complex and protracted. To begin with, a pardon did not mean either removal of the sentence or restoration of a rebel's estates, but it cancelled his death sentence and outlaw status, enabling him to receive care from kinfolk without threat of penalty. Before the pardon passed the great seal, however, there were criteria to be met. Petitioners had to appoint well-connected sureties of impeccable reputation who would guarantee their continued obedience. They were placed on good behaviour bonds and told where to live and with whom. When the terms had been arranged and the crown petitioned, subjects then had to wait upon the king's good grace.[6] Thus early in 1484 William Berkeley was bound in 2000 marks to the king, and ordered to live in a place appointed by him. Similar conditions applied to John St Lo, Nicholas Latimer, Walter Hungerford, the Gaynesfords and Thomas Lewkenor, who was banished from Kent 'without license of the king'.[7] Though the petitioners invoked the Almighty in their pledge to the sovereign, their subsequent activity made it clear that they were neither investing in his reign nor demonstrating their loyalty to the régime. Berkeley for one had fled England by early October 1484, seven months after his pardon was issued, forfeiting his bond and embarrassing his sureties, Sir Edward Berkeley and his brother-in-law, John, Lord Stourton, who were forced to pay up. The Brandons were granted mercy but the brothers fled to exile, while their father took sanctuary at Colchester allegedly because he feared for his life under Richard, but more likely because, with his sons, he continued to plot against the crown. Some, such as John Harcourt, ignored pardons secured by concerned family or friends, and remained in exile with Henry Tudor, though Harcourt's death in June 1484 suggests that illness as well as intransigence was at play.[8] Bishop Morton's friends at Balliol, Oxford, were early off the mark with their petition to Richard seeking pardon for one of their own, just four days after the king left the University for Southampton in late October 1483. Morton's pardon was in fact granted on 11 December 1484, though he remained in the Low Countries fomenting conspiracy.

The pardons reflect the rebels' own conduct as well as the crown's attitude towards them. Of the attainted Exeter gentry, for example, only John Trevelyan received a pardon: the others apparently neither petitioned nor were approached by the crown, though rebels from the east who remained in England received the king's mercy.[9] With Harcourt an early exception, it is hardly surprising that dissident exiles were not thus favoured, their presence with Henry Tudor a menacing reminder of an inevitable confrontation. Richard had already exercised the royal prerogative of mercy by granting 'all who withdrew from the rebels' cause . . . his full and general pardon' in an attempt to restore the status quo. Around a thousand servants used the period of amnesty to secure their copy for a fee, which (unlike the petitions of the attainted rebels which were sent directly to the king) were recorded in chancery in the first six months of 1484. Traditionally, the crown's friends as well as its enemies took advantage of grants of royal pardon, designed to cover a range of debts and illegal deals as well as treasonable offences.[10] As the majority of the nominees were men of rank and status, the general pardon of 1483 was thus quite out-of-step with others offered, say, during the political crises of Henry VI's reign in 1452, 1458 or 1460 reflecting, of course, the unprecedented nature of the rebellion. As well as seeking indemnity many wanted to be seen to be investing in the régime, others to regain their former standing after their revolt, underlining its significance to both the petitioners and the crown. Pardons were obtained by 12 nobles, 46 knights, 170 squires, 191 gentlemen, 57 merchants, 201 ecclesiastics and 201 yeomen; with groups of trustees and executors, widows and those unstyled comprising the shortfall.

A reversed Tudor rose, set in a garter as part of a border of a chronicle in Henry VII's possession.

Many were royal servants of the household, bureaucracy and estates, along with lesser officials who worked in the ports and towns; others were prelates and members of civic and religious institutions or servants of the aristocracy. Most were under suspicion, real or imagined, by the crown, and some doubtless felt they could be implicated by enemies; in view of the nature of the rising, all felt it wise to petition and indemnify themselves as a precaution.

Of the grants which allow full analysis, around two-thirds of the petitioners were from the south and East Anglia, including half the knights and two-thirds of the squires; 142 grants were recorded for the midlands and 89 for the north. The nobles who took up the offer include the Duke of Norfolk and his son, the Earl of Surrey; the aged Earl of Arundel and his son, Lord Maltravers; the eccentric social climber, William Berkeley, Earl of Nottingham, who was more interested in cashing in his share of the Mowbray inheritance for a marquisate than in any form of subterfuge; George Neville, Lord Bergavenny; John, Lord Stourton; Thomas West, Lord Lawarre; John Touchet, Lord Audley; John Sutton, Lord Dudley; Thomas, Lord Stanley; and Henry Percy, Earl of Northumberland.[11] There is a strong case for the disaffection of Stanley, Audley, and perhaps Northumberland and Lawarre; the others, especially Norfolk and Surrey, seemed fully committed to the new régime. While much time could be spent analysing the motives behind the pardons, the common link between the nobles was their affinity with, and service to, the former king. Indeed the rebellion, widely perceived as a groundswell of opposition from all ranks who had served Edward IV, made a pardon obligatory for the rest.

Collectively the figure includes six of Edward's knights of the body – Thomas Bourchier, Thomas Montgomery, Thomas Burgh, John Gresley, William Stanley and Charles Pilkington – and sixteen of his squires, including Robert Poyntz, John Courtenay, Edward Brampton, John Risley, James Haute and John Fortescue, together with a liberal number of king's carvers, gentlemen ushers and royal yeomen. Some, like Burgh, Brampton, Sir Humphrey Starkey and Sir John Wood, had served Edward at the council table, in bureaucracy and abroad; others, such as Sir Richard Croft, had combined active military service with household administration. Thomas Lygon and John Fineux represented the cream of the legal world as king's solicitors, while most were local governors and royal administrators. Conservatively, some 120 of the squires may thus be identified, with 31 justices of the peace, 30 sheriffs, 12 escheators and 24 customers among their number.[12] Likewise the gentlemen and merchant petitioners reinforce the trend with almost half their number occupied at court or in the counties, occasionally as peace commissioners or sheriffs, but most commonly as customers, collectors, bailiffs and the like. Those who represented the household include John Fitzherbert, the king's remembrancer; Richard Lee, the yeoman of the crown; and Peter Curtis, who had fallen from favour.[13] Some, like John Hayes, were royal receivers and stewards, while others were leading lawyers or wealthy merchants, such as Morgan Kidwelly, Thomas Kebell and John Brown. A solid proportion had narrowly avoided attainder such as the St Leger brothers, Thomas Audley and John Biconell, or had close kinsmen who rebelled; others had been implicated well before the rising, such as John Forster, who had lost a peace commission in its wake, or became disaffected during 1484, including James Blount, Fortescue and John Risley.[14] Several, including Bray and John Horde, had attended Margaret Beaufort or Lord Stanley; there were some of Buckingham's servants such as the Harpers and John Kymer who had most likely accompanied Thomas Brandon, Richard and Robert Morton, Stephen Calmady and John Halwell's brother, Nicholas, at Exeter.[15] Thirty-one of the merchants had been on the royal pay-roll, mainly as customers, and though none was listed as a rebel many of them, such as James Morton and Henry Colet (an intimate of Reginald Bray), might well have been involved.[16] In view of their support to the exiles, no doubt the merchant-customers scrambled to secure a pardon as insurance against penalty.

The church also played a significant role in the rebellion, which clearly left many ecclesiastics feeling vulnerable. The sanctuary rights offered by sacred houses, which could be extended for an indefinite period, held obvious attractions for outlaws during periods of crisis. Yet the church was also actively involved with a number of petitioners linked to centres of revolt, most notably David Hopton, Archdeacon of Exeter, and Thomas Nende, Abbot of Beaulieu. Others can be linked to specific families such as David Berkeley, prior of the Church of Peter and Paul in Plympton, Devon; John Bourchier, Archdeacon of Canterbury; and a deacon from the Brent family of East Malling.[17] The many petitions from Gloucestershire, Wiltshire and Hampshire highlight ecclesiastical feeling against the régime and the region's significance in this context. Lionel Woodville's sedition at Thornbury with Robert Morton, Archdeacon of Gloucester, probably also involved the latter's colleague, Henry Dene, prior of the monastery of Llanthony, Gloucestershire, and one of the late king's intimates. Dene obtained his pardon on 26 February as did Richard Chyne, Abbot of St Mary, Cirencester, and later the deacons and canons of the cathedral church there. Like Beaulieu, the abbey may well have given sanctuary to rebels in late October.[18] By far the most interesting pardons were secured by Thomas Rotherham and John Russell, archbishop and bishop, respectively (and past and present chancellors and keepers of the privy seal), and Oliver King, canon of the collegiate Church of Mary of Southwell, and Edward's secretary. All three were disaffected servants of the late king and of Edward V, and were themselves under suspicion, evidenced by the imprisonment of Rotherham and King in June 1483.[19]

While none of the yeomen was in service to Edward IV, many were implicated in sedition as tenants and servants of the gentry whose address often signalled their revolt. Sir Thomas Fulford, the Courtenays, Sir John Fogge, the Guildfords and Gaynesfords, Sir William Norris, the Hungerfords, Tocoteses and many more were among their masters. Others had been in service to Buckingham at Penshurst or Tonbridge in Kent and at his Essex manor, Writtle.[20] As itinerants they were ideal agents for spreading the word. In this context the pardons demonstrate that the rebellion cut across the levels of society, exposing scores of rebels from yeomen to knights and prelates. Through their various official positions, the knights and squires were able to reach large sections of the populace. The gentlemen, serving nobility or royalty as lawyers and escheators, often doubling as merchants and tax collectors, were also able to spread the news and organize themselves across the south. The church assisted with protection and practical help, as well as its own representation among rebel ranks. Equally, the yeomen acted as couriers and were ready for action at strategic points. Nowhere is the cross-section of rebels more evident than in the West Country where 181 pardons were granted to 5 knights, 36 squires, 40 gentlemen, 14 merchants, 39 ecclesiastics and 47 yeomen.

Rather than being primarily a roll-call of the disaffected, the pardons identify the common factor among the petitioners as service to Edward IV. In this sense the general pardon was as much a concession to public sentiment as a cheap and convenient way for the régime to offer patronage for 'the greater security' of the realm. In fact coming so soon after his coup the revolt was a mirror of political opinion which reflected Richard's urgent need to restore both his credibility in the south and confidence in his rule. Despite the pressing concerns at home, he also turned his attention to the exiles, many of whom were not, initially at least, as committed to Henry Tudor's cause as they were opposed to Richard's rule. The king, of course, was well aware of the pretender's enhanced status, and of the threat posed by the political exiles who gained steady support in the south. In fact soon after Edward's death, when Francis of Brittany relaxed the conditions of custody under which Henry Tudor was held and permitted Sir Edward Woodville, in flight from England, to join him, alarm bells rang and Richard wasted little time in sending envoys to Francis II to negotiate for Tudor's extradition. He also dispatched a cordial note to Louis XI, who feared a policy of rapprochement between the two. Indeed an Anglo-Breton alliance might also attract Maximilian of Austria and would be a major threat to France's security. None the less Louis replied in an upbeat fashion, offering his full support to the new monarch. While renewal of the truce between Brittany and England was important, Richard's agent Thomas Hutton was also to inquire how the land lay between Francis II and Edward Woodville, and to ascertain whether or not a Breton offensive seemed likely. Clearly the Tudor problem was also high on the agenda. In fact in July and August the duke dispatched his own envoys to Richard's court to remind the king that military assistance to Brittany was vital if he were to keep the pugnacious Louis XI from seizing the independent duchy: essential not just for Brittany's security, but England's also.

As for Henry Tudor, having embarked on his English invasion with Francis II's full consent and backing, he understood only too well his diminished value to Brittany as well as to France in their relations with England after the débâcle, and he no doubt welcomed the political refugees who represented his only hope of a second chance at the English crown. For their part, though they formed a loyal community tightly bound by experience and aspiration, their situation was far from ideal. As members of English élites long accustomed to wealth and position, they found themselves suddenly in exile, under sentence of attainder and bereft of family and friends. Lacking regular and reliable news many were doubtless fearful for the security of loved ones left at home, and felt isolated and vulnerable; for the first time in their lives they were dependent on charity for survival. The duke helped out with monthly allowances paid to Dorset, Sir Edward Woodville, John Halwell and the Willoughbys, totalling 800 livres. The colony also received from him 3,100 livres in June 1484, and further welcome assistance from civic and religious corporations, some of which was underwritten by Francis himself.

Snapshots of the community abroad reflect their collegiate spirit, piety and common goals as well as their hardships. They regularly attended mass at Rennes Cathedral, and their spiritual needs were succoured by cathedral clergy such as Piers Courtenay. In Vannes for only a year they seem not to have mixed with the Vantois, save for an unfortunate episode involving one of their number in which a local was murdered and his widow reimbursed by Francis for 200 livres. Henry was deeply obligated to the exiles to whom he doubtless offered his heart-felt thanks in early discussions with them at Rennes. There was, of course, great symbolic significance in the ceremony on that first Christmas Day in 1483 at Rennes Cathedral

Elizabeth of York.

when Henry pledged himself to Elizabeth of York, and the English exiles paid him formal homage as their future sovereign.[21] Nevertheless these months cannot have been easy for the pretender who was burdened with expectations on the one hand, yet largely stripped of hope on the other. They were little better for Richard. While the king was fully aware of the threat posed by the offshore rebels, his situation was complex, with numerous factors at play. If he had wanted to entice the gentry home early in 1484, or for that matter seriously cultivate those who had remained in England, he was in a bind. Having altered the traditional basis of power in the south with his creative policy, he could hardly remove his followers' props without alienating them. Conversely, in the face of increasing hostility, nor could he trust the rebels whose expertise he was forced to replace. Thus matters stood: without forty per cent of the household, the scheme Richard adopted to reinforce political society and the rewards used to confer political status proved in the short term untenable, and in the long term his undoing.

The men from the north quashed the revolt, indicted the traitors and before the dust had settled took over their estates. Within weeks of the crisis the king's policy had matured with many of his captains ensconced as royal retainers, local officials and landlords in those areas where they had resisted the rebels. Among those who had come south in May were the high-profile Sir Richard Radcliffe of Yorkshire, Lancashire's Sir Ralph Ashton and Sir Robert Brackenbury, all members of Gloucester's ducal affinity. Others joined Richard to confront the rebels in October and were promptly introduced into the regions: Sir Thomas Markenfield, Halneth Mauleverer and Edward Redmane in the south-west; in the central-south and further east Sir Christopher Ward and Sir John Saville, William Mirfield, Ralph Bigod, Sir Marmaduke Constable and Sir Robert Percy. By the end of the reign around three dozen northerners had been placed in the south. With the exception of Radcliffe and several others, the vast majority, like Brackenbury, were lesser gentry in their home counties whose patronage was thus quite out of context. Radcliffe, Ashton, Ward, Constable and Markenfield became Richard's knights of the body, and Mirfield, a king's knight, while John Huddleston, Edward Franke and Redmane were among his squires. Replacing Edward's core-affinity their duties were to guard the south against revolt and defend the realm against invasion. Great responsibility was theirs with the 'Black Knight', the brutish Ashton, appointed vice-constable of England on 24 October and empowered to try rebels without appeal and to snare those 'guilty of lèse majesté'; Percy became controller of the household, Ward, master of the harthounds, and Brackenbury, constable of the Tower. Most became fixtures in local government as sheriffs and peace commissioners. Whereas only three of Gloucester's retainers were justices in the southern counties before October, Huddleston and Radcliffe in Gloucestershire, and Ashton in Kent, from December the latter was joined by Constable and Bigod, and later by Sir Edward Stanley, Sir John Savage, Sir William Harrington, Richard Ashton, Robert Brackenbury and William Mauleverer.[22] The intended role of the imports is evident in Edward Redmane's commissions and offices: sheriff of Somerset and Dorset in November 1483, he was on the Wiltshire bench in December, and a commissioner of array, arrest, imprisonment, and oyer and terminer in Wiltshire, Dorset, Devon and Cornwall in 1484.[23]

Given traditional patterns of gentry service and the powerful alliance of interests at stake, it is little wonder that local society was scandalized by Gloucester's use of his northern affinity. Their outrage is recorded by the Crowland chronicler who railed against Richard's men 'whom he planted in every part of his dominions', to the 'shame' of the southerners who 'murmured ceaselessly and longed more each day for the return of their old lords in place of the tyranny of the present ones'.[24] Their presence, of course, was a constant reminder of unwelcome change: the removal of ruling families, of patronage and provenance. Though gentry circles turned on custom, connection and status, membership altered over time through extinction and attainder, or the reshuffling of a notable's following as his interests expanded across county borders. The king's retainers were also agents of change to suit royal need as well as satisfy their own burgeoning interests; thus the gentry were accustomed to different faces – but not in the fashion or with the speed of Richard's imports. As they were accompanied by their own kinsmen and clients, in some areas the social order was stood on its head as key gentry and their circles of influence were overturned by the new local leaders and their minions. In the case of absentee landlords like Sir Thomas Everingham who continued in service at Calais, and Constable who was often busy in the midlands, outsiders managed their interests, preventing a new order based on royal authority vested in the king's man from developing, and blocking off important channels of access and patronage for lesser gentry and smaller fry. Society's rage at the unprecedented action from above was also fuelled by instances of blatant self-serving as northerners, wearing their official caps, seized manors which on occasion they kept for themselves. In Kent, for instance, William Mauleverer retained the land of the deceased William Langley, even though it had been granted to Langley's widow. Strong-arm tactics were used by the sons of Sir Ralph Ashton in order to have their way with other Kent manors. Due to competing claims the Brandons' estates generated a number of tussles, though in view of the younger William's violent reputation the king's men probably got more than they bargained for. Instances of cattle-rustling and theft were also reported, and probably much else in the scurry to secure the forfeits.[25]

In truth Richard had cast his net more widely than the north for replacements, using midlanders and East Anglians as well as reliable locals who had shown him early support, and who could operate within their area of influence. The lawyer William Catesby, a former Hastings retainer, and John Kendal from Leicestershire and Warwickshire both made the inner sanctum of service, the former as a councillor, the latter as king's secretary, and became landowners in the south-west and south-east respectively. Norfolk's clients Sir James Tyrell and Gilbert Debenham welcomed Richard and prospered, while Tyrell's brother Thomas became master of the horse. West Country powers Sir Henry Bodrugan and Morgan Kidwelly also served the king, while others closely associated with the régime included Sir Richard Croft and his younger brother Richard, Avery Cornburgh, John Sapcote and Sir Thomas Montgomery. Most had been Edward's knights and squires of the body, and remained thus under Richard, though Bodrugan and Croft were newly created. Many others, of course, conducted local affairs: Edward Hardgill, Richard Lewkenor, James Haute, Sir Richard Harcourt and Sir Philip and John Courtenay, both of Richard's chamber, among them. The king's affinity was also reinforced by a number of northern peers with Lords Scrope of Masham, Lumley, Dacre, Fitzhugh, Scrope of Bolton and Lovell conspicuous in southern affairs. Lovell, for instance, already Richard's chamberlain, became chief butler of England, and Lord Scrope of Bolton, his councillor. Nor were a number of the southern and midland peers averse to the government with Lords Dinham, Grey of Codnor and Dudley all serving as Richard's councillors and Maltravers, Grey of Powys and Ferrers of Chartley prominent in royal service. Superficially at least other nobles backed Richard: his son-in-law the Earl of Huntingdon, his brother-in-law the Duke of Suffolk, and his nephew the Earl of Lincoln, along with the elderly Earls of Arundel and Kent and Viscount Lisle; all were among those who shared the spoils.

Thus others apart from Richard's northerners had a hand in changing the face of the south, and while the age-old prejudices between north and south occasioned by distance, custom, wealth and politics were inflamed in 1483, hostility was kindled not so much by regional bias as by royal interference with ruling élites.[26] The king's introduction of twenty-eight outsiders to replace Edward's knights of the body, who had long represented the king's rule in the

Sir Roger Tocotes (d. 1492). Bromham, Wilts.

counties and county concerns at court, was a grave mistake. When they took up residence Richard ordered local bailiffs, farmers and tenants to deliver up their rents, 'not failing hereof, as you will eschew our grievous displeasure'. Most paid little heed and when Marmaduke Constable settled into Buckingham's Kent lands, the locals soon made him aware that he was not among his own people. Yet as he had been 'deputed' by royal letters to live among them their loyalty, service and, of course, rents, were demanded. The locals maintained their rage, however, as the orders against liveries during the period attest. Hostility was not confined to Richard's northern servants. When Lord Dinham's brother Charles moved into John Halwell's forfeited Devon manors and Bodrugan was assigned rebel lands in Cornwall, royal letters declared both their right of entry and their tenants' obligations; yet the stern warning which accompanied the orders underlines the radical nature of the changes and the expectation of trouble even with the tenants of southern landlords. Letters of protection also accompanied royal agents in their task of rounding up the rebels. Thus when John Norris was taken before the king by the Duke of Norfolk in February 1484, all 'officers, ministers and subjects' were commanded upon their 'liegances' not to 'interrupt' royal interests or agents, suggesting that the rich bounty placed on the heads of Guildford, Lewkenor, Haute, William Cheyne and others in Kent was not altogether successful.[27]

The scale of offices and estates reissued after the rising best reflects the stature of those indicted in 1483 and the upheaval their replacement wrought. Thousands of pounds of prime property changed hands throughout the land, most of it in the south and East Anglia. The chief beneficiaries were Norfolk, who, apart from his Mowbray inheritance, acquired numerous estates from the Rivers and de Vere holdings in East Anglia, while his son, created Earl of Surrey, was favoured with an ostentatious annuity of £1,100 from duchy of Cornwall revenue. The duchy was also bled for the Earl of Lincoln's annuity of £176, a nice complement to his £300-worth of lands. Baronial members of Gloucester's affinity, Lords FitzHugh, Zouche and Scrope of Bolton were also blessed with grants in the south. In fact of land grants in Devon, Cornwall, Somerset and Dorset approaching £3,000, excluding the Duke of Norfolk's acquisitions, around £2,360 went to outsiders with a number of northern and midland lords as major beneficiaries. None the less gentry members of Richard's affinity came off best, Radcliffe obtaining Courtenay lands amounting to close on £500, with Markenfield and Everingham also richly endowed, the latter picking up St Leger's castles of Barnstaple and Torrington. Markenfield, with Radcliffe's brother Edward, John Nesfield and

Edward Redmane profited by the dispossession of Sir Robert Willoughby, Sir Roger Tocotes, Walter Hungerford and Richard Edgecombe to the tune of over £400, while in the south-east John Savage, William Harrington, William Mauleverer, Ashton and Brackenbury acquired the pick of the rebels' lands.[28] The plum offices were also theirs with some ten constableships in the south-west changing hands in a few weeks: Exeter, Old Sarum and Southampton were taken by Scrope, John Musgrave and John Hutton respectively. The latter, of only middling status in county Durham, was created a squire of the body and treated to most of William Berkeley's possessions in south-west Hampshire in an attempt to restore the king's rule in the county; his retainers, referred to by locals as 'the northern men', gained numerous grants in the New Forest. West midlanders also received meed for service, including Humphrey Stafford of Grafton, Thomas Stafford and Ralph Bannaster; as did a number of East Anglians and southerners, including Lords Dinham and Cobham, Ralph Willoughby, Sir James Tyrell, Sir Thomas Montgomery, Morgan Kidwelly and John Risley.[29] Where possible Richard enabled his servants to build on existing interests acquired through marriage or patrimony; thus Lovell obtained the Oxfordshire and Berkshire lands of Stonor and Norris, and augmented his interests in Wiltshire and Hampshire; the Earl of Northumberland, Brackenbury, Ashton and Mauleverer were likewise fortunate. As well as lands in the south, Lord Stanley acquired the north-west lands of Sir Roger Tocotes, as well as his interests in the Home Counties.[30]

The scale of their rewards in terms of offices and estates can most effectively be gauged, however, by an assessment of the attainted rebels' returns through Richard's reign. Few had direct access to their forfeited lands, though Hungerford was regranted some of his estates, William Uvedale was able to farm one of his manors, Nicholas Gaynesford received the revenues from a Kent estate, and Thomas Brewes obtained £10 from an Ipswich fee farm. In several cases the kinsmen of rebels received forfeited estates which effectively gave control back to the owner, thus Latimer, Thomas Fiennes, Richard Haute and the Gaynesfords received some assistance.[31] Concessions had also been made to some of the rebels' wives, including Anne Harcourt after her husband's death in exile, and Alexander Cheyne's wife, Florence, who was taken into the king's care 'for her good and virtuous disposition' and given the wardship of her husband's estates. Elizabeth Daubenay and Catherine Arundel were also given pensions from their former lands. Yet the rebels' gains were negligible considering the scale of their losses, and most could expect little, especially if their land were divided among Richard's retainers. Though a quirky grant saw John Rushe issued with a licence to resume his livelihood in trade, the rebels who petitioned for their estates all failed. A case in point concerns Thomas Lovell whose petition, recorded on 2 February 1485, was not supported. In terms of grants of local office the pattern was repeated;

none of the attainted rebels was restored to the bench in his principal county nor employed in estate management, though Brewes and John Wingfield bobbed up in odd commissions. The latter clawed his way back through the lordship of Norfolk, gaining a knighthood for his trouble, though the door to the household remained firmly shut.[32]

Facing mounting opposition on a number of fronts, Richard's most pressing task was to legitimize his rule. All but the most feeble-minded must have known that he had no grounds for his usurpation, yet it had been easier for the greater polity to accept the soft propaganda of would-be prophets such as Buckingham, backed by influential theologians, than to confront the reality of Richard's coup. Had he been able to accelerate the legal formalities to ratify his title he would surely have felt more secure six months on. Buckingham's rebellion, however, had put paid to his first parliament called for November 1483. It finally met at Westminster on 23 January, and although no records are extant, it was most likely packed with Ricardians and its speaker was none other than William Catesby, who was skilled in the art of counsel but unsure of the ways of parliament. Its legislation ratified Richard's title and right to the throne and attainted the rebels, and was sanctioned, according to the Crowland chronicler, through fear rather than faith. The aim of the *Titulus Regius* was to still men's minds and to assuage all doubts concerning his claim, which was his by right of his nephews' bastardy. Using propaganda reminiscent of the earlier attack on Dorset, it denounced Edward's court as having been corrupt, promiscuous and self-indulgent, in contrast to Richard's which was a model of virtue. Yet the king's deep insecurity is evident in an oath of loyalty to his son Edward, which he extracted from high-ranking officials, to be adhered to in the event of his death; this was followed by a public showing at Westminster of his 'title and right' before city notables, an event which was reproduced in major towns throughout the land.

Despite the formalities and the sideshow, the king's power-base diminished as the weeks slipped by, and he seemed to trust few of his servants in either the household or the regions, save for his northern affinity. His qualms over men such as Peter Curtis, temporarily removed from office in September 1483, are understandable. But there were many others who also never fully enjoyed the crown's confidence. Some were removed from the regions yet were retained at court under Richard's watchful eye; others remained as local governors yet left the household.[33] While the graft of his ducal connection on to the south had radically altered patterns of service, his ability to exploit remaining networks for gentry support had been undermined both by continuing conflict and his own insecurity. At a time when he needed to cultivate the locals, the king's behaviour may thus be explained. Already operating with reduced numbers, he relieved others at court including Sir William Huddesfield, Edward's attorney-general, Sir James Crowmer, John Lye, William Middleton, a gentleman usher of the chamber, and Edward's knight and squire of the body, Sir Thomas Montgomery and John Risley, respectively. On the other hand Thomas Fowler, John Sturgeon, Robert Pemberton, Thomas Wintershulle and Thomas Roger, lost county peace commissions though they remained in the chamber.[34] Fowler and Sturgeon were selected as sheriffs by Richard in November and should have been among his most trusted officials; but with other sheriffs such as John Barantyne and Ralph Willoughby, whose kin and colleagues were part of the early groundswell against him, and who themselves had lost office, his choices doubtless caused him great unease.

Indeed the king's position in the south became ever more tenuous. While the general pardon was both a conciliatory gesture and designed to bolster his credibility, his plantation experiment was a disaster with a hefty price, as increasingly the south viewed the scheme as the worst form of cronyism. In fact the post-rebellion carve-up affected many more than the rebels and their immediate circles. Richard's promotion of southern gentry who had been less favoured under Edward led to the heightened expectations of servants such as the Powderham Courtenays, Sir Philip and John, of spoils on a par with the outsiders, given the economic returns thought to be at the king's disposal. Yet their gains in Devon were modest and mean-spirited compared to those of northerners such as Everingham and Halneth Mauleverer, men of commensurate household status.[35] Of the thirteen southern servants rewarded with grants in Devon, Cornwall, Somerset and Dorset, Lords Cobham and Dinham and John Sapcote received a stake of around £360, while the rest, including Charles Dinham, Morgan Kidwelly and the customers Thomas Grayson, Richard's yeoman, and Thomas Baker, accounted for a meagre £280. The fact that southern servants obtained such a small share of the forfeits created enormous hostility, and from early 1484 Richard had also to contend with a disgruntled counter-class of former supporters who added theirs to the growing chorus of dissident voices. As his base in the south crumbled he was forced into an even greater reliance on, and patronage of, his old affinity who secured what little remained in Richard's treasury. To many his policies appeared moribund, and in numerous circles the notion that the king had forfeited the right to rule gained strength. In his attempt to restructure society using men from the north, it was not so much that Richard failed to appreciate the nature of political life in the south and the role of Edward IV's servants, but that he had no choice. The irony is that through his systematic colonization of the south Richard created the dysfunction he strove so hard to avoid.

CHAPTER 7

The Politics of Disaffection

Richard's take-over forced changes to Edward's regional policy, and Buckingham's rebellion caused him to experiment with existing loyalties. As king's lieutenant in the north he was part of the successful team that had maintained the balance of power from 1471 with Northumberland, Hastings, the Stanleys, the Woodvilles, the Duke of Norfolk and key baronial and gentry families. Gloucester had excelled as an administrator and at 'good lordship' while he consolidated his own interests. After his coup he broke with Edward's policy of devolution of power and created a council through which he brokered royal authority directly to the region. This incensed local powers, especially the Earl of Northumberland with his high hopes of regional hegemony, given Richard's newly elevated position. The earl was confirmed as warden-general of the Marches and acquired Buckingham's stewardship of England and the rich lordship of Holderness, but his actual role was not extended; Richard in fact retained the wardenship of the West March with Lord Dacre as his deputy. His son's death in the spring of 1484 forced the king to revise his conciliar policy and in the summer he chose his nephew John de la Pole, Earl of Lincoln, as his political heir to head the council. Admittedly Lincoln was a royal kinsman, yet he was almost landless in the north and his appointment was a slap in the face for Northumberland whose position made him by far the better candidate. As great powers for over a century, the Percies had always enjoyed strong local support and led formidable retinues. Their military exploits were renowned and in many quarters the Percy name conjured images of victories which, in fact, belied the reality of their situation for much of the fifteenth century. With the death of his adversary Warwick the Kingmaker in 1471, Percy was restored to the earldom and thus was able to rebuild his position, though Richard, as head of the Neville affinity in Yorkshire, was clearly the king's man in the region. While Gloucester and Henry Percy had shared an intense rivalry for regional control they had also co-operated when necessary, particularly after Edward's death, and during Richard's bid for power and the subsequent rebellion. Thus his treatment of Percy in 1484 confirms both his desire to retain control of the area and his uncertainty with his leading nobles. Still, at a time when he needed to shore up his position and invest proven agents with responsibility as his brother had done, he showed acute political naiveté which was to cost him dearly in 1485. Stung by Lincoln's promotion, Northumberland probably found his affinity attenuated as his men were tempted south by royal bounty.[1]

None the less Richard was aware of other, more obvious candidates for disaffection in the north-west. After Lord Stanley's imprisonment with Hastings in June, a detente of sorts had been reached through necessity, according to Vergil, as the king dreaded Stanley requital in Lancashire. Stanley and Gloucester had locked horns over competing interests in the north-west in the 1470s, and local history has it that Stanley was successful in that affair. While Richard was wary of their loyalty and fearful of their might, for their part the Stanleys may have felt challenged by Richard's officials in Lancashire, particularly their sworn enemies, the Harringtons of Hornby, and perhaps feared changes to the pecking order. In 1483 Buckingham's own revolt possibly created an ally for Richard in Stanley; certainly the family was warmly rewarded for its support: Thomas obtained £700 worth of far-flung estates and a £100 annuity, replaced Buckingham as constable of England, became a knight of the garter and then steward of the household, having joined Richard at the council table with his son, Lord Strange. His brother Sir William became chief justice of north Wales and constable of Caernarvon with a £600 stake in the Welsh borderland. Richard's generosity also extended to many of their clients who received annuities. Yet he was also careful not to expand Stanley's role and to reward his royal officials and retain his own offices. In Wales the king had deployed Sir Thomas Vaughan at Brecon, Richard Williams at Pembroke, and the Tyrells and John White in strategic positions along the south coast to bolster his position; parts of his dominion in the south-east were still lawless, however, while in the north Caernarvon under Sir William Stanley was fractious and Richard had to remind the locals to be 'at all seasons, aiding, obeying and assisting' the new sheriff, Sir Thomas Tunstall. In fact given that the Stanleys' domain now included north Wales, midland territory and the country between Shrewsbury and Lancaster, and that their military power was exceeded only by Norfolk's, the promotion of Thomas underlines Richard's vulnerability.[2] The fact that he was forced to favour the second most powerful magnate in the realm, whose stepson had just mounted an invasion from abroad, whose wife was an instigator of the plot and whose own loyalty was entirely suspect, created problems for the king which would have required a leap of faith to remedy. His other aristocratic replacement in south Wales was the politically inept former second Earl of Pembroke, William Herbert, who had lost his title under Edward, but rose again under Richard, marrying the king's natural daughter Katherine, and receiving into the bargain 1,000 marks a year and the office of chief justice of south Wales.

Elsewhere the king was also uncertain. The midlands had long proved unpredictable and for much of the century had lacked consistent aristocratic control. With Buckingham's death, the Stafford heir was a minor; so, too, was the Talbot Earl of Shrewsbury, and the demise of both the Hastings and Woodville factions left only minor peers, Lords Audley, Zouche, Grey of Codnor, Ferrers of Chartley and the octogenarian Dudley to rule the region for the crown. Buckingham had had little time to consolidate in the north-west midlands, which as he found out before his death had shown preference for the lordship of lesser nobles over major powers, and Richard was aware that a good deal of fine-tuning of local offices would be necessary, particularly in Staffordshire, as loyalties settled and men declared themselves. He was chary of Audley whose family had rebelled, of old Stafford retainers such as the Harpers, Hassalls, Bagots and Egertons, and of former Hastings men such as the latter's nephew and Edward's knight Sir John Ferrers, William Bassett and Humphrey Stanley, all of whom had been dropped from the bench after the rising. As the king was concerned to prevent the old Hastings affinity from rearing its head, he again chose to plant northerners in strategic midland counties. In Staffordshire Sir Thomas Wortley and Sir Marmaduke Constable were appointed to the shrievalty and Constable also acquired the Tutbury stewardship. Outsiders also padded the peace commissions in Staffordshire, including Norfolk and Edward, Viscount Lisle, doubtless to the chagrin of the locals as neither man had interests in the county.[3] Wortley's orders to the gentry against liveries underlines Richard's fear, and the fact that Dudley was the only local noble sufficiently trusted to lead commissions of array in 1484 is telling. Elsewhere, Richard's squire William Catesby was deemed suitable for securing the Hastings affinity outside duchy control, in Warwickshire and Northamptonshire.[4]

Despite the insecurity that shaped his policies, Richard took comfort from the support of nobles such as his chamberlain and confidant Viscount Lovell, whose substantial base in the Thames Valley and network of clients made him a valuable ally and crucial in the new order. Richly endowed in the north and midlands, Lovell held as his grandfather's heir numerous manors from Gloucestershire across to Hertfordshire.[5] Other asset-rich lords on whom Richard might call for aid were Viscount Lisle and Lords Bergavenny, Zouche, Scrope of Bolton, FitzHugh, Dacre and Ferrers, as well as an array of southern barons.[6] None the less John Howard, Duke of Norfolk, was the obvious choice as his mainstay in the south. The Howards' great rise through the century was largely facilitated by the marriage of John's father to a daughter of Thomas Mowbray. The eclipse of the de la Pole Dukes of Suffolk and the de Vere Earls of Oxford in East Anglia following the Yorkists' success also assisted their advancement. With Mowbray blood in his veins, John Howard quickly established a powerful circle in East

THE DUKE OF NORFOLKE KILLED AT BOSWORTH FEILD

Jockey of norfolk
For Dickon thy

be not too bold
master is bought
and sold

John Howard, Duke of Norfolk.

Anglia and at court where he was elevated to the peerage in the late 1460s for his singular ability in the household, at counsel and in battle. With impressive political and military credentials, he combined the traditions of the courtier-knight with the presence of a natural leader; having been an enormous asset to Edward, he was also vital to Richard in the new scheme as earl marshal of England. For his part, having been deprived of his share of the Mowbray interest under the late king, Howard owed Richard heavily for his dukedom in 1483. The exigencies of the period successfully tested his talents and he was a workhorse for the régime in 1484. On paper his power was considerable, with around a thousand men ready to serve him at short notice.

Nevertheless if Richard had hoped to exploit his networks for solid gentry support in East Anglia and the Home Counties he was sorely disappointed. While the duke provided him with Cobham, Debenham and the Tyrells from his clientage, most East Anglian gentry blew hot and cold or remained in eclipse, like the Pastons, cousins of Lady Beaufort, signifying not only Norfolk's failure to weld the former Mowbray affinity into a coherent political force but also the fine line that separated noble and gentry interests in 1483. The rebels Wingfield, Brandon and Brewes, old Mowbray clients, were interrelated; John Wingfield was the son-in-law of Lord Audley, first cousin of Mary Fitzlewis (the second wife of Earl Rivers), and a kinsman of Lord Stanley, while his brother-in-law was none other than Richard's henchman, Lord Scrope of Bolton, a local landowner of some note.[7] The king knew he could expect little from the likes of Stanley. Many who were connected with Beaufort-Stanley circles in the south and East Anglia had already declared their hand, or were under suspicion. As for Lovell, he had no more been able to prevent his 'cousin' Sir William Stonor and Sir William Norris and their people from rising, any more than Norfolk could rein in his disaffected associates in East Anglia. In fact Stonor may well have drawn into the revolt some of Lovell's own affinity.[8]

With much to occupy his thoughts at home, from early 1484 Richard was also prosecuting two wars abroad. One, waged with France and Brittany, was a diplomatic battle, which aimed at securing a treaty with the new French king, Charles VIII, on the one hand, and of obtaining Henry Tudor's extradition from the Breton duke on the other. Yet the protocol of diplomacy masked a spiteful naval war between Richard and Francis II, a direct result of the duke's support of Henry Tudor and his court, and the fear excited in Richard by Henry's Christmas covenant with the exiles. Piracy raged in the Channel with Devon and Cornish sailors hijacking a number of Breton vessels rich with booty, and also losing several of their own. The conflict escalated, necessitating safe-conducts for agents of both parties and prompting Richard's order to the Earl of Arundel's son and Lord Scrope in March to patrol the sea. Richard's concern was less about piracy than about the risk of treason spanning the Channel, linking Henry's court and the English coast. Attempts were made to frustrate Richard's negotiations with Brittany over Henry Tudor's surrender and his envoys needed safe-conducts to leave the realm unmolested, while Bretons required letters of passage to guarantee their safety at Dover or Sandwich. Primed for an invasion as early as May 1484 the king sent Cobham to Dover and Sandwich to foil an attack expected from Sir Edward Woodville. As a counter-measure, some weeks later Arundel was charged to extract an oath of loyalty to the king from all seafarers.[9] Fear of a second invasion by Tudor also caused Richard to intensify both his diplomatic and military pressure on the duke, and to this end he recruited the help of Maximilian and softened an ailing Francis with financial promises. The mercurial world of Breton politics had created two distinct factions, one of which favoured an alliance with England to counter French ambitions while the other sought to strengthen ties with France. Richard found an unexpected ally in the Breton treasurer, Pierre Landais, who believed that an Anglo-Breton alliance was desirable both for Brittany and himself. His influence with Francis had caused hostility in high places and such a deal would bolster his position with the duke and against his enemies in noble ranks. Then again, in view of the negotiations that held the promise of a successful outcome to the Tudor problem, Landais may also have believed that Henry Tudor had already made overtures for assistance to the French court. Happily for Landais the pro-English faction was currently in favour and an agreement reached on 8 June was formally declared two days later; it held until April 1485. To help mend fences the king dispatched John Grey, Lord Powys, from Southampton to Brittany with a thousand archers.[10]

As the truce with Brittany was being hammered out, relations between England and France deteriorated with fierce naval strikes occurring in June and July prompting fears of a French assault on the English garrison at Calais. Simultaneously Richard's anxiety over treasonable activity bridging the Channel materialized, and on 6 July Somerset squire James Newenham was tried with others for treason before Lord Scrope.[11] Only weeks earlier he had taken out a general pardon which, coupled with this later intrigue, indicates his collusion with the exiles. Still in July, Richard Edgecombe and several West Country merchants were the subject of a much more powerful commission at Exeter. Edgecombe, already implicated in the 1483 revolt, had avoided attainder by securing a pardon, though he remained in contact with the rebels abroad. Allegedly, he planned to send money to Sir Robert Willoughby, his neighbour across the Tamar, and to Piers Courtenay in Vannes with the aid of merchants

John Lenne of Launceston, John Belbury of Liskeard and John Toser, a dyer of Exiland. The sum involved – fifty-two pounds – was apparently intended to ease the plight of the cash-strapped rebels. Belbury and Toser, who were to travel in disguise as tin and wool merchants, were subsequently pardoned; Edgecombe and Lenne, however, were indicted, though the former managed to flee to Brittany having forfeited his lands and goods.[12]

Far more serious was the treason of William Collingbourne and John Turberville. The latter came from Friarmayne in Dorset and was related to Bishop John Morton whose hand was already guiding intrigue from his base in the Netherlands. Collingbourne, a serjeant of the pantry under Edward and an usher at his funeral, was sidelined under Richard. Quite possibly he was involved with Margaret Beaufort as his Wiltshire seat, Lydiard, was held by her. His kinsman John Darrell, in exile with Henry, whose family also held Beaufort land, was perhaps the go-between. On 10 July he met with others in Portsoken ward, London, and arranged to send Thomas Yate to Brittany to entice Henry Tudor to invade England by way of Poole on St Luke's Day, 18 October 1484, with eight pounds 'danger money'. Allegedly Yate was urged to plead a case for sending John Cheyne to Charles VIII to beg for his support of the invasion. Perhaps the courier who got lost and was waylaid in August in Normandy en route for Henry

John, Lord Cheyne KG (d. 1499). Salisbury Cathedral, Wilts.

Tudor in Brittany was Collingbourne's agent. In the event, Charles VIII spared the messenger both because of his destination and the possibility of news from the English court. As a companion piece to Collingbourne's treason, on 18 July he secured seditious verse to the doors of St Paul's in a brazen display of opposition to the king. Lampooning 'The Cat, the Rat and Lovell our Dog', who 'Rule all England under an hog', his doggerel indicates that by mid-1484 tempers in the south were still inflamed by Richard's rule and the use made of his powerful outsiders, William Catesby, Sir Richard Radcliffe and Viscount Lovell, in this instance. Shaken, the king made an example of Collingbourne in October in an effort to counter the disaffection, and he suffered the ghastly fate of hanging, castration and disembowelment. Though Henry Tudor did not take up the invitation to invade, the whole episode unnerved the king as his powerful commission into Collingbourne's treason, issued on 29 November, indicates.[13] Turberville made good his escape, possibly to Henry Tudor for he was knighted at Bosworth, and in the following weeks was bestowed with gifts 'for good and faithful service' performed at 'great costs and charges'. Yet sedition continued and only weeks before Collingbourne's death Thomas Grayson was ordered to arrest West Country men who had acted 'against their natural duty and liegance', while Robert Holand was assisted on 4 October in the arrest of unnamed rebels for treason.[14] Sir Henry Bodrugan finally ended Stephen Calmady's excursions abroad in the rebels' cause and confiscated his vessel on 21 November. Around this time Robert Redness from Yorkshire was captured in Sussex and his father John described as a rebel; so, too, were William Tyler and John Waller.[15]

Against this backdrop Richard expedited negotiations with Brittany for Henry Tudor's return through Pierre Landais, sending as his own envoy William Catesby, whose offering to St Vincent at Vannes Cathedral in September convinced Henry, already under house arrest, that his repatriation was imminent. Perhaps Richard had tempted Francis with the earldom of Richmond, the domain of Breton rulers until the close of the fourteenth century. Henry had long styled himself Earl of Richmond, even though he had lost the title six years after the death of his father Edmund Tudor in 1456. Clearly Landais had curried favour with his master on Richard's account, having been assured of the English king's assistance against his enemies. Whatever else, Morton, with his finger firmly on the pulse in Flanders, heard of the treaty either through his spies at Westminster or via Margaret Beaufort, and dispatched his young clerical colleague Christopher Urswick to Vannes to warn Henry of the Anglo-Breton treaty. Henry, in turn, sent Urswick to Charles VIII to gauge the mood. Charles was amenable and without delay Henry Tudor decamped to the French court. Interesting detail is provided by Vergil of Henry's dramatic flight to France. Unbeknown to almost all, at some point in September his uncle Jasper set out with several trusted notables from Vannes, ostensibly to visit Francis at Rennes, located near the French border; with French soil in sight, the small party scurried across into the French province of Anjou. Henry followed with a few companions two days later, allegedly on a visit to a sick friend. Disguised as a groom, he crossed the border thus coming under Charles VIII's protection. In an act that indicates both his magnanimity and fecklessness, Francis allowed the exiles safe passage into France, and in an audience with Edward Woodville, Edward Poynings and John Cheyne he promised to pay for the expedition, providing over 700 livres from his own pocket.[16]

Henry Tudor's position in international affairs now altered dramatically. While in Brittany he had caused Richard great anxiety, in France he posed an enormous threat as the court of Charles VIII was clearly prepared to pay far more than lip service to his political and dynastic aspirations. Henry's flight to France, apart from signalling Richard's complete failure at diplomacy with Brittany, gave Charles VIII a lever in his negotiations with England, and removed from Francis II the advantage he had held over Richard for support against the French. As for Richard, his only hope lay in the factionalism of the French court, for when Louis XI died on 30 August 1484, his son Charles was only thirteen years old and the government was in the hands of his elder sister Anne, the wife of Pierre, Lord of Beaujeu. His hope was soon extinguished, however, as the opposing faction, led by a nobleman of royal blood, Louis de Orléans, had forged an alliance with Francis II with the aim of sabotaging Richard's talks with Charles VIII, thereby undermining the government. With Henry's flight to France the plan of the Orléans party was thwarted, and much to Richard's distress the new government welcomed Tudor with alacrity.

Henry Tudor's enhanced status thus had an immediate and dramatic impact on English politics. The powerful backing of the French king, who acknowledged him as the heir to the English throne, gave immense heart to the exiles and their allies, and provided the stimulus they needed to engage in coherent and disciplined treason. Almost from his accession Richard's position had been defensive as he sought to counter the politics of disaffection; the opposition, however, seemed able exploit his mistakes as he attempted to regain control. With the quickening pace from October 1484 the rebels were able to call the play, on which royal policy was increasingly predicated. Within days of Henry's flight a rising which began in East Anglia crossed the Channel to Hammes, one of the Calais forts. Orchestrated by Morton in Flanders, it connected the de Vere and Mowbray affinities with Richard's own household. Sir William Brandon and his sons led an armed revolt at Colchester in Essex, involving Sir William Stonor and Thomas Nandyke, all of whom had rebelled in 1483; it also pulled in Robert Clifford and John Risley, Richard's squire. The conspiracy failed and on 2 November Brandon's sons Thomas and William, with Risley, made good their escape from East Mersea to Henry Tudor, while Brandon senior returned to sanctuary at Colchester. Though details of the plot are obscure, it certainly spilled over into Hertfordshire implicating a number of the Brandons' associates and lesser men who were brought to trial in Richard's second year. The royal manor of Ware was at its core and John Sturgeon, Richard's steward, lost his position to Robert Brackenbury. His replacement as sheriff, the northerner Robert Percy, magnifies the extent of disaffection in Essex and Hertfordshire.[17]

Several days before, on 28 October, Richard had ordered the return of the Earl of Oxford, who had been in custody at Hammes since 1475, having heard of a plot to rescue him. He sent his servant William Bolton to fetch the earl to England, though Brackenbury, sent to Dover to accompany them to the Tower, returned empty-handed: the captain of Hammes, James Blount, a former Hastings retainer, and the porter of Calais, John Fortescue, had defected to Henry Tudor's court, taking Oxford with them. In December the Hammes garrison who had remained loyal to Blount withstood an attack from the governor of Calais, Lord Dinham. Unhappily for Blount not all the garrison had managed to escape, his wife among them. In January Oxford and Thomas Brandon returned to Hammes where the latter led a force of thirty men into the castle to rescue the remaining garrison. Under fire from Oxford, stationed close by, the Calais force opted for a negotiated settlement with the earl, under the terms of which the disaffected could leave under safe-conduct. Oxford, Brandon, Blount's wife and the rest made for Henry Tudor's camp where they remained, their ranks having swelled to seventy-two.

The episodes at Colchester and Calais were closely linked. According to the indictment the Brandons were assisting Oxford and Henry Tudor. John Risley had been employed on the de Vere manor of Lavenham, while a number of lesser men were also de Vere annuitants. Significantly many of Oxford's de Vere estates, made over to Norfolk, were in Essex and doubtless the Brandons hoped to raise local support for the earl.[18] Fortescue's seat, Ponsbourne, was in a disaffected area of Hertfordshire, close to Ware. The address of John Forster, also of Ware, invites speculation. His role in the earlier intrigue was substantial – he was acting as an agent for his late master Lord Hastings and Elizabeth Woodville – and saw him in gaol with fellow prisoners Morton and Stanley in June 1483. Certainly Forster had no love for Richard. Half-starved in prison, he then had to meet the conditions of a stiff bond on his release. His close links with Morton indicate that he very likely played some role in the Colchester intrigue.[19] Directing the conspiracy from his residence in the Netherlands, Morton had strong ties with most of the rebels, including Brandon and Fortescue, who had attended his induction feast, as well as John Risley and William Stonor, and was in contact with government circles in England, his diocese in East Anglia, the exiles abroad and the Calais garrison. Around this time Robert Clifford's brother Roger was a prisoner at Exeter, so perhaps he had recruited in the west for Henry's invasion.[20] For Richard the episode was ominous. All too clearly it showed him Norfolk's inability to control East Anglia. Indeed John Scraton, father and son, the former who had served Norfolk, were involved in the plot, and it may be no coincidence that the duke took more of a back seat in official affairs in 1485. If, as Jean Molinet suggests, Blount sought Stanley's advice before the Hammes affair, then the episode was of grave significance for the crown. Molinet also suggests that both Oxford and Stanley at this point urged Henry Tudor to style himself king. From the time rebellion was first mooted in 1483 Henry and his supporters recognized his status as the claimant to the English throne. Certainly from November 1484 his entreaties for English support were signed 'H', a compromise on 'Henricus Rex' after the style of English kings, rather than his characteristic 'Henry de Richemont', indicating a new confidence to match his improved status.[21] And if former Mowbray and Hastings retainers, assisted by Stanley, tapping the de Vere network on behalf of Henry Tudor and converting most of the Hammes garrison into the bargain, were not bad enough for Richard, the disaffection had spread to the household, touching some of his closest servants.

Having intercepted a letter sent in November from Henry Tudor to his allies in England, the king was in no doubt that the Essex plot, like the earlier plan, anticipated an English invasion. Henry urged his 'good friends' to help him further his 'rightful claim, due and lineal inheritance of that crown', and to assist him in ridding the country of an 'unnatural tyrant'; they were to send word when all was in readiness for his journey to claim the crown. The king's proclamation issued on 7 December predictably traduced Tudor and his uncle, Dorset, Oxford and Sir Edward Woodville. According to Richard, Henry's aspirations to the English crown in which he had no 'interest, right or colour' were the result 'of his ambitious and insatiable covetousness'. In desperation he alerted every county in the kingdom in December that the exiles now 'confedered with our ancient enemies of France'.[22] Fearing an invasion by way of Harwich the town was placed on high alert, while Surrey, Middlesex and Hertfordshire were warned to resist the rebels at short notice should they arrive. Royal officials took a head-count of all able-bodied men to fight for the king, whose knights, squires and gentlemen were also ordered to array without exception if they wanted to 'avoid the king's high displeasure'. In Gloucestershire the Earl of Nottingham apparelled men with the accoutrements of war, and was to convey them in companies to the king to protect the realm against the 'malice' of the rebels and foreign enemies 'as the need arises'.[23]

The threat of invasion brought into focus the king's financial worries and called into question his policies and patronage. Though his rich gifts were a product of his insecurity, royal largesse even on Richard's scale could be justified if it produced the desired results; and he was, after all, fulfilling the chivalric ideal of the bountiful ruler. Even so, the political crisis was linked with his economic viability and as he had emptied his stocks without winning over the uncommitted and had also alienated many former supporters, his policies were, at best, ill-considered. According to the Crowland chronicler Richard was a spendthrift whose lavish celebrations, particularly in York, had greatly undermined his cash reserves. Buckingham's rebellion had thus created enormous financial strain with agents often footing the bill for their forays against the rebels: John Belle, for instance, a bailiff of Cambridge, answered Richard's plea for help 'with four men defensibly arrayed', and at his 'great cost' he attended the king 'all our journey in repressing of our rebels and traitors unto the time we came to our city of London'.[24] Not all the problems were of the king's making, however. Edward's death had left a depleted treasury, a war with Scotland and an imminent conflict with France. And after the rising the king worked hard at financial reform. Greatly assisted by his life grant from parliament of tonnage and poundage, he resuscitated the chamber finances and reviewed a range of administrative procedures as they related to crown revenues.

Nevertheless, when it came to paying for his military preparations from December 1484, the extent of his liquidity problem became clear. Pawning jewels and silverware to London merchants would not provide the sort of cash needed by the crown to outfit men for war in every county at short notice, and Richard was driven to exact loans from leaders throughout the realm.[25] Unpopular in the extreme, it was not a policy designed to win friends and influence, and at a time when the king needed all the support he could muster, it indicates his dire financial situation. Edward's use of benevolences or forced gifts to help finance his war with the Scots had met with stiff opposition, but at least Richard managed to avoid resorting to that measure. Indeed he had right on his side: the crown, after all, was under-resourced and under attack. Moreover subjects were to be reimbursed (that is, if Richard could honour the debt). Cogent propaganda was employed by special agents to inspire 'every true Englishman' in defence of the realm. None the less, despite Richard's use of local men in each county, such as Richard Croft and Thomas Fowler in Oxfordshire, Berkshire and

Buckinghamshire, those who paid often failed to meet the actual request, while many simply ignored the letters altogether: clearly not a good sign for the crown. While it was hoped to net around £10,000 with the first collection in February 1485, with subsequently higher returns, as a revenue-raiser it was a disaster. Men avoided payment simply because they could, or because they believed it was 'dead' money. Whatever else, with the crown under duress the failure of this financial expedient underlines Richard's political bankruptcy.[26]

The intrigue that bridged the Channel had inspired further defections to Paris of Buckingham's rebels, including Sir William Berkeley and the Brandons. Henry Tudor's court also attracted some of the brightest intellectual stars of the day including Richard Fox, then at the University of Paris, and a number of men through the Beaufort-Stanley connection, including Christopher Urswick who served as Henry's chaplain, Hugh Conway and Thomas Savage, who was Stanley's nephew and a great power in Cheshire. Braced for trouble, Richard was appalled by the defection of a number of his chamber servants: his squires of the body, John Risley, John Fortescue, Sir James Blount and William Benstead; several members of his household, and from the circle at Calais under the late Lord Hastings.[27] For Richard the Hammes treason underscored the susceptibility of Calais to French attack, and its potential as a tantalizing stepping-stone for an invasion of England. The position of Hammes Castle close to the French border had worried Lord Dinham at the time of Louis XI's death when whispers of a French attack were overheard. He had informed Richard of the vulnerability of the Calais forts and pushed for an alliance with Maximilian to strengthen England's hand against France. Richard was tardy in response, though he immediately tried to repair the damage, dispatching Sir James Tyrell to Flanders to negotiate with Maximilian, and probably to try to gain Morton's ear. Aware that the defection of the English soldiers of the Calais March provided the exiles with professional support, and conscious of the boost both to morale and to Henry's cause provided by their aristocratic recruit, the Earl of Oxford, Richard saw his only option as one of conciliation. On 16 November, two weeks after Oxford's defection, he offered James Blount a pardon and confirmation of his former posts; Morton received his pardon in December and on 27 January 1485, Thomas Brandon, Elizabeth Blount and the Hammes garrison were also pardoned. At the same time, having unearthed more of the Brandons' lands, Richard soon confiscated them with those of their associates, Roger Tocotes and Robert Willoughby.[28]

Indeed fear produced in Richard an odd carrot and stick approach as, desperate to regain the initiative, at times he appeared to conciliate his enemies and punish his

Richard III (1452–85).

allies. The household defections brought the wider Hastings network at Calais under suspicion. The Essex knight of the body Thomas Montgomery fell from grace at this time, presumably for his failure to keep Hammes loyal. Originally plied with Essex lands worth £412 and county offices, he lost his position at Guisnes deputizing for the gravely ill Lord Mountjoy, Blount's elder brother, and some of his Essex manors several months later. When it became clear that Mountjoy was dying neither Montgomery nor Sir Ralph Hastings, William's brother and a knight of the body who had been ear-marked for the job, were sufficiently trusted as replacements. Other Hastings retainers were suspect, such as Sir John Ferrers who was confirmed as a king's knight, yet had to pledge himself to remain in London in August 1484.[29] The ubiquitous James Tyrell was appointed lieutenant of Guisnes and Thomas Wortley, plucked from office in Staffordshire, was Blount's replacement as lieutenant of Hammes. As Hastings's brother-in-law Sir John Donne had already lost his post at the Calais fort of Ruysbank to Thomas Everingham after October 1483, Richard was at least confident of his three captains. Yet the governor of Calais, John Dinham, became another casualty. After the coup he had provoked the king by highlighting his officers' recent oath of allegiance to Edward V; despite showing concern over the security of Calais, and, moreover, paying for the relieving operation at Hammes, the king obviously held him responsible for the mutiny and appointed his natural son John, Duke of Gloucester, as captain with overriding authority. Despite a sweetener of £600 and patronage to his younger brother Charles, Dinham cannot have relished being sidelined. For Richard, disaffected members of the old Hastings network at Calais had at least shown their hand, while others had been neutralized, as he hoped, through replacement.[30]

In the event, John Dinham remained loyal to Richard. Yet as the king continued to trust fewer servants with increasing work, his power-base atrophied to such an extent that he no longer had the numbers for effective rule. In a ploy aimed at weakening Henry Tudor's position and making his own seem more desirable, the king offered pardons to around eight of the attainted 1483 rebels (including Tocotes though he was soon to forfeit more land), and two of the Colchester offenders, Robert Clifford and William Benstead. On 12 January Sir John Fogge and Sir Richard Woodville were bound to honour their sovereign lord, to behave themselves and to part with steep bonds of 1,000 marks; in return Fogge recouped some of his lands and received his pardon in February, Woodville in March.[31] Indeed Richard's trump card was to be his conciliation of the Woodvilles, designed to break the spirit of the exiles. To this end he used other tactics. At his Christmas court in 1484 Richard made a fuss of his niece, Princess Elizabeth, in a crass display according to the Crowland chronicler in which Elizabeth was garbed in similar fashion to Anne Neville, the king's wife. This was food for speculation, and after the death of the queen in March 1485, rumours spread, particularly within the Neville compound, that Richard had poisoned her in order to wed either Elizabeth or her younger sister, Cecily. More salacious was the tattle that he had already bedded the young Elizabeth and fathered a child, and that he had also poisoned Anne's elder sister. Though he hotly denied such talk, he had indeed secured the girls' release from sanctuary on 1 March 1484, probably at that stage with a view to marrying them off, sooner rather than later, to dash his rival's dynastic plans, and counter this dangerous new dimension to Henry's cause. Indeed what would become of the prince if Richard married, or at least married off, the princess, thus removing the linchpin of his Yorkist support? Moreover, the king's own position was looking decidedly shaky after the death of his son in 1484. As the fruit even from an immediate union would not ripen for the greater part of a generation, Richard was under pressure to nominate an heir presumptive. According to John Rous, the choice was between his two nephews; allegedly he favoured first Clarence's son, the Earl of Warwick, then later chose the Earl of Lincoln. As the claim of the former to the throne was stronger than his uncle's, it is easy to see why Richard may well have opted for the latter. None the less in these circumstances a marriage with his niece had obvious attractions.[32]

As it was, the reaction of his henchmen to the persistent rumours of his intended match ended his vacillation. As the Crowland chronicler has it, those most hostile were those who had been best rewarded: William Catesby and Richard Radcliffe, who told the king point blank that such a union would cause a mutiny among his northern servants. Ostensibly, the council feared the image problem facing Richard among his public if the match occurred. The real reason, according to Crowland, was fear of a Woodville vendetta over the destruction of their kin. Most likely, mercenary reasons were uppermost in men's minds: Richard's affinity would lose greatly with a Woodville resurgence. Those who had garnered fabulous wealth and power under the new régime did not want to see their position and privileges diminish. Richard thus had no option; it was not a time for obstinacy. He next persuaded Elizabeth Woodville to woo the Marquess of Dorset back to Westminster, as his presence with his uncle Edward at Henry's court was a major block to an accord. In the event, Dorset may already have had flight in mind as in February 1485 his agent, Roger Machado, formerly Richard III's herald, had been busy on Dorset's behalf in Flanders, his alleged destination. In what must have been a black moment for the exiles, Dorset stole away under cover of darkness, but was overtaken by Humphrey Cheyne and Mathew Baker at Lihons-sur-Santerre, on his way to France's northern border, Henry Tudor having obtained Charles VIII's permission to apprehend the miscreant.[33]

While Dorset had hoped to join Richard's camp he was in the minority, as many royal servants who saw the new reign in did not last the distance, John Biconell, William Courtenay and the customer, Thomas Croft, among them. The latter possibly joined Henry in Paris, the former were in Tudor's camp at Bosworth. A number in fact deserted Richard at the eleventh hour, while he in turn became more suspicious than ever: of his squire, for instance, John Mortimer, who lost his royal stewardship in Gloucestershire in February 1485, and later answered to Henry's authority at Bosworth. Peter Curtis, a conspirator from 1483 who regained his post as keeper of the great wardrobe, had vacated it by mid-May 1485 and was in sanctuary at Westminster, perhaps having received word from Robert Skerne, his brother-in-law in Paris, of Henry's imminent arrival. Robert Morton, his co-conspirator, was described at this time as 'king's rebel', along with John Peke and Watkin Williams. Reginald Bray collected cash to recruit men in England; others sent aid to the exiles or managed to escape themselves.[34] Added to this Richard was still dogged by intrigue as men prepared for the invasion. Peterhouse College, Cambridgeshire, with which John Morton had close ties and from which he drew his retinue, was the focus of a conspiracy involving two of its fellows. Another intrigue, centred perhaps at Winchelsea, Sussex, involved the Fienneses (a family involved in 1483), Thomas and Roger and probably their brother and Richard's knight of the body, Robert, together with Richard Sackville, John Devenish and Richard Culpepper, who had served Richard as commissioner of array in 1484. All were bound in £100 to attend the king when summoned, and to 'have them from henceforward as true liegemen . . . towards our said lord'.[35]

Henry Tudor also knew deep despair. When word reached him that Richard had more than an avuncular interest in Elizabeth, he was reportedly 'pinched by the very stomach'. While he had found an alternative bride, the daughter of William Herbert, Earl of Pembroke (d. 1469) whose care he had known in Wales, it was imperative to urge Charles VIII to immediate action in his cause. His credibility and thus much of his support depended on the French king's backing, and in the fickle world of diplomacy a sudden realignment of French interests could easily destroy his position as rapidly as it had facilitated his rise. He had only to reflect on the Anglo-Breton truce brokered by Maximilian, to which Richard had just put his seal, for confirmation of the volatile world of international relations. Yet Charles also felt the urgency of the moment; ever since the English claimant had entered his territory, his council had feared an imminent English strike. Henry consulted with Philippe de Commynes, the Flemish diplomat at the French court, on the best way to expedite matters. Most probably the king's visit to Normandy in March 1485 for the opening of the parliament at Rouen provided the occasion for Charles finally to honour his assurances. On 4 May his request to the Norman assembly on Henry's behalf for money to enable him to claim the English throne was met with a positive response, and Henry returned to Paris early in June, well pleased with the outcome.[36]

Reminiscent of 1483, plans were made behind closed doors and agents were dispatched with crucial intelligence, bravely leaving the coast under cover of darkness. This time the Norman capital rather than Vannes was the centre for conspiracy with clerics such as Urswick and Fox, already adept in diplomacy, scurrying between Morton in Flanders, the exiles in Rouen and Charles VIII's court. Agents for Henry on both sides of the Channel secured allies and took soundings, while Richard may well have employed agents provocateurs in his desperation to gauge the mood and trap the unwitting. Allegedly Urswick even crossed the Channel to lobby support from the great Northumberland, though the meeting apparently did not happen. Among Henry's Welsh

Stone representation of the Red Dragon of Cadwaladr, adopted by Henry Tudor to highlight reputed descent from ancient British kings.

contacts were the Morgan brothers, John, a lawyer, and Trahaiarn, who urged him to hurry his journey. He gained heart from his mother who had long championed his cause, raising money and men and securing a final commitment from Lord Stanley on his behalf. Indeed Stanley, his brother Sir William and Gilbert Talbot, uncle of the young Earl of Shrewsbury, had finally come round to Henry on 3 May, according to 'The Song of Lady Bessy', bringing in the north-west and north-west midlands with them. Before the crossing Tudor also heard of Stanley's conversion of his nephew, John Savage, and that the most formidable chieftain in Carmarthenshire, Rhys ap Thomas, might also come across. Northumberland was an unknown quantity. Word must have reached Henry of his disaffection under Richard, though if in fact Urswick had attempted an audience with him in England, his failure must have chilled all hearts.

By 9 June a suspicious Richard had stationed himself at Nottingham Castle whose location allowed him to keep an eye on his enemies as well as his allies and to gather together his followers for the upcoming fight. At the apex of the midlands, he was close to Stanley strongholds and to those powerful families whose allegiance had been to the House of Stafford, to his brother via Hastings through the Honour of Tutbury, or to the late lord chamberlain in his role outside the duchy. While there were many others to whom the gentry might answer, Richard feared most the formidable coalition of disaffected powers led by the Beaufort-Stanley circle, which could well have defeated him in 1483. There was danger of course in leaving the rebels in the south to their own devices; choice, however, was not a luxury he could afford. He had done what he could to secure the realm, ordering a general muster on 22 June, and allocating to his lieutenants specific tasks: Brackenbury was to guard the Tower with a strong contingent while Lovell was to supervise naval and military preparations for the south coast at Southampton. Norfolk was at Framlingham in Suffolk where he hoped to realize his full strength at the muster. Northumberland was in charge of the northern levies, while Stanley had left the royal entourage at Nottingham ostensibly to array for the king in the north-west. In Wales the Earl of Huntingdon supervised the activity of Williams, White, the Vaughans and his other captains. As the rebels could well make landfall at Milford Haven in Pembrokeshire or at a number of other points in south Wales, the area was kept under close surveillance. Though the crown had granted cash to Rhys ap Thomas to help him recruit, the king was clearly unaware that he was dissembling. But he believed he had more to fear from the major nobles than dissident local powers. He may not have been at all sure of Northumberland. Indeed as late as 16 August citizens of York sought information from the king himself of his military requirements, indicating that the earl had been dragging his feet in the matter of the royal muster.[37] None the less Stanley remained the king's main worry. The king had only approved his withdrawal to Lancashire on condition that his son, Lord Strange, and the former Hastings retainer and powerful Caernarvonshire squire William Griffith, remain with him as hostages, thereby hoping to clip Stanley's wings if treason were in the wind. He recalled the great seal from Chancellor Russell in London which he received in the chapel at Nottingham Castle on the evening of 1 August. Thus it was that Richard waited for his adversary to show himself.

CHAPTER 8
To Claim the Crown

Bosworth really was an enormous gamble. When Henry Tudor's flotilla made landfall on 7 August at Milford Sound in Pembrokeshire, his prospects looked bleak. His arrival was met without fanfare or indeed any sign of serious support – a worrying sign for the rebels as the locals would soon have broadcast the news. The pretender's force can have been no more than five thousand strong, and though he was served by some distinguished Frenchmen, according to Molinet the vast majority of his force consisted of a motley crew of French conscripts, mercenaries and ex-convicts. Not exclusively French, however, it also included his Breton allies who had followed him to France, and allegedly a thousand Scots led by Alexander Bruce and John of Haddington. While Henry lacked impressive manpower, he had considerable expertise at his disposal in Sir Edward Woodville, as former admiral of England, the Earls of Oxford and Pembroke, whose military savvy had ensured their prominence in campaigns, and his executive French captain, Philibert de Chandée. Moreover he had the discipline provided by the soldiers of the Hammes garrison. Though the driving force in 1485 was the same as it had been in 1483, the crucial difference which gave 1485 its soul lay in the unity of Henry and his band of exiles. He had an heroic and potent force of between four hundred and five hundred men who were inspirational in the field under the command of Richard Guildford, newly created master of the ordnance: Edward Courtenay, Thomas Arundel, John Cheyne, Edward Poynings, Robert Willoughby, John Halwell, Giles Daubenay, the Brandons, John Fortescue, James Blount, John Risley and Richard Edgecombe among them. They fought alongside David Owen, the bastard son of Owen Tudor; David Phillip, formerly in Lady Beaufort's service; the old Lancastrian campaigner, Sir Edmund Montfort, in exile since 1471, and John Williams.

A considered move saw the insurgents strike camp at Dale on the evening of the seventh, while at sunrise they were on the road to Haverfordwest, and thence to Cardigan, a Lancastrian stronghold whose viceroy had not been replaced after

Sir Richard Edgecombe (d. 1489), from a painting in his home, Cothele House, Cornwall, depicting his tomb at Morlaix, Brittany.

Buckingham's death. They had determined to cross the mountains of central Wales through Welshpool and travel on to Shropshire, where they could rally their allies to the bold standard of the Red Dragon, before crossing the Severn and marching on London. The rebels reached Shrewsbury around the 15th, and paced themselves through Newport, Stafford, Lichfield and Tamworth, making Atherstone in Warwickshire by 21 August, in all a distance of some 170 miles.[1] Early on, Henry had informed Lord Stanley of his plan, and sent word to Lady Beaufort and Gilbert Talbot. Rather than a pitched battle, the leaders probably envisaged the same sort of rebellion that had been planned for 1483: a series of co-ordinated risings, but on a much larger scale across the country and this time with powerful aristocratic support. Yet much was uncertain. To achieve the victory that had eluded the rebels in 1483, the independent Welsh powers had to be won over, the Stanleys and their friends had to honour their commitment and the south had to translate its good wishes into practical assistance. Though Henry had strong support in the south, he was vulnerable almost everywhere else. The north-east was very much uncharted territory, while the midlands contained many independent-minded gentry whose commitment was still a matter for conjecture. Despite the promises of support, it can only have been with trepidation that Henry, now styling himself King of England, forged ahead with his host, the only certainty being that Richard would have at his disposal the might and resources of the nation.

At Haverfordwest the news was grim: while Jasper Tudor learnt of allies in Pembroke, word came in that neither Sir John Savage nor Rhys ap Thomas would muster for Tudor and had declared for the king. At Cardigan the rebels heard that Walter Herbert had recruited for the royal banner and was fast approaching from Carmarthen. Accustomed to the fickle nature of politics, Henry must have imagined that his support could easily evaporate not because of treachery as much as the inability of potential allies to match promises with action. Richard had kept a tight rein on Herbert and Rhys (and in fact had taken custody of the latter's son); in addition to their own retinues both had also marshalled levies in the southern shires.[2] John Savage, who had been arrested in May in Pembroke and committed to Richard Williams's custody, was soon at liberty, but under great pressure from the king. Then, of course, Stanley's son, Lord Strange, was a hostage in Richard's camp. Dispirited but not defeated, Henry bestowed knighthood on a number of his company: John Cheyne, John Halwell, Edward Poynings, James Blount, John Fortescue, William Tyler, David Owen and his French captain, de Chandée. He also appealed directly to the national pride of the men of Cardigan, Caernarvon and elsewhere, such as John ap Maredudd, seeking to exploit the strong anti-English sentiment among people who had long hoped for deliverance from their overlords. Henry could propagandize the Tudor cause with the help of Welsh poets such as Robin Ddu who predicted a glorious future for Wales in the pretender's hands. Thus he spoke to Welshmen of delivering the kingdom from 'that odious tyrant' and of his urgent need of their help, 'wherein you shall cause us in time to come to be your singular good lord'. Whether or not John ap Maredudd answered the call is not known. Yet men such as Owen Lloyd, Richard ap Philip and Adam ap Jankyn of Cardigan rallied to Henry's banner along with Richard Griffith, a landowner of note in west Wales.[3] It was some days, however, before his efforts achieved solid results. On 14 August the pretender wrote to the Shropshire leader Sir Roger Kynaston, the uncle of John Grey, Lord Powys, who was in Brittany in June 1484. Henry's letter to Kynaston suggests that an understanding existed between himself and Grey, whose support he may

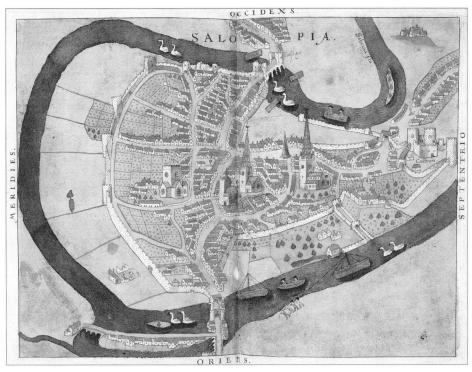

A sixteenth-century map of the town of Shrewsbury.

have been able to canvass abroad.[4] Grey was an immensely important ally who could greatly assist the rebels' passage through the perilous border counties.

Approaching Shrewsbury Henry's spirits rose as Rhys ap Thomas (allegedly bribed into action with the promise of rewards) came in behind him with a force, according to tradition, of more than 1,800 men; Walter Herbert, who had been shadowing the army with Rhys, also fell in behind his standard. The swollen company passed the night of the 16th on Long Mountain, with Welshpool away to the east, before striking out for Shrewsbury.[5] Though the city only reluctantly threw open its gates to the rebels after some arm-twisting applied to its bailiffs by Sir William Stanley's men, Stanley authority was a potent force and eminent Englishmen now came in freely behind the Tudor standard: Gilbert Talbot, with 500 men; Sir Richard Corbet, William Stanley's stepson, with 800 more; Shropshire squire Humphrey Cotes and Roger Acton; and Sir William Stanley himself, with a full complement perhaps some three thousand strong from Cheshire and north Wales, who most probably met Henry at Stafford on 17 August. Within hours Henry was transformed from a mere pretender to a credible claimant with a formidable following. The rebel army had made Lichfield by the 19th, with Lord Stanley close by but taking care to keep his

Effigies of Simon Digby (d. 1519), and his wife, Elizabeth Arundel. Westminster Abbey.

distance lest scouts alert the king, thereby jeopardizing his hostage son's safety. The Stanley name also brought credit in the form of the Lancashire knights Sir Robert Tunstall, Sir Hugh Persall, Sir Piers Legh and Cheshire's Sir John Savage, who had finally managed to shake off Richard's spies; all of them brought sizeable companies. Others from the midlands followed suit: the powerful Staffordshire squire Humphrey Stanley, John Hanley from Worcestershire, Henry Vere of Northamptonshire, and John Hardwick of Lindley, 'a small man, but brave and active', who proved invaluable to Henry's captains with his broad knowledge of the landscape. Exploits, real or imagined, became part of local lore. Sir Thomas Ferrers was said to have given Henry Tudor the keys to the ordnance room at Tamworth Castle, and the pick of the weapons for his use at Bosworth. The Digbys of Warwickshire and Leicestershire allegedly committed all seven brothers to Henry's standard; Simon gained special mention as a defector from Richard on the eve of the battle, who brought with him information about the royal strategy with which Henry could later outwit his opponents.[6]

Richard heard of Henry's arrival on 11 August from his constable at Pembroke, Richard Williams, and immediately summoned his captains and alerted his sheriffs and commissioners of array. Apprised of events by 13 or 14 August, the Duke of Norfolk ordered a muster at Bury St Edmunds for the 16th, and informed clients including Sir John Paston that 'the king's enemies be on land', and to array 'such a company of men as you can easily make up at my expense', to meet 'as upon Tuesday night'. With Stanley, as he hoped, recruiting at Lathom in west Lancashire, and Northumberland busy at Beverley in Yorkshire, Richard may have felt pleased with Huntingdon and his agents in Wales who seemed to have mastered the situation.[7] Any complacency over Henry Tudor's low-key arrival, however, gave way to fury and fear when he learnt of the duplicity of Rhys ap Thomas, Walter Herbert and other Welsh powers who had joined the rebels. Not only had Huntingdon failed him, but Henry's arrival at Lichfield at the head of a formidable host clearly meant treachery of the worst kind from his most powerful allies. Closeted with his henchmen high in the midlands, the king expedited the royal muster and on 21 August departed Leicester to intercept the rebels who were moving along Watling Street, en route for London. It was in the vicinity of Market Bosworth that the combatants engaged, at Redemoor, on 22 August.

The exiles and their allies had recruited well, and when firm news of Henry Tudor's landing reached the south, men began a series of strenuous marches to join the insurgents. Unsure of Henry's plans, confusion doubtless marred their effective organization for the best part of a week, with scouts and couriers abroad for both parties. None the less a number of the southern gentry and their companies caught up with the rebel army at Atherstone in Warwickshire on the eve of the battle, including Walter Hungerford and Thomas Bourchier, who had been imprisoned in the Tower of London yet managed to evade Sir Robert Brackenbury when summoned to Richard's side at Leicester. Those who made the trek from the south included old campaigners from 1483: Sir Amyas Paulet, Robert Poyntz, Sir William Norris, Nicholas Gaynesford, Richard Haute, Anthony Kene, the Wingfields and Thomas Lovell; they joined new rebels-in-arms such as Reginald Bray, Thomas Croft, Sir William Carew and Robert Harcourt, whose father had died abroad. For others it was also too late, as both Lionel Woodville and Sir Thomas Lewkenor were dead by August. The ageing war-horse Sir William Brandon did not take the field, remaining in sanctuary until after the battle. Likewise Sir John Fogge, by then around sixty, seems not to have given battle, while Sir William Berkeley and Sir Thomas Arundel actually made Bosworth but died within weeks of the fight.[8]

Men from the south flocked to the cause with their own servants and clients or, like John Biconell, John Carew and William Courtenay, absconded to the pretender with levies raised by royal command. Overlapping circles of influence and intrigue characterized the rebels' camp as men sought to renew their links with the exiles. Margaret Beaufort's lawyers, Biconell, John Heron and William Hody, all from warrior stock who had known the rigours of civil war, found legal associates who had followed Henry, such as Richard Pigot and William Case, and of course their own powerful patron, Sir Giles Daubenay. From the Beaufort-Stanley-Stafford circle, members of the Horde and Harper families who had also been abroad caught up with their brothers and colleagues like Bray, Beaufort's agent in England, and Hugh Conway, her messenger to Brittany, as well as Robert Skerne, also involved with the Curtis-Morton circle. Other Stafford clients were at Bosworth including the Darrells and William Treffry, the latter who sought out his comrades from the Bodmin incursion, Thomas Arundel and Edward Courtenay. The Hastings interests were represented by the Blounts, Humphrey Stanley, Sir Thomas Ferrers of Tamworth, Fortescue, Risley and others, while Woodville contacts are too numerous to name. Ecclesiastical representation was also high, and though John Morton's scouts Richard Fox and Christopher Urswick did not take the field, cathedral clergy with martial skills such as Piers Courtenay actually engaged. Thomas Croft, Robert Harcourt, Hungerford,

Richard III's banner at Bosworth.

Bourchier and the Norrises joined forces with Sir William Berkeley, Sir William Stonor, Edmund Hampden and the intrepid John Cheyne, and though there was little time for reminiscence before battle, their camaraderie must have been palpable, and a boost to flagging morale in the certainty of Richard's mighty host. Their greatest bond, of course, lay in their service to the late king, Edward IV, whose memory Richard Guildford in his role as captain doubtless invoked. In the tradition of a true warrior-knight, Guildford enjoined his men to display courage, honour and fidelity in the fight against injustice and dishonour. Later, Henry began battle with a vow of resolve in the face of the enemy, with allowance made for the will of God, reinforcing the justice of their cause and the inveterate wickedness of their foe. According to the chronicler Edward Hall, Henry claimed the Almighty's support against his enemy, being 'an homicide and murderer of his own blood and progeny, an extreme destroyer of his nobility, and to his and our country . . . a burden intolerable'. He capitalized on Richard's plantation policy, using it to stress the common bond he shared with his men. For just as Gloucester 'keepeth me from the crown and regiment of this noble realm', likewise his imports 'occupy your lands, cut down your woods and destroy your manors, letting your wives and children range abroad for their living'; it was fiery rhetoric designed to kindle in his followers both a passion for conquest and the heat of blood-lust.[9]

The rebels may have had the momentum, yet Richard had both the numbers and the strategic advantage, and his defeat at Bosworth upset expectation. While the evidence points to a vast royal host, its numbers far exceeded its commitment. Added to this the king was caught off balance. Still reeling from the knowledge of certain defections, he was anxious over the loyalty of major allies. As it happened a number of nobles including Lovell, Dinham, Audley and Huntingdon may not have made the field in time, while others including Lords Scrope of Bolton and Masham, Greystoke and Fitzhugh could well have joined Northumberland's flag. The Duke of Norfolk and the Earl of Oxford were the first to engage, and under a ferocious counter-attack from Henry's French recruits, Norfolk was soon on the defensive, and subsequently killed. It probably came as no surprise to the king to see both Lord Stanley and Northumberland hold aloof, which should have counselled caution, yet Richard determined to lead the charge on the young pretender despite the ominous presence of Sir William Stanley. As the king drove in hard, slaying Henry's standard-bearer William Brandon, Sir Thomas Arundel and others closed ranks as the huge warrior-knight John Cheyne attempted to block Richard's advance. Committed to the moment, Richard managed to unhorse Cheyne, glancing the top of his helmet in the charge, and wounded several others in savage hand-to-hand combat in his desperation to cut down his rival. Nevertheless it was all over for the king, who found himself caught between the forces of Henry Tudor and Sir William Stanley, who now entered the fray.

After a valiant fight, Richard became the victim, according to Molinet, of a throng of Welsh pikemen, whose assault on him continued until well after his life was extinguished.[10] Surprisingly, in view of the ferocity of the battle, William Brandon appears to have been the only casualty among Henry's bodyguard.

In the aftermath of Bosworth, rewards for the victors came thick and fast. In genuine appreciation of their outstanding service abroad and as a boost to morale, Henry had knighted a number of his most faithful captains, including Edward Courtenay and William Willoughby, before the battle; after his victory prayer, he dubbed a number of others, including Gilbert Talbot who had been wounded in the fight, Robert Poyntz and John Biconell, with Edward Poynings being made a knight banneret.[11] Praise was given to his standard-bearer William Brandon, whose family had been stalwarts throughout, and who had died a hero's death clinging to his standard even after he was cruelly felled by Richard; to Anthony Brown, whose brother George was beheaded in 1483; and to Robert Harcourt, whose father lay buried in Breton soil. From September the new administration was busy stamping royal patronage in the form of gifts, grants and offices, as well as confirmations. Peter Curtis, who suffered 'great persecution, jeopardies, pains, robberies and losses . . . for our sake and quarrel', received prime offices in Leicestershire; Stephen Calmady, a ship 'in recompense of the great jeopardies, tribulation and losses sustained . . . when he was in the parts beyond the sea'; Anthony Brown, a stewardship in Surrey; and William Cheyne, Sir George Brown's old offices in Kent. Henry's French and Scottish captains, the Morgans, Rhys ap Thomas, the Savages, Digbys, Harpers, Hassalls, John Kymer, Edmund Hampden, Walter Courtenay, William Froste and many more were recipients of royal largesse.[12] Henry also thanked scores of lesser men, the servants of John Cheyne, Edward Poynings, John Welles and Giles Daubenay, who had been in exile with their masters, and others who had fallen in behind the Red Dragon on the march to Bosworth, such as the Caernarvonshire gentleman William Anneon, John Punch of Shrewsbury, Staffordshire's Thomas Gaywood and from Warwickshire James Kayley. His bounty extended to those guilty by association, such as Sir William Stonor's kinsman Walter Elmes, who had lost county office under Richard; crucial allies from 1483 like Lewis Caerleon, the queen's physician who had assisted in the Beaufort-Woodville intrigue, John Forster, Oliver King, Hugh Conway and Christopher Urswick; and of course the major players, the Stanleys, the Earl of Oxford, Henry's uncle Jasper Tudor, and his most loyal supporter, his mother Margaret Beaufort, among them.[13]

As a usurper, even one who had slain Richard in battle, whose stepfather had become the mightiest lay power in the realm, and whose marriage to Princess Elizabeth in January 1486 cemented his alliance with the Yorkists, Henry's position was remarkably fragile. A novice at kingship and far more au fait with French than with English governance, his immediate tasks on assuming the throne were to establish a symmetry of views within the polity, to embrace old allies and make new friends; his coronation on 30 October was the perfect venue for honours and assurances. Henry's greatest gifts went to the true believers: his uncle Jasper, who gained the dukedom of Bedford and restoration of the earldom of Pembroke, and his

Henry VII.

mother, who received duchy of Exeter estates in the midlands and the west, and part of the Honour of Richmond. Stanley, whose loyalty was never had for the wanting, received the earldom of Derby and the constableship of England, as well as profits through his wife's custody of Stafford lands during the minority of Buckingham's son and heir; Sir William Stanley resumed most of his offices in north Wales and became chamberlain of the household. In addition, the Earls of Oxford, Ormond and Devon were restored. Far from spoiling the rest, Henry also spared the rod. The Earl of Wiltshire who had supported Richard was forgiven; as was the young Earl of Shrewsbury who received his lands in 1486. The Earl of Westmorland, whose son was taken into royal custody, was placed on a bond, while Northumberland, after a brief spell in prison, was soon returned as king's lieutenant in the north. As vital accessories to Henry's rule, their power stretched in an arc from south Wales to East Anglia. In the 1490s Thomas Howard, Earl of Surrey, was prominent in the north, while through the 1480s Henry Bourchier, Earl of Essex, became a force in the south-east and East Anglia and the Earl of Devon was formidable in the south-west.

As well as providing an index of allies, the new king's bounty reflects the make-up of the early Tudor court and household, showing his dependence on the

Yorkist affinity and the strong personal monarchy of Edward IV. In his first parliament of 7 November attainders were reversed and in due course men such as John Welles received their patrimony, while others including Giles Daubenay, Robert Willoughby, and John Cheyne were ennobled. Henry reserved for his truest knights the highest honours: Cheyne, Guildford, Willoughby, Edgecombe and Risley became knights of the body along with crucial friends in England, Thomas Bourchier, William Uvedale, Reginald Bray, William Stonor and William Norris. Thomas Lovell and Richard Nanfan, initially king's squires, also became Henry's knights with Lovell joining Cheyne and Daubenay in the prestigious Order of the Garter.[14] With powerful aristocratic support Henry turned most often to his friends from exile to serve him in the country, in council and at court, and as the reign progressed they came to embody more fully both the high politics of the court and the business of the household where they wielded immense power. Indeed the lord chamberlain, lord steward, chancellor of the exchequer, treasurer and under-treasurer of the chamber, master of the ordnance, master of the mint, controller, marshal of the household, and chief carver were all from among their ranks.[15] They also served in the chamber, supervising guests or handing out gifts, but mainly catering to the royal whim, at the table, in the wardrobe, and as companions at rest and at play. In fact Henry's fondness for the hunt and the hawk invited the same sort of off-the-record, informal counsel that Edward had enjoyed and at which he had excelled. Initially Daubenay as master of the harthounds was most often in the chase at Eltham, Kenilworth or Richmond, or part of the festivities at the Earl of Oxford's estate, Hedingham. The Marquess of Dorset also joined in the fun, but since his fall from grace in France his companionship in games seems to have been almost all Henry required of him. Squires of the body Thomas Brandon, Mathew Baker, the Welshman Hugh Vaughan, Roland de Veleville (perhaps Henry's bastard son) and Guillaume de la Ryvers, two of his foreign servants, delighted visitors with their skill at the joust and their savvy as hosts at sumptuous feasts and lavish courtly celebrations.[16]

Well placed to offer the king armchair advice or to relay gossip, a number of servants also provided Henry with formal counsel. Initially senior courtiers had tutored him in high politics, and as diplomats they guided him on policy, procedure and protocol. He sat at the table with old friends from 1483, most often Giles Daubenay, Sir John and Sir Richard Guildford, Lovell, Bray, Uvedale, Risley, John Morton and Richard Fox, who assisted him in the art of governance and the business of statecraft. They shone as diplomats, most particularly Daubenay, who was invaluable in promoting Henry's interests overseas. He may well have had a hand in securing for the king a truce with France in October 1485, and in the commercial treaty signed with Brittany in July 1486. He was certainly

Keep of Kenilworth Castle, Warwickshire.

involved in talks with the aides of both Maximilian and Ferdinand of Spain in 1486 and 1487 as France stepped up its campaign to absorb Brittany, and with Christopher Urswick he adopted a peace-keeping role for Henry. In the event Brittany collapsed in 1488 and at St Aubin du Cormier, Sir Edward Woodville, rather a loose cannon at Henry's court, was killed in battle fighting for the duchy. In 1489, when Henry's diplomacy finally gave way to military action, a force of six thousand men under the command of Robert, Lord Willoughby, was sent in to assist the ailing Bretons. Nevertheless France claimed the duchy in 1491.[17]

The same men continued to take the king's rule to the country, resuming their positions in local government and on royal estates, and were crucial to Henry in building bridges to ruling élites and lesser folk, as well as promoting would-be servants.[18] Daubenay was even more attractive, after 1485, in the patronage stakes with numerous perks in his gift as the greatest office-holder in his region, while Sir Richard Guildford displayed the sort of good lordship the locals had been

Robert, Lord Willoughby de Broke KG (d. 1501). Carlington, Cornwall.

deprived of under Richard.[19] They were confirmed as stewards, constables and keepers on royal estates, and were, needless to say, Henry's first choice as sheriffs across the south with Sir Roger Tocotes, Sir Robert Poyntz, Sir William Stonor, Sir Edward Berkeley, John Halwell, Richard Nanfan, Nicholas Gaynesford and William Cheyne occupying the office in 1485.[20] As the reign progressed and the household grew, the king maintained his circle, even after his ordinance of around 1495 relieving knights and squires of domestic duties, partly through his retainers' positions on crown lands and in local office, though of course his intimates remained constant in counsel, administration and diplomacy.[21]

As they had responded to the chivalrous culture of Edward's court, so they were Henry's warrior-knights and sentinels of the realm. Lords Daubenay, Willoughby and Cheyne won high praise on continental campaigns: Daubenay was deployed to Flanders with Sir Edward Poynings and Sir Walter Hungerford; Willoughby and Cheyne to Brittany with Sir Richard Edgecombe and Sir John Arundel as the Franco-Breton crisis escalated. They had already shown their mettle within the realm during early attempts at Yorkist restoration, the first whiff of which occurred in 1486 and was led by Francis, Viscount Lovell. Far more serious was the conflict that escalated to the Battle of Stoke in 1487, generally viewed as the last battle of the Wars of the Roses, which crushed the opposition centred on Lambert Simnel masquerading as the Earl of Warwick, with the aid of Lovell, the Earl of Lincoln and the dowager Duchess of Burgundy, Margaret of York. Henry's massive host, numbering as many as fifteen thousand, was led by the retinues of Oxford, Shrewsbury, Viscount Lisle and others, while

Henry VII and Elizabeth of York, with their children, kneel before St George.

an impressive array of lords and gentlemen made up the field. Gilbert Talbot, John Cheyne and William Stonor, created bannerets, distinguished themselves and after the fight (in which Lincoln was killed and Lovell disappeared) partook of the spoils.

While Henry's early years were fraught with tension and intrigue, his achievements at Stoke Field and in the following months were crucial in enabling him to consolidate his rule, and though still uneasy in office and vulnerable to intrigue, his wife's coronation at the end of 1487 reflected the broadening base of the Tudor régime. By 1489 his success was evident in the massive, morale-boosting host which collected to counter a revolt in Yorkshire, during which the Earl of Northumberland was brutally murdered while gathering royal taxes. Assembled for the king were thirty nobles or their deputies, including the Earls of Derby, Essex, Oxford, Shrewsbury, Surrey and Wiltshire, and Lords Cobham, Lawarre, Hastings, Powys, St Amand, Zouche and Dudley. More impressive still were the 200 or so independent knights and squires, many of whom had provided Henry with critical support in 1483, 1485 and 1487, with Stonor, Tocotes and Robert Harcourt among the 'Earl of Derby's folks', Sir William Norris riding with Lord Strange, and Sir Roger Lewkenor, Sir John St Lo and Sir Thomas Lovell, who could on occasion raise up to 1,300 men. Given that many of Henry's captains were serving abroad, the tally is all the more remarkable. Though the incursion fizzled out, the fact that the heavy-weights answered Henry's call attests his broad military base.[22] Whether or not the full-scale mobilization was window-dressing or sheer indulgence by the king cannot be known. None the less the overwhelming response to his call, particularly among the lesser nobility, indicates that by 1489 he had entered a comfort zone of aristocratic solidarity.

CHAPTER 9
1483 in Perspective

Buckingham's rebellion is remarkable in a number of respects: in its nature, content and context it was unique in English political history. Most significantly, and rather ironically, though it was initially ineffectual it was the catalyst that brought down a dynasty. The rebellion was a symptom of a society in crisis: an evocation of outrage against a usurping king, a perceived child-killer. But more than this it was an attempt to restore the status quo. Conversely, the Battle of Bosworth was the product of escalating conflict caused by Richard's response to the crisis. In the event the crisis was resolved, the status quo restored, and Richard ultimately defeated simply by numbers. Yet the last Plantagenet had never enjoyed the support of the south, though he tried hard to represent the interests of the realm. In general his rule upset time-honoured patterns of royal service, custom and tradition, in particular the political developments that gained strength from the late 1460s, in which the royal affinity united king's rule in the country, most effectively across the south. The rebellion was possible only because of the role of its leaders in a polity that was becoming increasingly inclusive, increasingly king-centred, and whose relationship with its sovereign was increasingly personal. Its leaders were, of course, king's knights and squires: men at the heart of the polity and at the head of ruling élites.

The stability of Edward's second rule followed a recognition of structural weakness within the polity itself and a self-conscious reformation at the heart of government. Inspired leadership and sound policy were crucial elements in restoring peace, assisted by a political culture that had proved itself to be both resilient and flexible. Of course the relative absence of competing magnates and the prominence of powerful gentry created a healthy climate for kingship in the 1470s. Nevertheless, the power and authority vested in the monarch had remained intact throughout this period of the Wars of the Roses, along with the form of consensual government between king and nobles which had long characterized English politics. Yet as the process by which the middle man, the magnate, was eliminated from relations between the lesser nobility – barons, knights and squires – and the king gained pace, so Edward regained firm control of the country. It is not surprising that during the conflict in 1469 to 1471, for instance, Edward had most support from the household in the south-east, an area largely free from magnate rivalries, and by 1483 he had long since mastered his affinity. It is in this context that Buckingham's rebellion can best be understood. Its very occurrence demonstrates the strengths rather than the weaknesses of the polity after Edward's death.

As Richard III had failed with his brother's men, so Henry VII won their support, learnt from them, ruled with them and promoted them. Through his senior councillors and leading officials, often one and the same, he maintained strong personal rule. In many ways the new king perpetuated and enhanced the traditions of the late medieval polity as he built on old foundations. For effective control after his usurpation he needed to broaden his political base and, following Edward's lead, under his direction the court grew apace absorbing new allies as well as old friends, enabling him to satisfy the wishes of the broader political community while retaining the services of his closest advisors. It allowed him to defuse tension and reduce court intrigue, and to include former Ricardians, thereby escaping much opprobrium from otherwise disgruntled servants.[1] Change, however, did occur in the creation of the privy chamber under the groom of the stool to minister royal needs, as household knights and squires were relieved of their domestic duties. Naturally the king's ear grew more difficult to obtain for the broader affinity outside the private world of the privy chamber. To help counter this effect Henry reworked the policy used so effectively by Edward of investing the gentry with powerful office on crown lands and promoting their interests as king's men, thereby maintaining his link with the country. Recent work has shown that the stewards also added a military dimension to king's rule through their power to retain for the crown what were virtually standing armies in the country. Of course Buckingham's rebels as constables and stewards had thus raised the south in 1483, albeit against rather than for the crown.[2]

Like Edward, Henry ruled partly with the aid of a new nobility created from old gentry families: independent and powerful men with leadership qualities who served him well. As Edward had Hastings, so Henry had Daubenay; both chamberlains of the household and lieutenants of Calais.[3] As men who helped to bring down one dynasty, they were integral members of the next. Indeed Buckingham's rebels remained at the heart of the polity, vindicating Henry's judgement and facilitating his gradual introduction to kingship. Of course not all was to his liking; and not all his servants returned his trust. Sir William Stanley, for instance, the first chamberlain of the household, was executed in 1495 for his alleged involvement in the Perkin Warbeck affair; a pretender's attempt to pass for Edward's younger son, Richard of York. The Cornish tax revolt in 1497 led to the execution of Lord Audley, and the suspicion that Daubenay as king's agent and regional power was tardy in response for the crown. Early in the next century

William, Lord Courtenay, fell from grace, as did Thomas, Marquess of Dorset, and Sir James Hobart, Henry's attorney-general. Both Daubenay and Sir Richard Guildford were thought to have engaged in corrupt activity, and were given a smart rebuke. Guildford resigned in disgrace, though Daubenay, ever the survivor, won back high favour. As always jealousies existed in the fertile environment of the court where local interests met high politics and so much turned on connection and favour. In his later years Henry's rule became both harsh and in many circles unpopular as he grappled with intrigue and fear surrounding the succession after the death of his eldest son Arthur in 1502. Yet the crises and conflict should not obscure his very real achievements. There is no small measure of truth in Vergil's depiction of Henry as a peace-maker, though it is hard to reconcile the 'myth' which was in the making even before his death with the harsh realities of his rule. None the less the Tudor propagandists had rich material with which to work. Henry's reign did eventually end, chapter and verse, the dynastic conflict of the Wars of the Roses; the king did restore stability after a period of immense upheaval; his marriage with the Yorkist princess did appease Yorkist sentiment; and moreover he did produce an heir who acceded to the throne in Vergil's own time. It all came at a cost, however. During his last years he was worn down by life, and his queen, his uncle and many of his friends such as John Cheyne, Robert Willoughby, Richard Edgecombe and Giles Daubenay had predeceased him. Despite the trials of his later years, he may well have reflected on his early battles and gained some comfort from the knowledge that by the end of his second year he had countered the greatest challenge to his rule with the aid of 'his true knights', the very men who proved to be Richard III's nemesis in their pursuit of the 'true and rightful life'.

Notes

CHAPTER ONE

1. J. Gairdner, *History of the Life and Reign of Richard the Third* (New York, rev. edn, Greenwood Press, 1969), p. 133. Gairdner was the first to use the title 'Buckingham's Rebellion'; see also P.M. Kendall, *Richard the Third* (London, Allen and Unwin, 1955), p. 273, who uses the phrase 'Buckingham's revolt'.

2. *British Library Harleian MS 433*, ed. R. Horrox and P.W. Hammond (4 vols, Gloucester, Alan Sutton Publishing, 1979–83) (hereafter *BLHM*); R. Horrox, 'British Library Harleian Manuscript 433', *The Ricardian*, 5 (1979), 87–91; C. Ross, *Richard III* (London, Eyre Methuen, 1981), p. 170.

3. Public Record Office, C67/51.

4. *Rotuli Parliamentorum*, ed. J. Strachey (6 vols, London, Record Commissioners, 1767–83), vol. 6, pp. 244–51; in general see G.R. Elton, 'The Rolls of Parliament 1449–1547', *The Historical Journal*, 22 (1979), 1–29.

5. For the indictment at Torrington, Devon RO, ECA Book 51. The document concerning the Bodmin inquisition taken before Lord Scrope of Bolton, which came to light at the end of the nineteenth century among the papers of the Le Grice family, is now to be found in a Memoranda Book among the Borlase papers held at the Royal Institution of Cornwall: Ms BV. 1/4; see also I. Arthurson, N. Kingwell, 'The Proclamation of Henry Tudor as King of England, 3 November 1483', *Historical Research*, 150 (1990), 100–6.

6. PRO, C81/1392/6; *Calendar of the Close Rolls Preserved in the Public Record Office* (London, HMSO, 1892–1963), *1476–85*, no. 1171 (hereafter *CCR*).

7. *Extracts from the Municipal Records of the City of York during the Reigns of Edward IV, Edward V and Richard III*, ed. R. Davies (Gloucester, rev. edn, Trowbridge & Esher, 1976), pp. 152–3, 214–15; Elton, 'The Rolls of Parliament', pp. 119–20.

8. *Paston Letters and Papers of the Fifteenth Century*, ed. N. Davis (2 vols, Oxford, Clarendon Press, 1971–76), vol. 2, no. 799.

9. *Plumpton Correspondence*, ed. T. Stapleton (Camden Society, old series, 4, 1839), p. 45; R.A. Griffiths, *Sir Rhys ap Thomas and his family: a study in the Wars of the Roses and early Tudor politics* (Cardiff, University of Wales Press, 1993), pp. 5–6, 37.

10. *Calendar of the Patent Rolls Preserved in the Public Record Office* (London, HMSO, 1891–1982), *1476–85*, p. 371 (hereafter *CPR*). The indictment states that the rebels had unlawfully arrayed 'per mandatum . . . Henry Duke of Buckingham': Royal Institution of Cornwall, BV. 1/4.

11. Philippe de Commynes, *Memoirs: the Reign of Louis XI, 1461–83*, ed. M. Jones (Harmondsworth,

Penguin Books, 1972), pp. 26, 35, 344–5, 353–4, 396–7; B.A. Pocquet du Haut-Jussé, *François II, Duc de Bretagne et L'Angleterre, 1458–88* (Paris, 1929), pp. 251–3; R.A. Griffiths, R.S. Thomas, *The Making of the Tudor Dynasty* (Gloucester, Alan Sutton Publishing, 1985), pp. 102–3.

12. Lord Macaulay, *History of England to the Death of William III* (4 vols, London, rev. edn, Heron Books, 1967), vol. 1, p. 29.

13. *Chroniques de Jean Molinet (1474–1506)*, ed. G. Doutrepont, O. Jodogne (3 vols, Académie Royale de Belgique. Classe des Lettres et des Sciences Morales et Politiques. Collection des Anciens Auteurs Belges. Brussels, 1935–7), vol. 1, p. 431.

14. Dominic Mancini's work captured the attention of English historians in 1936 when it appeared in an edition by C.A.J. Armstrong. It is likely that Mancini was in England from the summer of 1482 until shortly after Richard's coronation on 6 July 1483, at the behest of his patron, Angelo Cato, Archbishop of Vienne: Dominic Mancini, *The Usurpation of Richard III*, ed. C.A.J. Armstrong (Oxford, Clarendon Press, 1969).

15. *The Crowland Chronicle Continuations, 1459–1486*, ed. N. Pronay and J. Cox (London, Alan Sutton Publishing, 1986), p. 163.

16. R.F. Green, 'Historical Notes of a London Citizen, 1483–1488', *English Historical Review*, 96 (1981), 585–90 (hereafter *EHR*). *The Chronicle of Fabian, which he nameth the Concordance of Histories newly perused and continued from the beginnyng of King Henry the Seventh to th' End of Queen Mary* (London, 1559). For a modern edition see *The New Chronicles of England and France by Robert Fabyan, named by himself the Concordance of Histories*, ed. H. Ellis (London, 1811). *The Great Chronicle of London*, ed. A.H. Thomas and I.D. Thornley (London, G.W. Jones, 1938), p. 234.

17. While St Leger is mentioned in both the *Crowland Chronicle* and *The Great Chronicle*, the latter is the first chronicle to mention Brown, Clifford and Ramney.

18. *The Great Chronicle*, ed. A.H. Thomas and I.D. Thornley, p. 234.

19. 'John Rous's account of the reign of Richard III', in A. Hanham, *Richard III and his Early Historians, 1483–1535* (Oxford, Clarendon Press, 1975), pp. 122–3.

20. P.B. Farrer and A.F. Sutton, 'The Duke of Buckingham's sons, October 1483–August 1485', *The Ricardian*, 78 (1982), 88–9.

21. *The 'Anglica Historia' of Polydore Vergil, AD 1485–1537*, ed. D. Hay (Camden Society, new series, 74, 1950).

22. Philippe de Commynes, *Memoirs*, pp. 355, 397; Ross, *Richard III*, pp. xxiv, xxxi, xlvi–xlvii.

23. C. Rawcliffe, 'Henry VII and Edward, Duke of Buckingham: the Repression of an "Overmighty Subject"', *Bulletin of the Institute of Historical Research*, 53 (1980), 114–18; D. Hay, 'The Manuscript of Polydore Vergil's "Anglica Historia"', *EHR*, 54 (1939), 247–8, for opinions suppressed for political reasons; see also A. Gransden, *Historical Writing in England, c. 1307 to the Early Sixteenth Century* (London, Routledge and Kegan Paul, 1982), p. 444.

24. *The 'Anglica Historia' of Polydore Vergil*, ed. D. Hay, p. 199; 'Vitellius A XVI' comments that Dorset escaped around the time of Richard's coronation, and 'for whom King Richard made narrow and busy search': 'Vitellius A XVI', p. 191.

25. *The 'Anglica Historia' of Polydore Vergil*, ed. D. Hay, pp. 196–7, 200. As Bray died in 1503, it is possible that Vergil had direct contact with him soon after his arrival at the English court in 1502.

26. Edward Hall, *The Union of the Two Noble and Illustre Families of Lancastre and York*, ed. H. Ellis (London, 1550) (Facsimile, 1970), 'The Tragical Doings of King Richard the Third', ff. IIIIr–Vv.

27. E. Hall, in Shakespeare, *King Richard III*, ed. A. Hammond (London, Methuen & Co.

Ltd, 1981), ff. xxxix–r; xl–r (hereafter, Hall, in Shakespeare); *The 'Anglica Historia' of Polydore Vergil*, ed. D. Hay, p. 199.

28. Hall, in Shakespeare, ff. xl–r; for quotation, introd., *King Richard III*, ed. A. Hammond, p. 87. Hall has copied Vergil's error here in naming Humphrey Bannaster, instead of Ralph Bannaster.

29. Raphael Holinshed, *Chronicles of England, Scotland and Ireland*, ed. H. Ellis (6 vols, New York, reprint of 1807–8 edn, A.M.S. Press, *c*. 1976), vol. 3, p. 421.

30. J. Stow, *The Annales of England* (London, 1592); for Scott cited by Stow, see A.E. Conway, 'The Maidstone Sector of Buckingham's Rebellion, October 18, 1483', *Archaeologia Cantiana*, being *Transactions of the Kent Archaeological Society*, 37 (1925), 105.

31. See M.J. Bennett, *The Battle of Bosworth* (Gloucester, Alan Sutton Publishing, 1985), pp. 10–11 and Appendix V. The origin of 'Buckingham Betrayd by Banaster' is uncertain, and though it was set down in the eighteenth century, elements suggest that it could well have derived from the early sixteenth-century oral tradition; 'Murdering of Edward the Fourth his Sons' is probably extant from 1659 and based on a 1612 edition; the earliest surviving text of the 'Song of Lady Bessy' is from around 1600; see *Bishop Percy's Folio Manuscript: Ballads and Romances*, ed. J.W. Hales, F.J. Furnivall (3 vols, London, 1868).

32. *Bishop Percy's Folio Manuscript*, ed. J.W. Hales, F.J. Furnivall, vol. 3, pp. 163–6.

33. Sir George Buck, *History of the Life and Reign of King Richard the Third* (1619), ed. A.N. Kincaid (Gloucester, Alan Sutton Publishing, 1982), pp. 25, 64–5. Like Hall, Buck has copied Vergil's error in naming Humphrey rather than Ralph Bannaster.

34. C.A. Halsted, *Richard III as Duke of Gloucester and King of England* (2 vols, London,

Longman, Brown, Green and Longmans, 1844); Ross, *Richard III*, p. l; A.R. Myers, 'Richard III and Historical Tradition', *History*, 53 (1968), 196.

35. Halsted, *Richard III as Duke of Gloucester*, vol. 2, pp. 181–2, 238–40, 264.

36. L. Gill, 'William Caxton and the Rebellion of 1483', *EHR*, 112 (1997), 113–18.

CHAPTER TWO

1. See R. Horrox, 'Richard III and London', *The Ricardian*, 85 (1984), 322–3; *CCR, 1476–85*, no. 473.

2. M. Hicks, 'Richard, Duke of Gloucester and the North', *Richard III and the North*, ed. R. Horrox (Gloucester, Alan Sutton Publishing, 1986), p. 14.

3. See appendix 3 for the official list of rebels and appendix 4 for the sample of fifty-five knights, squires and gentlemen on whom the discussion is based.

4. *Victoria County History* (hereafter *VCH*) *Wilts*, vol. 4, p. 409; vol. 10, pp. 238–42; vol. 11, p. 110; vol. 13, p. 222; *The Crowland Chronicle Continuations*, ed. J. Pronay and N. Cox, p. 153.

5. For direct grants of duchy of Lancaster lands see *VCH Wilts*, vol. 8, p. 235; vol. 9, pp. 176–8; vol. 11, pp. 109, 139, 145, 168–70, 173, 210, 240; *VCH Berks*, vol. 4, p. 533; for duchy of Cornwall, see *VCH Glos*, vol. 11, p. 16; *VCH Somerset*, vol. 3, pp. 122–3; *VCH Wilts*, vol. 11, pp. 109, 139; *CPR, 1467–77*, p. 283.

6. M. Hicks, *False, Fleeting, Perjur'd Clarence* (Stroud, Alan Sutton Publishing, 1980), appendix II, pp. 206–7; see also *CPR, 1461–67*, pp. 198–9, 212–13, 226, 328, 331, 362, 366, 388, 452–5, 484; *CPR, 1467–77*, pp. 88, 330, 457–8.

7. M. Hicks, 'The Changing Role of the Wydevilles in Yorkist Politics to 1483', *Patronage, Pedigree and Power in Late Medieval England*, ed. C. Ross (Stroud, Alan Sutton Publishing, 1979), pp. 73–4.

8. M. Sayer, 'Norfolk Involvement in Dynastic Conflict 1467–1471 and 1483–1487', *Norfolk Archaeology*, 36 (1977), 315–16; M.J. Tucker, 'The Life of Thomas Howard, Earl of Surrey and Second Duke of Norfolk, 1443–1524', PhD thesis, Northwestern University (1962), pp. 3–4; J.M. Robinson, *The Dukes of Norfolk* (Oxford, Oxford University Press, 1982), pp. 1–6.

9. Rawcliffe, *The Staffords, Earls of Stafford and Dukes of Buckingham, 1394–1521* (Cambridge, Cambridge University Press, 1977), appendix A and B; A. J. Collinson, *The History and Antiquities of the County of Somerset* (3 vols, London, 1892), vol. 1, p. 228; vol. 3, p. 56; *VCH Glos*, vol. 3, p. 481; vol. 4, pp. 5, 41; *VCH Surrey*, vol. 3, p. 449; vol. 4, pp. 28, 324, 327, 329; 'Some Observations relating to Four Deeds from the Muniment Room of Maxstoke Castle, co. Warwick', ed. T.W. King, *Archaeologia*, 38 (1860), 278.

10. See in general K. Mertes, 'Aristocracy', *Fifteenth Century Attitudes: Perceptions of society in late medieval England*, ed. R. Horrox (Cambridge, Cambridge University Press, 1994), pp. 42–60; S.J. Payling, 'The politics of family: late medieval marriage contracts', *The McFarlane Legacy: Studies in Late Medieval Politics and Society*, ed. R.H. Britnell, A.J. Pollard (Stroud, Alan Sutton Publishing, 1995), pp. 21–47, especially pp. 21–5; see also *Kingsford's Stonor Letters and Papers, 1290–1483*, ed. C. Carpenter (Cambridge, Cambridge University Press, 1996), pp. xxxii–xxxiii.

11. See S.J. Payling, *Political Society in Lancastrian England, The Greater Gentry of Nottinghamshire* (Oxford, Oxford University Press, 1991), pp. 1–4, for a useful discussion on gentry wealth; *BLHM*, vol. 1, pp. 101, 116, 174, 176, 188, 193, 198, 207, 236, 250, 269, 277; vol. 2, pp. 31–7, 55–6, 58, 77, 83, 108–9, 126, 137, 181; *CPR, 1476–85*, pp. 54–6, 63, 424, 433, 454, 471, 476, 478, 481, 487, 501; *CCR, 1476–85*, no.

175; *Calendar of Inquisitions Post Mortem, Henry VII* (London, HMSO, 1898), vol. 1, nos 30, 55, 161, 181–4, 210, 212–13, 215, 217, 222, 239, 961, 973, 977, 1030–1, 1129, 1175 (hereafter *CIPM*); PRO, PROB 11/9, f. 223v; *The Stonor Letters and Papers, 1290–1483*, ed. C.L. Kingsford (2 vols, Camden Society, third series, 1919), vol. 1, pp. xi–xvi; G. Ormerod, 'A Memoir on the Lancashire House of Le Noreis or Norres', *Historic Society of Lancashire and Cheshire Transactions*, 2 (1850), 159 and *passim*; W.D. Cooper, 'Pedigree of the Lewkenor Family', *Sussex Archaeological Collections*, 3 (1850), 89–102; S. Bolton, 'Sir John Fogge of Ashford', *The Ricardian*, 69 (1980), 202–3; J.R. Dunlop, 'Pedigree of the Family of Crioll, or Kyriell, of co. Kent', *Miscellanea Genealogica et Heraldica*, 6 (fifth series, 1926–7), 259; G. Waters, 'The Gloucester Scene – August 1483', *Richard III, Crown and People*, ed. J. Petre (Gloucester, Alan Sutton Publishing, 1985), pp. 241–3; H. Kleineke, 'The Reburial Expenses of Sir Thomas Arundell', *The Ricardian*, 141 (1998), 288.

12. I.D. Rowney, 'The Staffordshire Political Community 1440–1500', PhD thesis, University of Keele (1981), *passim*; E. Acheson, 'The Leicestershire Gentry in the Fifteenth Century, *c.* 1422–1485', PhD thesis, University of New England (1989), *passim*; see C. Carpenter, 'Gentry and Community in Medieval England', *Journal of British Studies*, 33 (1994), 340–80, for an excellent critique of gentry works, especially pp. 349–50, for useful comments on regional élites.

13. J.C. Wedgwood, *History of Parliament: Biographies of the Members of the Commons House, 1439–1509* (London, HMSO, 1936), pp. 550, 600, 875, 944; W.E. Hampton, *Memorials of the Wars of the Roses* (Gloucester, Alan Sutton Publishing, 1979), no. 331; for Daubenay's contacts, *CCR, 1476–85*, nos 548, 754, 760, 923.

14. *CIPM*, no. 413; *Stonor Letters and Papers*,

ed. C.L. Kingsford, vol. 1, nos 75, 87, 89, 94, 110, 115, 116; vol. 2, nos 179, 182, 197; C. Carpenter, 'The Stonor Circle in the Fifteenth Century', *Rulers and Ruled in Late Medieval England: Essays presented to Gerald Harriss*, ed. R.E. Archer and S. Walker (London, The Hambledon Press, 1995), pp. 178–87.

15. PRO, PROB 11/5, f. 241v; PRO, PROB 11/11, ff. 21v–r; PRO, PROB 11/17, f. 225r; L.F. Salzman, 'Sussex Domesday Tenants: The Family of Chesney or Cheyney', *Sussex Archaeological Collections*, 65 (1924), 20–54; C.S. Gilbert, *An Historical Survey of the County of Cornwall* (2 vols, London, Longman, Hurst, Rees, Orme and Brown, 1817–20), vol. 2, pp. 468–70, 533; *The Complete Peerage of England, Scotland, Ireland, Great Britain and the United Kingdom*, ed. V. Gibbs, H.A. Doubleday, D. Warrand, Thomas, Lord Howard de Walden, and G. White (13 vols, London, St Catherine's Press, 1910–59), vol. 12, part II, p. 660; *VCH Wilts*, vol. 8, p. 151; Conway, 'The Maidstone Sector of Buckingham's Rebellion, October 18, 1483', p. 115; Hampton, *Memorials*, no. 154; *VCH Hants*, vol. 4, p. 337; *CIPM*, no. 1140; Wedgwood, *History of Parliament*, p. 245.

16. PRO, PROB 11/6, f. 106r; PRO, PROB 11/7, f. 191v; PRO, PROB 11/8, ff. 235r–236v; PRO, PROB 11/8, f. 255r; *CCR, 1476–85*, nos 389, 749, 979, 989. By the later fifteenth century these connections were of decades' standing. In the 1440s John Norris and Thomas Stonor were both trustees with the 1st Duke of Buckingham, with Sir Robert Harcourt (d. 1470) and his brother, Sir Richard (d. 1486?); see also R.A. Griffiths, *The Reign of King Henry VI: The Exercise of Royal Authority, 1422–1461* (London, Ernest Benn Ltd, 1981), pp. 70–1.

17. For Berkeley-Gloucester, *CCR, 1476–85*, no. 473; see also nos 42, 311, 719, 748, 1370; PRO, PROB 11/10, f. 102v; PRO, PROB 11/7, f. 31r; PRO, PROB 11/8, f. 319r; PRO, PROB 11/9, f. 223v; see also *CIPM*, nos 392, 681.

18. *Stonor Letters and Papers*, ed. C.L. Kingsford, vol. 2, nos 285, 320.

19. PRO, PROB 11/8, ff. 319v–320v; PRO, PROB 11/6, f. 130v–r; PRO, PROB 11/3, f. 11r; A.F. Sutton, 'The Court and its Culture in the Reign of Richard III', *Richard III: A Medieval Kingship*, ed. J. Gillingham (London, Collins and Brown Ltd, 1993), p. 81.

20. See, for example, Carpenter, 'The Stonor Circle in the Fifteenth Century', pp. 190–1.

21. *Stonor Letters and Papers*, ed. C.L. Kingsford, vol. 1, no. 141; see also S.J. Payling, 'Murder, Motive and Punishment in Fifteenth Century England', *EHR*, 113 (1998), 1–2, 16–17.

22. *CPR, 1476–85*, pp. 370–1; *CCR, 1476–85*, no. 1242.

23. *Stonor Letters and Papers*, ed. C.L. Kingsford, vol. 2, nos 287, 288, 313, 319; Wedgwood, *History of Parliament*, p. 815. Estates may well have been at the heart of his conflict with Gloucester through his marriage with Anne Neville, daughter of John, Marquess Montagu, brother of the deceased Earl of Warwick and a cousin of Gloucester, whose ward she most likely was: *Stonor Letters and Papers*, ed. C.L. Kingsford, vol. 1, p. xxiii.

24. *CIPM*, nos 30, 181.

25. B.P. Wolffe, 'The Management of English Royal Estates under Yorkist Kings', *EHR*, 278 (1956), 3, 6–9; B.P. Wolffe, *The Royal Demesne in English History* (London, Allen and Unwin, 1971), pp. 160–1.

26. The Courtenays had been foresters of the chase of Dartmoor, stewards of the borough and manor of Bradninch and of all duchy lands in Devon and held the office of warden of the stannery: A.L. Rowse, *Tudor Cornwall* (London, Macmillan and Company Ltd, 1969), p. 114; for Arundel, *CPR, 1461–67*, p. 23.

27. In February 1483 Daubenay became constable of Bridgwater, held by Edward IV's mother, Cecily, Duchess of York. Berkeley was

constable of Southampton; Stonor, steward of numerous royal manors in Buckinghamshire; Nicholas Gaynesford was a constable in Surrey; Sir John Fogge the same in Kent and also supervisor of hunting in Sussex; St Leger was a custodian of the king's park at Guildford in the east, and of Torrington in the west; while Lewkenor became constable of Bodiam and also keeper of the park there: *CPR, 1461–67*, pp. 23–4, 220; *CPR, 1467–77*, pp. 297–8; *CPR, 1476–85*, pp. 35, 337, 444, 535; for Berkeley, 'Financial Memoranda of the Reign of Edward V: Longleat Miscellaneous Manuscript', Book II, ed. R. Horrox, *Camden Miscellany*, 22 (fourth series, London, 1987), 233–4; for Fogge, Norris and Stonor, Wedgwood, *History of Parliament*, pp. 340, 640, 815; see also *BLHM*, vol. 1, p. 101; *VCH Surrey*, vol. 3, pp. 3, 335; *VCH Sussex*, vol. 7, pp. 257–8; vol. 9, p. 263.

28. Gaynesford received Lord Clifford's Surrey lands in 1462, and Fogge the keepership of the Earl of Oxford's estates; in 1478 Sir George Brown received the stewardship of Witley, Kent, forfeited by Jasper Tudor, Earl of Pembroke, while John St Lo received a number of the Earl of Wiltshire's forfeited West Country estates. Then again, many others profited from Clarence's downfall in 1478 including his clients St Leger and William Norris, as stewards of his estates, with another client, St Lo, who was confirmed in offices he had recently received. For Fogge and Gaynesford, Wedgwood, *History of Parliament*, pp. 340–1, 368; *CPR, 1475–85*, pp. 87, 91, 157.

29. *CPR, 1461–67*, p. 43; *CPR, 1467–77*, p. 83; *CPR, 1476–85*, pp. 88, 177, 416; *CCR, 1476–85*, no. 859; Wedgwood, *History of Parliament*, pp. 341, 640.

30. R. Somerville, *History of the Duchy of Lancaster* (London, 1953), pp. 428, 605, 615–16, 621, 637; *VCH Wilts*, vol. 4, p. 442; vol. 13, p. 222; *VCH Somerset*, vol. 2, p. 565; *VCH Berks*, vol. 2, p. 139; vol. 3, pp. 24, 528; *BLHM*, vol. 1, p. 9.

31. PRO, PROB 11/7, f. 86v; PRO, PROB 11/6, f. 40; *The Coronation of Richard III: the Extant Documents*, ed. A.F. Sutton and P.W. Hammond (Stroud, Alan Sutton Publishing, 1983), pp. 316, 378; for Norris and Stonor, Wedgwood, *History of Parliament*, pp. 640, 814–15; see also *Stonor Letters and Papers*, ed. C.L. Kingsford, vol. 1, pp. xxx–xxxi, xxxiii and no. 79. Stonor's father, Thomas, had been in service to George Neville, Archbishop of York, from the late 1460s, and Sir William's marriage with Anne Neville obviously opened up this circle for him. Then again, Stonor's father had married the natural daughter of William, Duke of Suffolk.

32. *CIPM*, nos 331, 548; Gilbert, *An Historical Survey*, vol. 2, p. 888. Berkeley was steward of the Salisbury lands on the Isle of Wight: P.A. Johnson, *Duke Richard of York, 1411–1460* (Oxford, Oxford University Press, 1988), appendix III.

33. G. Waters, 'The Gloucester Scene – August 1483', pp. 241–3; Rawcliffe, *The Staffords*, appendix B, pp. 74, 203, 205, 210, 212; appendix C, p. 227; appendix D, p. 235; Somerville, *Duchy of Lancaster*, p. 608; 'The Account of the Great Household of Humphrey, First Duke of Buckingham, for the year 1452–3', ed. M.H. Harris, *Camden Miscellany*, 29 (fourth series, London, 1984), 11–53.

34. K.B. McFarlane, 'Bastard Feudalism', reprinted in *England in the Fifteenth Century*, ed. G.L. Harriss (London, The Hambledon Press, 1981), p. 31.

35. Conway, 'The Maidstone Sector of Buckingham's Rebellion, October 18, 1483', p. 108; Rawcliffe, *The Staffords*, p. 33.

36. PRO, PROB 11/7, ff. 190v–191r; PRO, PROB 11/7, f. 182v; PRO, PROB 11/9, f. 83v; PRO, PROB 11/11, f. 213r; *CCR, 1476–85*, nos 647, 664, 667, 748–9, 829, 1370; *CPR, 1467–77*, p. 339; C.H. Cooper, *Memoir of Margaret Countess of Richmond and Derby* (Cambridge, Cambridge University Press, 1874), p. 50.

37. See D.A. Luckett, 'Crown Patronage and Political Morality in Early Tudor England: The Case of Giles, Lord Daubenay', *EHR*, 110 (1995), 581–2, for Daubenay's 'lordship' during Henry VII's early years, which equally applied to Daubenay and some others in the years prior to 1483.

38. The queen's relatives were often first in line for rich preferment. Sir Edward Woodville was granted the supervision of Portsmouth and the custody of the castle, forest and warren of Porchester, with the offices of porter, 'artiller', watchman and groom in his gift: Hampton, *Memorials*, no. 352; *CPR, 1467–77*, pp. 366, 339; Somerville, *Duchy of Lancaster*, p. 418; K. Houghton, 'Theory and Practice in Borough Elections to Parliament during the Later Fifteenth Century', *Bulletin of the Institute of Historical Research*, 39 (1966), 137.

39. Ross, *Richard III*, pp. 106–7; R. Virgoe, 'Sir John Risley 1443–1512: Courtier and Councillor', *Norfolk Archaeology*, 38 (1982), 142.

40. *VCH Berks*, vol. 3, p. 12; *VCH Surrey*, vol. 1, p. 365; *The Travels of Leo of Rozmital*, ed. M. Letts (Cambridge, Cambridge University Press, 1957), p. 55; for quotation, E.W. Ives, *The Common Lawyers of Pre-Reformation England* (Cambridge, Cambridge University Press, 1983), p. 374.

41. Families with a tradition of service as royal retainers include the Hungerfords, Bourchiers, Norrises, Lovells, Browns, Arundels, Cheynes, Treffrys, Edgecombes, Nanfans, St Los, Fiennesses, Tocoteses, Harcourts, Wingfields, Hampdens and Trevelyans: Griffiths, *The Reign of King Henry VI*, pp. 82, 263, n. 10, 303, 309, 337, 340–1, 493, 633–4, 815; G.L. Harriss, *Cardinal Beaufort* (Oxford, Oxford University Press, 1988), pp. 72–3, 158, 235; J.S. Roskell, *Parliament and Politics in Late Medieval England* (3 vols, London, 1981–3), vol. 2, pp. 96, 105, 118, 122, 127; vol. 3, p. 174.

42. *Paston Letters and Papers*, ed. N. Davis, vol. 1, no. 383; A.R. Myers, *The Household of Edward IV* (Manchester, Manchester University Press, 1959), p. 41; Ross, *Richard III*, pp. 105–6.

43. D.A.L. Morgan, 'The House of policy: the political role of the late Plantagenet household, 1422–1485', *The English at Court: From the Wars of the Roses to the Civil War*, ed. D. Starkey (London, 1987), p. 58; *The Coronation of Richard III*, ed. A.F. Sutton and P.W. Hammond, p. 312.

44. S.J. Gunn, 'The Courtiers of Henry VII', *EHR*, 108 (1993), 35–6, for a valuable discussion on the households of Henry VII and Queen Elizabeth.

45. Morgan, 'The House of Policy', pp. 55–6, 63–4; D.A.L. Morgan, 'The King's Affinity in the Polity of Yorkist England', *Transactions of the Royal Historical Society*, 23 (1973), 18–19; S.J. Gunn, *Early Tudor Government, 1485– 1558* (New York, St Martin's Press, 1995), pp. 24–7.

46. Gunn, 'The Courtiers of Henry VII', p. 28.

47. Morgan, 'The House of Policy', pp. 59, 69–70.

CHAPTER THREE

1. *VCH Oxon*, vol. 4, p. 21; vol. 10, p. 7; *VCH Berks*, vol. 2, p. 138; vol. 3, p. 12; *Historie of the Arrivall of King Edward IV in England and the final Recoverye of his Kingdomes from Henry VI, AD 1471*, ed. J. Bruce, Camden Society, 1 (original series, London, 1838), p. 74; C. Ross, *Edward IV* (London, Eyre Methuen, 1974), pp. 57–8.

2. A. Goodman, *A History of England from Edward II to James I* (London, Routledge and Kegan Paul, 1977), pp. 55–6.

3. *The Chronicles of the White Rose of York*, ed. J.A. Giles (London, 1845), pp. 28–9; *Historie of the Arrivall of King Edward IV*, ed. J. Bruce, pp. 22–3; J. Warkworth, 'A Chronicle of the First Thirteen Years of the Reign of King

Edward the Fourth', ed. J.O. Haliwell, Camden Society (original series, London, 1893), p. 16; P.W. Hammond, *The Battles of Barnet and Tewkesbury* (Stroud, Alan Sutton Publishing, 1990), pp. 17, 32; Hicks, *False, Fleeting Perjur'd Clarence*, p. 72; Ross, *Edward IV*, p. 169.

4. C.L. Scofield, *The Life and Reign of Edward the Fourth, King of England and of France and Lord of Ireland* (2 vols, London, rev. edn, Frank Cass and Company Limited, 1967), vol. 1, pp. 219–20.

5. *CPR,1452–61*, pp. 402, 407, 489, 495, 559, 602–3, 613; *CPR,1461–67*, pp. 28–34, 38, 102; Scofield, *The Life and Reign of Edward the Fourth*, vol. 1, pp. 42, n. 3, 179–80, 480.

6. *CPR, 1461–67*, pp. 36–9, 65–6, 98–100, 132, 304; 'Gregory's Chronicle', *The Historical Collections of a Citizen of London*, ed. J. Gairdner (London, 1876), pp. 223–6; Scofield, *The Life and Reign of Edward the Fourth*, vol. 1, pp. 231–4, 250–3; C. Ross, *The Wars of the Roses* (London, Book Club Associates, 1976), p. 55; Ross, *Edward IV*, pp. 46–62.

7. Hampton, *Memorials*, no. 141; Wedgwood, *History of Parliament*, pp. 420, 888; J.M. Wingfield, *Some Records of the Wingfield Family* (London, John Murray Limited, 1925), pp. 18–19. Among Thomas Stonor's papers was an official Yorkist account of the first battle of St Albans; see *Stonor Letters and Papers*, ed. C.L. Kingsford, vol. 1, p. xxiii and no. 59.

8. *Paston Letters and Papers*, ed. N. Davis, vol. 1, no. 354; vol. 2, nos 609, 613; *Stonor Letters and Papers*, ed. C.L. Kingsford, vol. 1, pp. xxiii–xxvi; Sayer, 'Norfolk Involvement in Dynastic Conflict', pp. 307–9, 311–12; R. Virgoe, 'An Election Dispute of 1483', *Historical Research*, 60 (1987), 35; Virgoe, 'Sir John Risley, 1443–1512', p. 142; Hicks, *False, Fleeting, Perjur'd Clarence*, appendix 3; Morgan, 'The King's Affinity in the Polity of Yorkist England', p. 7.

9. *CPR, 1467–77*, pp. 217–18; *CPR, 1476–85*, p. 87; *CCR, 1468–76*, no. 962; M. Cherry, 'The Courtenay Earls of Devon: The Formation and Disintegration of a Late Medieval Aristocratic Affinity', *Southern History*, 1 (1979), 77, 94–6; Hicks, *False, Fleeting, Perjur'd Clarence*, pp. 139, 170, appendix 3; J.A.F. Thomson, 'The Courtenay Family in the Yorkist Period', *Bulletin of the Institute of Historical Research*, 14 (1972), *passim*. Clarence's retainers included Richard Nanfan, Sir Nicholas Latimer, Sir Robert Willoughby, James Norris, the Courtenays of Powderham, Sir Hugh Courtenay of Boconnoc, William Twynyho, Roger Tocotes, John Halwell, Richard Edgecombe, John St Lo, Edward Hungerford, Sir John Arundel of Lanherne, and almost certainly Sir Thomas St Leger.

10. *The Travels of Leo of Rozmital*, ed. M. Letts, pp. 58–9.

11. PRO, KB 9/320; *CPR, 1461–67*, p. 529; *Plumpton Correspondence*, ed. T. Stapleton, pp. 19–20, 30; Warkworth, 'A Chronicle of the First Thirteen Years of the Reign of King Edward the Fourth', ed. J.O. Haliwell, pp. 6, 11–12; H.T. Evans, *Wales in the Wars of the Roses* (Cambridge, Cambridge University Press, 1915), pp. 165–6; Ross, *Edward IV*, pp. 72–3, 77, 91, 119, 122–4.

12. *CPR, 1467–77*, pp. 42–3. The prototype of the manifesto was circulated in 1450 and used again in 1460. Others attacked in 1469 include the Earl of Pembroke, Humphrey Stafford, Earl of Devon (d. 1469) and Lord Audley: Scofield, *The Life and Reign of Edward the Fourth*, vol. 1, pp. 492–3; Morgan, 'The King's Affinity in the Polity of Yorkist England', p. 9.

13. Bennett, *The Battle of Bosworth*, p. 28.

14. M.J. Bennett, 'Edward III's Entail and the Succession to the Crown, 1376–1471', *EHR*, 113 (1998), 603–4.

15. *CPR, 1467–77*, p. 200; Thomson, 'The Courtenay Family in the Yorkist Period', p. 234; R.P. Chope, 'The Last of the Dynhams', *Report*

and Transactions of the Devonshire Association, 50 (1918), 451; Wedgwood, *History of Parliament*, pp. 122, 402; Hampton, *Memorials*, no. 329.

16. *CPR, 1467–77*, pp. 251, 267, 298; *Lists and Indexes No. IX: Lists of Sheriffs for England and Wales* (London, PRO, 1898), pp. 22, 36, 50, 55, 124, 137, 143; Wedgwood, *History of Parliament*, pp. 122, 402; Thomson, 'The Courtenay Family in the Yorkist Period', pp. 234, 237; Hampton, *Memorials*, no. 31; Sayer, 'Norfolk Involvement in Dynastic Conflict', pp. 310–11. Both dukes had served Edward in the earlier Lincolnshire campaign: M.A. Hicks, 'The 1468 Statute of Livery', *Historical Research*, 64 (1991), 26; Hicks, *False, Fleeting, Perjur'd Clarence*, p. 90.

17. Fogge's importance as a captain is evident after Towton when he was in charge of the muster at Beverley, and had the 'rule of the Country' in Kent: Ross, *Edward IV*, pp. 35–6, 323.

18. Hammond, *The Battles of Barnet and Tewkesbury*, pp. 34, 44, 70; Morgan, 'The King's Affinity in the Polity of Yorkist England', pp. 10–11; Hampton, *Memorials*, no. 297.

19. *CPR, 1467–77*, pp. 267, 609–10; Hampton, *Memorials*, nos 329, 404; Somerville, *History of the Duchy of Lancaster*, p. 631; Thomson, 'The Courtenay Family in the Yorkist Period', pp. 237–8; Sayer, 'Norfolk Involvement in Dynastic Conflict', p. 314.

20. BL, Stowe MS 440, f. 68; Scofield, *The Life and Reign of Edward the Fourth*, vol. 2, p. 200; C.F. Richmond, 'Fauconberg's Kentish rising of May 1471', *EHR*, 85 (1970), 689; Hampton, *Memorials*, no. 141.

21. Hicks, *False, Fleeting, Perjur'd Clarence*, pp. 101–4; Ross, *Edward IV*, pp. 154–60.

22. *CPR, 1467–77*, pp. 366, 414; *The Complete Peerage*, ed. V. Gibbs, H.A. Doubleday *et al.*, vol. 12, p. 356; D.E. Lowe, 'Patronage and Politics: Edward IV, the Wydevilles and the council of the Prince of Wales, 1471–83',

Bulletin of the Board of Celtic Studies, 29 (1981), 551–3; N. Orme, 'The Education of Edward V', *Bulletin of the Institute of Historical Research*, 57 (1984), 122.

23. Lowe, 'Patronage and Politics', pp. 557–60; Orme, 'The Education of Edward V' p. 124; Hicks, 'The Changing Role of the Wydevilles in Yorkist Politics to 1483', p. 78.

24. Ross, *Edward IV*, pp. 334–5; Rawcliffe, *The Staffords*, pp. 30–1.

25. Sir George Brown (almost exclusively Edward's servant), Sir William Knyvet, the Gaynesfords, Sir Nicholas Latimer, John Twynyho and Sir Roger Tocotes distanced themselves from Clarence and received, among others, Woodville or Stafford patronage: *Paston Letters and Papers*, ed. N. Davis, vol. 1, no. 312; Virgoe, 'An Election Dispute of 1483', p. 32, n. 45; Hicks, *False, Fleeting, Perjur'd Clarence*, appendix 3.

26. Morgan, 'The House of Policy', pp. 63–5; Morgan, 'The King's Affinity in the Polity of Yorkist England', pp. 18–19; Lowe, 'Patronage and Politics', pp. 550, 552, 557–8; A.J. Pollard, *The Wars of the Roses* (London, Macmillan Education Ltd, 1988), p. 99; Hicks, 'The Changing Role of the Wydevilles in Yorkist Politics to 1483', pp. 63, 71.

27. *CPR, 1476–85*, pp. 21, 160, 571; *Sheriffs, Lists and Indexes*, pp. 22, 36, 55, 87, 124; *VCH Surrey*, vol. 4, p. 275; Thomson, 'The Courtenay Family in the Yorkist Period', p. 235. Daubenay at just twenty-three in 1474 became both a justice and sheriff in Devon, Somerset and elsewhere; Willoughby and Nanfan were sheriffs of Cornwall in 1478 and 1479, respectively; Berkeley and Uvedale (the latter just twenty-five in 1479), the same in Hampshire in 1476 and 1479 (the former was also sheriff of Somerset-Dorset in 1477); John Cheyne and Walter Hungerford also obtained the office in Wiltshire. Edward Courtenay was a commissioner in 1477 and sheriff of Devon in

1478, while Arundel rose to great heights as a squire of the body. The Gaynesfords used their Woodville links to obtain the seat of Guildford between 1473 and 1475, in the queen's gift, and to assist them to the shrievalty four times from 1474 to 1482. Likewise the Hautes dominated the shrievalty, with Sir William in office in 1474 and 1482, and Richard in 1477 and 1481. St Leger and Bourchier, both king's kinsmen, were also among the most solid regional powers.

28. *Stonor Letters and Papers*, ed. C.L. Kingsford, vol. 1, p. xxxii and vol. 2, nos 230, 285.

29. Appointed with Dorset in the west were Devon's Robert Willoughby and John Halwell; in Dorset Thomas St Leger, Nicholas Latimer, William Berkeley and William Uvedale; in Cornwall Edward Courtenay and Richard Nanfan; in Wiltshire Roger Tocotes, John Cheyne and Walter Hungerford; in Somerset Giles Daubenay; in Oxfordshire-Berkshire William Stonor and William Norris; in Kent with Earl Rivers, John Fogge and John Scott; and in Sussex with the Earl of Arundel, Thomas and Richard Lewkenor: *CPR, 1476–85*, p. 353.

30. Ross, *Edward IV*, pp. 97, 99; Morgan, 'The House of Policy', p. 65; Hicks, 'The Changing Role of the Wydevilles in Yorkist Politics to 1483', pp. 80–1.

31. See, for example, *CCR, 1476–85*, nos 719, 748–9, 1258, 1370.

32. See Bennett, *The Battle of Bosworth*, pp. 26, 152–3.

33. G.L. Harriss, 'The King and his Subjects', *Fifteenth Century Attitudes*, ed. R. Horrox, p. 21 and Harriss, 'The Dimensions of Politics', *The McFarlane Legacy*, ed. R.H. Britnell, A.J. Pollard, pp. 7–11; R. Horrox, 'Service', *Fifteenth Century Attitudes*, ed. R. Horrox, pp. 71–5; C. Richmond, 'After McFarlane', *History* (1983), 57–9; T.B. Pugh, 'The Magnates, knights and gentry', *Fifteenth Century England, 1399–1509*, ed. S.B.

Chrimes, C.D. Ross, R.A. Griffiths (Manchester, Stanley Bertram, 1972), pp. 86–128.

CHAPTER FOUR

1. Pollard, *Richard III and the Princes in the Tower*, pp. 74–83; R. Britnell, *The Closing of the Middle Ages? England, 1471–1529* (Oxford, Blackwell Publishers Ltd, 1997), p. 11.

2. *The Crowland Chronicle Continuations*, ed. J. Pronay and N. Cox, pp. 155, 157; *The Usurpation of Richard III*, ed. C.A.J. Armstrong, pp. 73, 75–7; *The Coronation of Richard III*, ed. A.F. Sutton and P.W. Hammond, p. 16; see Bennett, *The Battle of Bosworth*, p. 181, n. 6, for the Woodvilles' manor of Grafton Regis.

3. *Extracts from the Municipal Records of the City of York*, ed. R. Davies, p. 149.

4. *The Crowland Chronicle Continuations*, ed. J. Pronay and N. Cox, p. 159; *The 'Anglica Historia' of Polydore Vergil*, ed. D. Hay, p. 180; *The Great Chronicle*, ed. A.H. Thomas and I.D. Thornley, p. 231; *The Usurpation of Richard III*, ed. C.A.J. Armstrong, p. 91.

5. *The Crowland Chronicle Continuations*, ed. J. Pronay and N. Cox, p. 157; *The Usurpation of Richard III*, ed. C.A.J. Armstrong, p. 77: Richard 'accused them of conspiring his death and of preparing ambushes both in the capital and on the road'.

6. Hanham, *Richard III and his Early Historians, 1483–1535*, pp. 25–6, for details on Forster and Lord Hastings; Wedgwood, *History of Parliament*, p. 346: Forster had transferred the stewardship of St Albans to Hastings in February, 1483.

7. *BLHM*, vol. 1, pp. 9–10, 13–14, 17, 31, 66, 69, 72; vol. 2, pp. 2–3; Griffiths, *Sir Rhys ap Thomas*, p. 37.

8. J.G. Bellamy, *The Law of Treason in England in the Later Middle Ages* (Cambridge, Cambridge University Press, 1970), pp. 160, 170–1; Gairdner, *Life and Reign of Richard the Third*, p. 136. The office had been held traditionally by

the Bohuns whence it passed to Thomas of Woodstock, Duke of Gloucester (d. 1397), and through him to the Staffords.

9. Rawcliffe, *The Staffords*, pp. 20–7; 'Gregory's Chronicle', ed. J. Gairdner, p. 207.

10. *CPR, 1461–67*, p. 298; BL, Add. MS 6113, f. 74; Scofield, *The Life and Reign of Edward the Fourth*, vol. 1, pp. 297, n. 2, 375–8, 417, 503; vol. 2, p. 38.

11. Hanham, *Richard III and his Early Historians, 1483–1535*, p. 122.

12. Hall, *The Union of the Two Noble and Illustre Families of Lancastre and York*, ed. H. Ellis, p. 375; see also *The Coronation of Richard III*, ed. A.F. Sutton and P.W. Hammond, pp. 246–7.

13. *Stonor Letters and Papers*, ed. C.L. Kingsford, vol. 2, nos 330, 331.

14. For knighthood, St Leger and Cheyne, *The Coronation of Richard III*, ed. A.F. Sutton and P.W. Hammond, pp. 199, 272, 304, 312, 321, 390–1. Cheyne was selected by the barons of the Cinque Ports for the honour. For Stonor, Wedgwood, *History of Parliament*, p. 815. One hundred and four knights representing ninety-six families attended the king's coronation; see BL, Add. MS 6113, ff. 19–19b; see also Kleineke, 'The Reburial Expenses of Sir Thomas Arundell', p. 289.

15. Sir Thomas More, *The History of King Richard III*, ed. R.S. Sylvester (New Haven, Yale University Press, 1976), p. 84; Hampton, *Memorials*, no. 141. Ferrers had served Edward IV and was a nephew of Lord Hastings: Horrox, *Richard III*, p. 101.

16. *BLHM*, vol. 1, p. xxiii; 'An extract relating to the burial of King Edward IV', *Archaeologia*, vol. 1 (1770), pp. 350–3; Horrox, *Richard III*, pp. 146, 264.

17. *Rotuli Parliamentorum*, ed. J. Strachey, vol. 6, pp. 245–6.

18. *BLHM*, vol. 1, pp. xxiii–xxiv and vol. 3, p. 1.

19. PRO, E404/78/2/27; for Cheyne and Curtis, *The Coronation of Richard III*, ed. A.F.

Sutton and P.W. Hammond, pp. 137, 139, 321; for Lovekyn, A.F. Sutton, 'George Lovekyn, Tailor to Three Kings of England, 1470–1504', *Costume* (1981), 4.

20. Stow, *Annales*, p. 460; *BLHM*, vol. 1, p. 107.

21. For Dynham, Cornburgh and Cheyne, *BLHM*, vol. 1, pp. 42, 124, 177; for Sapcote, Horrox, *Richard III*, pp. 104–5.

22. For Haute's annuity, *BLHM*, vol. 1, p. 48; for gentry favoured at this time, *BLHM*, vol. 1, pp. 51, 71, 76–9, 86–8, 99, 191.

23. In the south-west, Thomas St Leger (despite losing other patronage), Robert Willoughby, Giles Daubenay, Thomas Arundel, Nicholas Latimer, John St Lo, Richard Beauchamp, William Berkeley, Roger Tocotes, William Uvedale, Edward Courtenay, and William Twynyho; from the south-east, John Guildford, Thomas Lewkenor and his uncle Richard, John Wood, William Brandon, William Knyvet and Nicholas Gaynesford; in the central-south, John and William Norris, Thomas Delamare, Richard Harcourt and William Stonor.

24. *The Usurpation of Richard III*, ed. C.A.J. Armstrong, p. 93. George Cely had heard a report that the king had died soon after 13 June, while the boy's physician, John Argentine, claimed that young Edward was 'like a victim prepared for sacrifice': Pollard, *The Princes in the Tower*, pp. 7, 123; Horrox, *Richard III*, pp. 149–50.

25. PRO, C81/1392/1.

26. *BLHM*, vol. 2, pp. 7, 23–4. The Mortons had held land in Buckingham's lordship of Thornbury since at least the 1420s. Robert Morton was well placed to conspire with his uncle and Buckingham, with whom he was connected through his mother, along with Bishop Woodville. Morton also had access to powerful people and information in London, and as master of the rolls he had inhabited a 'tower within a Tower': see G. Waters, 'Morton

Connections in Gloucestershire', *The Ricardian*, 46 (1974), 17–18; see also A.E. Fuller, 'Cirencester Documents', *Transactions of the Bristol and Gloucester Archaeological Society*, 29 (1895–6), 124.

27. *Rotuli Parliamentorum*, ed. J. Strachey, vol. 6, p. 245.

28. In a testimony given by Thomas, Earl of Derby, regarding the consanguinity of Henry VII, Derby states that he had heard Margaret Beaufort and others discuss the kinship of Henry Tudor and Princess Elizabeth, and their wish for a dispensation: *Calendar of Entries in the Papal Registers relating to Great Britain and Ireland, 1484–1492*, ed. J.A. Twemlow (1960), vol. 14, p. 18; Griffiths, Thomas, *The Making of the Tudor Dynasty*, pp. 88, 91; M.K. Jones, M.G. Underwood, *The King's Mother: Lady Margaret Beaufort, Countess of Richmond and Derby* (Cambridge, Cambridge University Press, 1992), pp. 61–2.

29. PRO, SC1/44/75; *CPR, 1476–85*, p. 465; *BLHM*, vol. 1, p. 4.

30. *The Crowland Chronicle Continuations*, ed. J. Pronay and N. Cox, p. 163; Pollard, *Richard III and the Princes in the Tower*, p. 111; J.A.F. Thomson, 'Bishop Lionel Woodville and Richard III', *Bulletin of the Institute of Historical Research*, 59 (1986), 133.

31. Horrox, *Richard III*, p. 152.

32. Bennett, *The Battle of Bosworth*, pp. 47–8.

33. Gairdner, *Life and Reign of Richard the Third*, p. 133; Kendall, *Richard the Third*, p. 267.

34. For the Ashmolean MS and The Divisie Chronicle, see Pollard, *Richard III and the Princes in the Tower*, p. 123; Ross, *Richard III*, p. 104.

35. *The Crowland Chronicle Continuations*, ed. J. Pronay and N. Cox, p. 163.

36. *Plumpton Correspondence*, p. 45.

37. *The Great Chronicle*, ed. A.H. Thomas and I.D. Thornley, pp. 234–5; *The Crowland Chronicle Continuations*, ed. J. Pronay and N. Cox, p. 165;

The 'Anglica Historia' of Polydore Vergil, ed. D. Hay, pp. 198–9. A manuscript held by S. Garbet provides some interesting information on Ralph Bannaster: *The History of Wem*, ed. J. Thornhill (Shrewsbury, 1982), p. 363.

38. Hampton, *Memorials*, no. 328.

39. Horrox, *Richard III*, pp. 106–8.

CHAPTER FIVE

1. Griffiths, Thomas, *The Making of the Tudor Dynasty*, p. 99; Griffiths, *Sir Rhys ap Thomas*, pp. 4–5, 37; C. Carpenter, *The Wars of the Roses: Politics and the constitution in England, c. 1437–1509* (Cambridge, Cambridge University Press, 1997), p. 213; Horrox, *Richard III*, pp. 162–4.

2. *Extracts from the Municipal Records of the City of York*, ed. R. Davies, p. 177; PRO, SC1/46/102; *Stonor Letters and Papers*, ed. C.L. Kingsford, vol. 2, no. 333; *Household Books of John Duke of Norfolk*, ed. J.P. Collier (London, 1844) p. 471; *CCR, 1476–85*, no. 1171; *Plumpton Correspondence*, ed. T. Stapleton, pp. 44–5; *The Itinerary of Richard III*, ed. R. Edwards (London, Alan Sutton Publishing, 1983), p. 9; Kendall, *Richard the Third*, p. 271; Horrox, *Richard III*, pp. 154–6, 161; M.K. Jones, 'Richard III as a Soldier', *Richard III: A Medieval Kingship*, ed. J. Gillingham, pp. 93–4. In relation to Strange's retinue, though large, this must be an exaggeration.

3. Arthurson, Kingwell, 'The Proclamation of Henry Tudor', pp. 101–3.

4. *The Itinerary of Richard III*, ed. R. Edwards, p. 9.

5. *Household Books of John Duke of Norfolk*, ed. J.P. Collier, pp. 70–1, 472; *The Great Chronicle*, ed. A.H. Thomas and I.D. Thornley, pp. 234–6; Stow, *Annales*, p. 775; Horrox, *Richard III*, pp. 155, 161; Conway, 'The Maidstone Sector of Buckingham's Rebellion, October 18, 1483', p. 115.

6. For Plymouth and Saltash, *BLHM*, vol. 2, pp. 34–5; for Gloucester, *BLHM*, vol. 2, p. 45; for oath of loyalty imposed on Kent, *BLHM*, vol. 2, pp. 75–6; for wearing liveries and for conflict within rebel strongholds, *BLHM*, vol. 2, pp. 69, 75–7, 81–3, 86–7, 110, 116, 124–6, 129; see also Conway, 'The Maidstone Sector of Buckingham's Rebellion, October 18, 1483', p. 108; Ross, *Richard III*, pp. 196–9; Horrox, *Richard III*, pp. 158, 277.

7. R. Horrox has convincingly argued that especially in regard to Exeter, the centres of revolt taken from the act of attainder may have been no more than a matter of convenience for the commissioners who compiled the act, and that there must surely have been other indictments, though none is extant. None the less, in regard to Exeter as an 'umbrella' for the other centres, it may be significant that an inventory taken at St Peter's Cathedral on 6 September 1506 revealed the standards of both the Duke of Buckingham and the Earl of Devon, lending credence to the idea of Exeter as a rallying point; see G. Oliver, *Lives of the Bishops of Exeter and A History of the Cathedral* (Exeter, 1861), p. 328; Horrox, *Richard III*, pp. 154, n. 63, 157; Griffiths, Thomas, *The Making of the Tudor Dynasty*, p. 102.

8. The Torrington attainders include the Marquess of Dorset, Piers Courtenay, Bishop of Exeter, Thomas St Leger, Thomas Arundel, John Halwell, Robert Willoughby and Walter Courtenay; while the Bodmin indictment also includes Piers Courtenay and Thomas Arundel, along with Edward Courtenay and John Treffry. Those who avoided attainder in the indictments include Sir Thomas Fulford, Sir John Crocker, Thomas Greenfield, Hugh Lutterell, Robert Burnaby, William Chilson, Ralph Arundell, Geoffrey Beauchamp, Remfry Densell, John Rosogan and Thomas Borlase.

9. For Combe PRO, KB 950/46; for Richard's visit to Canterbury in January 1484 during which he supervised the fitting-out of ships to guard the coast against French attack: *VCH Kent*, vol. 3, p. 296; see also Conway, 'The Maidstone Sector of Buckingham's Rebellion, October 18, 1483', p. 108; Horrox, *Richard III*, pp. 156–8; 'Financial Memoranda of the Reign of Edward V', ed. R. Horrox, p. 233, for Berkeley as constable of Southampton; for Edward Berkeley who was a parker at Clarendon, and bailiff in and sheriff of Southampton, PRO, C67/51/3 and Wedgwood, *History of Parliament*, p. 68.

10. Conway, 'The Maidstone Sector of Buckingham's Rebellion, October 18, 1483', p. 107.

11. *Rotuli Parliamentorum*, ed. J. Strachey, vol. 6, pp. 245–6; BL, Stowe MS 440, ff. 50–75; *Materials for the History of the Reign of Henry VII*, ed. W. Campbell, Rolls Series (2 vols, London, HMSO, 1873–7), vol. 1, p. 272; Griffiths, Thomas, *The Making of the Tudor Dynasty*, p. 108.

12. *BLHM*, vol. 2, pp. 31–4, 39–40, 43, 54–6, 59, 78, 121–2, 125; Borlase, *The Descent, Name and Arms of Borlase of Borlase*, p. 30; see also W. Lake, *A Complete Parochial History of the County of Cornwall* (2 vols, London, 1867), vol. 1, p. 227.

13. *Materials for the History of the Reign of Henry VII*, ed. W. Campbell, vol. 1, pp. 8, 39, 56, 67, 272 and *passim*; Wedgwood, *History of Parliament*, p. 429 and Rawcliffe, *The Staffords*, pp. 205–6, 215–16, for Harper; see also Griffiths, Thomas, *The Making of the Tudor Dynasty*, p. 108; for William Brown PRO, C67/51/26; for Edward Brown PRO, C67/51/27; for John Brown PRO, C67/51/17.

14. The Woodvilles were represented by the Marquess of Dorset and his son at Exeter; Bishop Lionel Woodville at Salisbury, Sir Richard Woodville at Newbury; in Kent, their kinsmen John Fogge, Richard Haute and the Guildfords.

15. *CIPM*, no. 794. John Rushe's son, Robert, predeceased him.

16. *CPR, 1476–85*, p. 415; *CCR, 1476–85*, nos 1218, 1225, 1353.

17. *BLHM*, vol. 2, pp. 39–40; Horrox, *Richard III*, pp. 160–1.

18. See appendix 3 for the attainders.

19. Fogge had been constable of Rochester; St Leger, keeper of Guildford in Kent and held the castle and manor of Torrington in Devon; Lewkenor had custody of Bodiam, Sussex; Berkeley was constable of Southampton; Cheyne of Christchurch, as well as keeper of New Forest, and steward of royal lands in Poole; John Halwell was constable of Plympton.

20. For Alexander Cheyne of West Shifford, Berkshire PRO, C67/51/6; for Norris senior PRO, C67/51/26; for Roger Cheyne PRO, C67/51/14; for John Kentwood PRO, C67/51/15; for Anthony Brown PRO, C67/51/14; for Elizabeth Brown PRO, C67/51/11; for Heron PRO, C67/51/8; for Baker PRO, C67/51/15; for Bray PRO, C67/51/11; see also Horrox, *Richard III*, pp. 159–60; for Bampton and Case, *Rotuli Parliamentorum*, ed. J. Strachey, vol. 6, p. 246; for associates and servants of rebel gentry: PRO, C67/51/9, PRO, C67/51/5; PRO, C67/51/17; PRO, C67/51/18; PRO, C67/51/31, PRO, C67/51/23, PRO, C67/51/26; PRO, C67/51/33.

21. Kymer and Cheyne were rewarded by Henry VII in the same grant in 1485: *Materials for the History of the Reign of Henry VII*, ed. W. Campbell, vol. 1, pp. 66, 202, 285; for Kymer, *BLHM*, vol. 2, p. 85; for Robert Brent, *CPR, 1476–85*, pp. 71, 207; for Brandon PRO, C67/51/14; for Croft PRO, C67/51/7; see also C.S.L. Davies, 'The Alleged "Sack of Bristol": International Ramifications of Breton Privateering, 1484–5' *Historical Research*, 67 (1994), 237–8, for some interesting comments on the possible activity of Thomas Croft in 1484; for Hassall, Flasby and Morton, 'Financial Memoranda of the Reign of Edward V', ed. R. Horrox, p. 227; see also Rawcliffe, *The Staffords*, p. 208.

22. PRO, KB/950/60, PRO, KB/950/62; *BLHM*, vol. 1, p. 155; *BLHM*, vol. 2, p. 145.

23. Woodville was dead by 1 December 1484. For Poyntz PRO, C67/51/10; *VCH, Hants*, vol. 3, p. 143; for Guildford and Brown, *CPR, 1476–85*, p. 465; *The Coronation of Richard III*, ed. A.F. Sutton and P.W. Hammond, p. 400; Gairdner, *Richard the Third*, p. 159; for Woodville, H.E. Salter, 'Registrum Annalium Collegi Mertonensis, 1483–1531', *Oxford Historical Society*, 75 (1921), 41; J.A.F. Thomson, 'Bishop Lionel Woodville and Richard III', *Bulletin of the Institute of Historical Research*, 59 (1986), 132–3, 135. C. Richmond, '1485 and all that, or just what was going on at the Battle of Bosworth?', *Richard III: Loyalty, Lordship and Law*, ed. P.W. Hammond (London, Richard III and Yorkist History Trust, 1986), pp. 198–9.

24. R. Virgoe, 'The Crown, Magnates, and Local Government in Fifteenth-Century East Anglia', *The Crown and Local Communities in England and France in the Fifteenth Century*, ed. J.R.L. Highfield and R. Jeffs (Gloucester, Alan Sutton Publishing, 1981), pp. 75–6; Britnell, *The Closing of the Middle Ages?*, pp. 85–7.

25. See appendix 4 for the sample of fifty-five knights, squires and gentlemen. The squires of the body who lost peace commissions under Richard are Thomas Croft and Thomas Fowler (Oxfordshire), Thomas Darcy (Essex), John Wikes (Gloucestershire), John Sturgeon (Hampshire); John Risley and John Fortescue rebelled in 1484.

26. The counties selected are Cornwall, Devonshire, Somerset-Dorset, Gloucestershire, Wiltshire, Hampshire, Oxfordshire-Berkshire, Kent, Surrey-Sussex, Norfolk-Suffolk: *Lists of Sheriffs for England and Wales*, pp. 2–153; W.A. Morris, 'The Sheriff during the Reign of Edward III', *The English Government at Work, 1327–1336*, ed. J.F. Willard, W.A. Morris, W.H. Dunham Jr (3 vols, Harvard, 1947), vol. 2, pp. 47–8; Virgoe, 'The Crown and Local Communities', p. 73; *CPR, 1476–85*, pp. 553–77; in general see J.R. Lander, *English Justices of the Peace, 1461–1509* (Gloucester, Alan Sutton Publishing, 1989).

27. Most were men of influence: John Biconell, William Hody, Sir William Paulet, Sir John Newton, John Newburgh, Stonor's cousin Walter Elmes, John Brocas, John Denton and William Beselles among them.

28. Courtenay became a knight of the body under Richard, yet may also have suffered through Richard's promotion of his northern servants in the south-west: Horrox, *Richard III*, p. 288; Thomson, 'The Courtenay Family in the Yorkist Period', pp. 237–8. Sir Alexander Baynham was a kinsman of Thomas Baynham, who moved in the Poyntz-Berkeley circle; Nicholas Crowmer of Great Torrington, Devon, mixed with St Leger and was related to Sir James Crowmer of Tunstall, Kent (whose relations with Richard III 'were not amiable'), while Thomas Kingston, who was knighted by Richard, and Henry Long, a local lawyer with Hungerford connections, had served Edward IV in the west on various local commissions but received little under Richard. For Baynham and Cromer, *BLHM*, vol. 4, pp. 12, 54; for Kingston, *BLHM*, vol. 4, p. 113; for Long, Wedgwood, *History of Parliament*, p. 550.

29. Stowell was on numerous commissions through the 1470s in Somerset including the April 1483 subsidy commission: *CPR, 1476–85*, p. 353, and was associated with Daubenay; see *The Registers of Robert Stillington, Bishop of Bath and Wells, 1466–1491*, and Richard Fox, *Bishop of Bath and Wells, 1492–1494*, ed. H.C. Maxwell Lyte, 52 (1937), no. 235; for Colowe see Wedgwood, *History of Parliament*, p. 148 and *CPR, 1476–85*, pp. 571–2. Somerset's Thomas Tremayle was a serjeant-at-law by 1468. He had represented Bridport, Bridgwater and Lyme Regis, and as a legal careerist he was a justice in Berkshire, Oxfordshire, Worcestershire, Gloucestershire and Staffordshire: Wedgwood, *History of Parliament*, pp. 867–8. Chokke, the son of Sir Richard, justice of the common pleas (d. 1483) was beginning to make his mark in 1483; while Fitzjames was a local lawyer of more modest

office; J.P. of Somerset and of the quorum in 1479: Wedgwood, *History of Parliament*, p. 373.

30. For Daubenay, *CPR, 1476–85*, pp. 47, 177, 337; *The Coronation of Richard III*, ed. A.F. Sutton and P.W. Hammond, p. 332; for Gorges, Hampton, *Memorials*, no. 276.

31. Brent remained off the bench until July 1484, while Scott, father-in-law of Edward Poynings, and named as a rebel by Stow, despite being a king's councillor and treasurer of the household, was clearly involved in later trouble as his bond to Richard in March 1485 indicates: *CCR, 1476–85*, no. 1408; Conway, 'The Maidstone Sector of Buckingham's Rebellion, October 18, 1483', p. 105.

32. For Appleton, S. Cunningham, 'Henry VII and Rebellion in North-Eastern England, 1485–1492: Bonds of Allegiance and the Establishment of Tudor Authority', *Northern History*, 32 (1996), 60; see also Carpenter, 'The Stonor Circle in the Fifteenth Century', pp. 193–4, 198.

33. Horrox, *Richard III*, p. 266.

34. Ross, *Richard III*, pp. 105, 110; Horrox, *Richard III*, pp. 167–70.

35. For Bartholomew St Leger PRO, C67/51/27; for Appleton PRO, C67/51/29.

36. *Stonor Letters and Papers*, ed. C.L. Kingsford, vol. 1, p. xxxii; Ross, *Richard III*, pp. 110–11.

37. Ross, *Richard III*, pp. 112–13; see also C. Richmond, '1483: The Year of Decision (or Taking the Throne)', *Richard III: A Medieval Kingship*, ed. J. Gillingham, p. 39.

CHAPTER SIX

1. Wolffe, 'The Management of English Royal Estates', p. 193; Pollard, *Richard III and the Princes in the Tower*, pp. 144–5.

2. *BLHM*, vol. 2, p. 110; *CCR, 1476–85*, no. 1380; *Materials for the History of the Reign of Henry VII*, ed. W. Campbell, vol. 1, p. 131.

3. Two knights, Richard Enderby and John

Donne were indicted but apparently talked their way out of attainder.

4. *CPR, 1476–85*, pp. 369–72, 375, 412–13, 415; R.L. Storey, *The End of the House of Lancaster*, (Gloucester, rev. edn, Alan Sutton Publishing, 1986), Appendix II; K. Dockray, *Richard III: A Reader in History* (Gloucester, Alan Sutton Publishing, 1988), p. 105; Horrox, *Richard III*, pp. 273–4.

5. Incidentally in 1471 Sir William Norris had been pardoned by word of mouth: *Stonor Letters and Papers*, ed. C.L. Kingsford, vol. 1, no. 115; PRO, C81/1531/48; see also Richmond, '1485 and all that', p. 198, n. 9.

6. See for example Sir Thomas Delamare's pardon in which those people 'owing him favour or affection' could 'receive or cherish him with vitailles': *BLHM*, vol. 2, pp. 206–7.

7. For St Lo, *CCR, 1476–85*, no. 1244; for Lewkenor, *CCR, 1476–85*, nos 1242, 1258; for Hungerford, *CCR, 1476–85*, no. 1245; for Latimer, *CCR, 1476–85*, no. 1243; for Berkeley, *CCR, 1476–85*, no. 1412; see also *BLHM*, vol. 1, p. 181.

8. See the petition of Sir Roger Tocotes in which he promised fealty to the king: PRO, C/81/1531/20; for Berkeley PRO, C81/1392/27; *CCR*, nos 1393, 1412; for the Brandons PRO, C67/51/5, PRO, C67/51/14; *CPR, 1476–85*, pp. 423, 526; *Materials for the History of the Reign of Henry VII*, ed. W. Campbell, vol. 1, pp. 124–5; for Harcourt, *BLHM*, vol. 1, p. 181; for Morton, R.C. Hairsine, 'Oxford University and the Life and Legend of Richard III', *Richard III, Crown and People*, ed. J. Petre (Gloucester, Alan Sutton Publishing, 1985), p. 310; C.S.L. Davies, 'Bishop John Morton, the Holy See and the Accession of Henry VII', *EHR*, 102 (1987), 9; *CPR, 1476–85*, p. 535; *BLHM*, vol. 1, p. 243.

9. Horrox, *Richard III*, p. 275, n. 14.

10. At least one hundred more pardons were obtained out of chancery during the period: *BLHM*, vol. 1, pp. 165–276; *CPR, 1476–85*, pp. 369–498; Storey, *The End of the House of Lancaster*, Appendix II.

11. *CPR, 1476–85*, p. 500; for Norfolk PRO, C67/51/11; for Surrey PRO, C67/51/18; for the Earl of Arundel and Lord Maltravers PRO, C67/51/3; for Berkeley PRO, C67/51/9; for Bergavenny PRO, C67/51/5; for Stourton PRO, C67/51/7; for Lawarre PRO, C67/51/20; for Audley PRO, C67/51/1; for Dudley PRO, C67/51/4; for Stanley PRO, C67/51/14; for Northumberland PRO, C67/51/16.

12. For Bourchier PRO, C67/51/11; for Montgomery PRO, C67/51/29; for Burgh PRO, C67/51/29; for Gresley PRO, C67/51/28; for William Stanley PRO, C67/51/7; for Pilkington PRO, C67/51/32; for Poyntz PRO, C67/51/10; for John Courtenay PRO, C67/51/7; for Brampton PRO, C67/51/18; for Risley PRO, C67/51/13; for Haute PRO, C67/51/30; for Fortescue PRO, C67/51/10; for Starkey PRO, C67/51/29; for Wood PRO, C67/51/16; for Lygon PRO, C67/51/10; for Fineux PRO, C67/51/12.

13. For Curtis PRO, C67/51/6; for Fitzherbert PRO, C67/51/16; for Lee PRO, C67/51/27.

14. For Hayes PRO, C67/51/34; for Kidwelly PRO, C67/51/15; for Kebell PRO, C67/51/21; for Brown PRO, C67/51/17; for Bartholomew St Leger PRO, C67/51/27; for James St Leger PRO, C67/51/27; for Audley PRO, C67/51/1; for Biconell PRO, C67/51/12; for Forster PRO, C67/51/20; for James Blount PRO, C67/51/18.

15. For Bray PRO, C67/51/11; for Horde PRO, C67/51/26; for Richard Harper PRO, C67/51/8; for William Harper PRO, C67/51/4; for Kymer PRO, C67/51/2; for Brandon PRO, C67/51/14; for Richard and Robert Morton PRO, C67/51/3 and PRO, C67/51/10, respectively; for Stephen Calmady C67/51/31; for Nicholas Halwell C67/51/16.

16. These were the men with 'discoverable' connections with the former king; doubtless many more were minor officials in the ports and towns.

17. For Hopton PRO, C67/51/20; for Nende

PRO, C67/51/29; for David Berkeley PRO, C67/51/12; for John Bourchier PRO, C67/51/28; for Brent PRO, C67/51/27.

18. Waters, 'Morton connections in Gloucester', p. 17; 'The will and Inventory of Robert Morton, AD 1486–1488', ed. E.M. Thompson, *Journal of the British Archaeological Association*, 33 (1877), 308; for Henry Dene's pardon PRO, C67/51/12; for Chyne PRO, C67/51/8; for deacons and canons of St Mary's, Cirencester PRO, C67/51/26; see also 'The Will of Henry Dene, Archbishop of Canterbury, Deceased 15 February, 1502–3', *Archaeological Journal*, 18 (1861), 256–7. Dene apparently owed his preferment to John Morton.

19. For Rotherham PRO, C67/51/6; for Russell PRO, C67/51/6; for King PRO, C67/51/7.

20. See for example PRO, C67/51/2, PRO, C67/51/5, PRO, C67/51/9, PRO, C67/51/18, PRO, C67/51/21, PRO, C67/51/8, PRO, C67/51/21, PRO, C67/51/23, PRO, C67/51/25, PRO, C67/51/2, PRO, C67/51/27.

21. Griffiths, Thomas, *The Making of the Tudor Dynasty*, pp. 96–8, 105–9; D.A. Luckett, 'The rise and fall of a noble dynasty: Henry VII and the Lords Willoughby de Broke', *Historical Research*, 69 (1996), 256.

22. Ratcliffe of Sedbury, Yorkshire and of Cumberland was created a knight of the body in October 1483, and Ashton by March 1484. Huddleston and Franke were squires of the body by September and October respectively. Markenfield became a knight of the body soon after: K. Dockray, 'Richard III and the Yorkshire Gentry', *Richard III: Loyalty, Lordship and Law*, ed. P.W. Hammond, pp. 47–8; Pollard, *Richard III and the Princes in the Tower*, p. 84; for peace commissions, *CPR, 1476–85*, pp. 561–3; for Ward, *BLHM*, vol. 1, p. 149.

23. *CPR, 1476–85*, pp. 371, 399, 488, 493, 577; *Sheriffs, Lists and Indexes*, p. 124.

24. *The Crowland Chronicle Continuations*, ed. J. Pronay and N. Cox, p. 171.

25. Horrox, *Richard III*, pp. 286–7, 289.

26. Carpenter, *The Wars of the Roses*, pp. 214–15.

27. For Constable, *BLHM*, vol. 2, pp. 81, 124; see *BLHM*, vol. 2, pp. 82, 110, 116, 126, 129, for other instances of warnings to tenants of new landlords; for Bodrugan, *BLHM*, vol. 2, p. 124; for Norris, *BLHM*, vol. 2, p. 91; for bounty, *BLHM*, vol. 2, p. 48.

28. *BLHM*, vol. 3, pp. 139–55, for rebels' forfeits to northern servants.

29. *BLHM*, vol. 1, pp. 102, 113, 117–18, 125, 130, 136–7, 140, 149, 161, 188; *BLHM*, vol. 2, p. 58; *VCH, Wilts*, vol. 4, p. 437; *VCH, Hants*, vol. 4, p. 608; vol. 10, p. 242; Pollard, *Richard III and the Princes in the Tower*, p. 145.

30. *BLHM*, vol. 1, p. 196; vol. 3, pp. 148–9; M.K. Jones, 'Richard III and Lady Margaret Beaufort: A Re-assessment', *Richard III: Loyalty, Lordship and Law*, ed. P.W. Hammond, pp. 28–9; E.B. de Fonblanque, *Annals of the House of Percy from the Conquest to the Opening of the Nineteenth Century* (2 vols, London, 1887), vol. 1, pp. 269–79; R. Jeffs, 'The Poynings–Percy Dispute', *BIHR*, 34 (1961), 148–64.

31. *CPR, 1476–85*, p. 527; *CCR, 1476–85*, nos 1243, 1379; *The Coronation of Richard III*, ed. A.F. Sutton and P.W. Hammond, pp. 308–9; Horrox, *Richard III*, pp. 274–5; see Ross, *Richard III*, pp. 119–20, who says that about one-third of the rebels received at least part of their estates; this is debatable.

32. For assistance to rebels' wives, *BLHM*, vol. 1, pp. 117, 150, 250; Buckingham's widow, Katherine, also received an annuity of 200 marks for life from the lordship of Tonbridge in Kent: *BLHM*, vol. 1, p. 213; for Rushe, *BLHM*, vol. 2, p. 134; see also Sayer, 'Norfolk Involvement in Dynastic Conflict', p. 318.

33. For Curtis who was again dismissed and entered sanctuary at Westminster in 1485, *BLHM*, vol. 2, p. 7.

34. Wedgwood, *History of Parliament*, pp. 242, 564, 591, 717–18; PRO, E404/78/3/29.

35. Horrox, *Richard III*, pp. 288–9.

CHAPTER SEVEN

1. Bennett, *The Battle of Bosworth*, pp. 72–4.

2. Bennett, *The Battle of Bosworth*, p. 76; Griffiths, Thomas, *The Making of the Tudor Dynasty*, p. 137.

3. Rowney, 'The Staffordshire Political Community 1440–1500', p. 127; Carpenter, *The Wars of the Roses*, p. 211.

4. For Wortley, *BLHM*, vol. 2, p. 44.

5. Lovell was the son of the Northamptonshire-based John Lord Lovell. His grandfather was Sir William Lovell, seventh Baron Lovell of Tichmarsh and Minster Lovell (d. 1455): *CCR, 1476–85*, no. 284; *VCH Berks*, vol. 3, p. 442; *VCH Wilts*, vol. 9, pp. 81, 176, 178; vol. 11, pp. 240–1; *VCH Glos*, vol. 6, p. 108; Collinson, *The History and Antiquities of the County of Somerset*, vol. 1, p. 227; vol. 2, p. 55; vol. 3, pp. 167, 475.

6. *VCH Glos*, vol. 8, p. 13; vol. 10, p. 209; vol. 11, p. 66; *VCH Wilts*, vol. 9, p. 122; *VCH Sussex*, vol. 7, pp. 3–4; *VCH Surrey*, vol. 3, *passim*; *VCH Essex*, vol. 4, p. 253.

7. PRO, PROB 11/11, ff. 211v–212r; PRO, PROB 11/11, ff. 87v–r; Hampton, *Memorials*, nos 287, 290.

8. Carpenter, 'The Stonor Circle in the Fifteenth Century', pp. 197–8.

9. For Woodville, *BLHM*, vol. 2, pp. 169, 178, 183; Hampton, *Memorials*, no. 151; A. Grant, 'Foreign Affairs under Richard III', *Richard III: A Medieval Kingship*, ed. J. Gillingham, p. 118; Ross, *Richard III*, pp. 196–9.

10. For Powys, *CPR, 1476–85*, p. 547; see also Griffiths, Thomas, *The Making of the Tudor Dynasty*, pp. 110–11; Davies, 'The Alleged "Sack of Bristol"', pp. 230–3; J.M. Currin, 'Persuasions to Peace: The Luxembourg–Marigny–Gaguin Embassy and the State of Anglo-French Relations, 1489–90', *EHR*, 113 (1998), 882–3. Davies contends that some sort of naval encounter occurred between Bretons and Bristolians towards the end of 1484, led by Jean de Coetanlem, and assisted by the French admiral; see also Davies, 'Richard III, Brittany, and Henry Tudor, 1483–1485', *Nottingham Medieval Studies*, 37 (1993), 110–22, in which he argues that Richard may not have sent military aid to Brittany until June 1485.

11. PRO, C81/1392/12; *CPR, 1476–85*, pp. 492–3.

12. PRO, C81/1392/26; *CPR, 1476–85*, pp. 456, 492; *BLHM*, vol. 1, p. 245; *The Crowland Chronicle Continuations*, ed. J. Pronay and N. Cox, pp. 180–1; Horrox, *Richard III*, pp. 275–6.

13. PRO, C81/1531/58; *CPR, 1476–85*, pp. 519–20; *Materials for the History of the Reign of Henry VII*, ed. W. Campbell, vol. 1, p. 61; Bellamy, *The Law of Treason in England*, Appendix III, pp. 237–8 for Collingbourne's indictment; Gairdner, *Life and Reign of Richard the Third*, p. 187; Griffiths, Thomas, *The Making of the Tudor Dynasty*, p. 111. The date, incidentally, is significant and lends credence to 18 October 1483 as the acknowledged date of the 1483 risings.

14. *BLHM*, vol. 2, pp. 164–5; Horrox, *Richard III*, p. 277.

15. For Calmady PRO, C82/55/6, and see Horrox, *Richard III*, p. 159; *BLHM*, vol. 2, pp. 36–7; for Tyler, *BLHM*, vol. 1, p. 155; for Waller, *BLHM*, vol. 2, p. 109.

16. Griffiths, Thomas, *The Making of the Tudor Dynasty*, p. 117.

17. Virgoe, 'Sir John Risley 1443–1512: Courtier and Councillor', p. 143; Ross, *Richard III*, p. 108; Davies, 'Bishop John Morton', pp. 6–7; Horrox, *Richard III*, pp. 279–82.

18. Virgoe, 'Sir John Risley 1443–1512: Courtier and Councillor', p. 142.

19. For Forster PRO, C67/51/20; Bennett, *The*

Battle of Bosworth, p. 41.

20. Gairdner, *Life and Reign of Richard the Third*, pp. 199–200; Horrox, *Richard III*, p. 280.

21. Griffiths, Thomas, *The Making of the Tudor Dynasty*, pp. 125–6.

22. Griffiths, Thomas, *The Making of the Tudor Dynasty*, p. 120; Ross, *Richard III*, p. 206.

23. *BLHM*, vol. 2, pp. 182–3; vol. 3, pp. 124–6.

24. PRO, E404/78/2/24. Others in the southwest dipped into their own reserves to help round up the rebels for which they were to be reimbursed: Horrox, *Richard III*, pp. 299–302.

25. *BLHM*, vol. 3, pp. 128–33.

26. Horrox, *Richard III*, p. 307.

27. Virgoe, 'Sir John Risley 1443–1512: Courtier and Councillor', pp. 142–3; *CPR, 1476–85*, p. 379; Horrox, *Richard III*, p. 282. Benstead received a pardon in March 1485: *CPR, 1476–85*, p. 543.

28. *BLHM*, vol. 2, pp. 78, 183, 203–4, 220; *CPR, 1476–85*, p. 535; Horrox, *Richard III*, pp. 281–2.

29. *CCR, 1476–85*, no. 1317.

30. Horrox, *Richard III*, pp. 140, 291–3.

31. *CPR, 1476–85*, pp. 511, 543; Horrox, *Richard III*, p. 293.

32. Hampton, *Memorials*, no. 187; Horrox, *Richard III*, pp. 298–9.

33. *BLHM*, vol. 1, p. 268; Griffiths, Thomas, *The Making of the Tudor Dynasty*, pp. 126–7.

34. *BLHM*, vol. 1, p. 287; for Morton, Peke and Williams, *BLHM*, vol. 2, pp. 196, 214–15.

35. *CCR, 1476–85*, no. 1456; Davies, 'Bishop John Morton', pp. 9–10; Hampton, *Memorials*, no. 301.

36. Griffiths, Thomas, *The Making of the Tudor Dynasty*, pp. 127–8.

37. Ross, *Richard III*, p. 214.

Chapter Eight

1. Ross, *Richard III*, p. 210.

2. Ross, *Richard III*, p. 212.

3. *CPR, 1476–85*, p. 32; *Materials for the History of the Reign of Henry VII*, ed. W. Campbell, vol. 1, p. 164; Bennett, *The Battle of Bosworth*, p. 87; Griffiths, Thomas, *The Making of the Tudor Dynasty*, pp. 142–3.

4. Griffiths, Thomas, *The Making of the Tudor Dynasty*, p. 146.

5. Griffiths, *Sir Rhys ap Thomas*, pp. 40–3.

6. Hampton, *Memorials*, nos 259, 283, 319, 322, 838.

7. Ross, *Richard III*, pp. 212–13; Bennett, *The Battle of Bosworth*, p. 89.

8. Sayer, 'Norfolk Involvement in Dynastic Conflict', p. 319; Hampton, *Memorials*, nos 12, 86, 252; *The Coronation of Richard III*, ed. A.F. Sutton and P.W. Hammond, pp. 316–17, 367.

9. Bennett, *The Battle of Bosworth*, p. 107.

10. For Arundel, *The Ballad of Bosworth Field*, line 235; *The Coronation of Richard III*, ed. A.F. Sutton and P.W. Hammond, p. 304; for Cheyne, Hampton, *Memorials*, no. 343; Pollard, *Richard III and the Princes in the Tower*, pp. 171–2.

11. *Materials for the History of the Reign of Henry VII*, ed. W. Campbell, vol. 1, pp. 100–1, 131, 329; for Talbot, Wedgwood, *History of Parliament*, p. 838; for Willoughby, Wedgwood, *History of Parliament*, p. 952; for Poyntz, Hampton, *Memorials*, no. 86; for Poynings, Conway, 'The Maidstone Sector of Buckingham's Rebellion, October 18, 1483', p. 110.

12. *Materials for the History of the Reign of Henry VII*, ed. W. Campbell, vol. 1, pp. 27, 56, 63, 175, 301, 320, 450, 549.

13. For Anneon, Conway and the servants of rebels, *Materials for the History of the Reign of Henry VII*, ed. W. Campbell, vol. 1, pp. 22, 100, 151, 272, 404, 440; for Kayley, Caerleon and Welles's servant, *CPR, 1485–94*, pp. 53, 75, 138.

14. *Materials for the History of the Reign of Henry VII*, ed. W. Campbell, vol. 1, pp. 344, 506, 521; M.J. Bennett, 'Henry VII and the Northern Rising of 1489', *EHR*, 105 (1990), 42; D. Luckett, 'Crown Office and Licensed

Retinues in the Reign of Henry VII', *Rulers and Ruled in Late Medieval England*, ed. R.E. Archer, S. Walker, pp. 224, 227, 231; Gunn, 'The Courtiers of Henry VII', pp. 27–8.

15. Daubenay replaced Sir William Stanley as lord chamberlain after the latter's execution for treason in 1495.

16. Gunn, 'The Courtiers of Henry VII', pp. 27, 29.

17. Griffiths, Thomas, *The Making of the Tudor Dynasty*, pp. 171–2; Gunn, 'The Courtiers of Henry VII', pp. 42–3; Currin, 'Persuasions to Peace', p. 883.

18. R. Horrox, 'Caterpillars of the Commonwealth? Courtiers in Late Medieval England', *Rulers and Ruled in Late Medieval England*, ed. R.E. Archer, S. Walker, p. 11.

19. Gunn, 'The Courtiers of Henry VII', p. 29; Luckett, 'Crown Patronage and Political Morality in Early Tudor England', pp. 581–2.

20. Harcourt obtained the stewardship of Warwick and Spenser lands in Oxford and elsewhere formerly held by his father; John Cheyne resumed in office in Wiltshire and Hampshire and also received some of Sir William Berkeley's positions. Walter Hungerford resumed hereditary positions on duchy of Lancaster estates in Wiltshire: Luckett, 'Crown Office and Licensed Retinues in the Reign of Henry VII', *Rulers and Ruled in Late Medieval England*, ed. R.E. Archer, S. Walker, pp. 232, 235; *Materials for the History of the Reign of Henry VII*, ed. W. Campbell, vol. 1, pp. 43, 66–7, 344, 357, 399, 548–9.

21. Luckett, 'Crown Office and Licensed Retinues in the Reign of Henry VII', *Rulers and Ruled in Late Medieval England*, ed. R.E. Archer, S. Walker, pp. 223–6; see also D. Luckett, 'Henry VII and the South-Western Escheators', 'The Reign of Henry VII', ed. B. Thompson, *Harlaxton Medieval Studies*, 5 (Stamford, Paul Watkins, 1995), pp. 54–64.

22. M.J. Bennett, *Lambert Simnel and the Battle of Stoke* (Gloucester, Alan Sutton Publishing, 1987), p. 95; Bennett, 'Henry VII and the Northern Rising of 1489', pp. 39, 51, 54–5; Luckett, 'Crown Office and Licensed Retinues', p. 230; Carpenter, *The Wars of the Roses*, p. 222.

CHAPTER NINE

1. Gunn, 'The Courtiers of Henry VII', pp. 41–2.

2. Gunn, *Early Tudor Government*, pp. 38–42; Luckett, 'Crown Office and Licensed Retinues', pp. 225–38.

3. Gunn, 'The Courtiers of Henry VII', pp. 27–9; Luckett, 'Crown Office and Licensed Retinues', pp. 224–5.

Bibliographical Notes

CHAPTER 1: TALES OF REBELLION

G.R. Elton, *The Sources of History: Studies in the Uses of Historical Evidence* (London, Hodder and Stoughton Ltd, 1969) provides an invaluable guide to the various classes of official material for the period, while the introduction to *British Library Harleian MS 433*, ed. R. Horrox, P.W. Hammond (4 vols, Gloucester, Alan Sutton Publishing, 1979–83), is also essential reading. C.L. Kingsford, *English Historical Literature in the Fifteenth Century* (Oxford, Clarendon Press, 1913) and A. Gransden, *Historical Writing in England II, c. 1307 to the Early Sixteenth Century* (London, Routledge and Kegan Paul, 1982) introduce the chronicle sources, while A. Hanham, *Richard III and his Early Historians 1483–1535* (Oxford, Clarendon Press, 1975) is a key work for the period. Eloquent insights are provided by C. Ross, *Richard III* (London, Eyre Methuen, 1981), M.J. Bennett, *The Battle of Bosworth* (Gloucester, Alan Sutton Publishing, 1985) and R. Horrox, *Richard III: A Study of Service* (Cambridge, Cambridge University Press, 1989). More recent historiographical discussion is presented in C. Carpenter, *The Wars of the Roses* (Cambridge, Cambridge University Press, 1997), ch. 10.

CHAPTER 2: KINGS, LORDS AND LANDLORDS

Numerous county and family histories have provided the framework for the discussion. Most valuable is the Victoria County History collection, which provides detail, context and often pertinent analysis. Accessible and instructive work on the leading figures is found in C. Ross, *Edward IV* (London, Eyre Methuen, 1974) and Ross, *Richard III*, M. Hicks, 'Richard, Duke of Gloucester and the North', in *Richard III and the North*, ed. R. Horrox (Gloucester, Alan Sutton Publishing, 1986), R. Horrox, *Richard III: A Study of Service*, M. Hicks, *False, Fleeting, Perjur'd Clarence* (Stroud, Alan Sutton Publishing, 1980) and Hicks, 'The Changing Role of the Wydevilles in Yorkist Politics to 1483', in *Patronage, Pedigree and Power in Late Medieval England*, ed. C. Ross (Stroud, Alan Sutton Publishing, 1979), and C. Rawcliffe, *The Staffords, Earls of Stafford and Dukes of Buckingham, 1394–1521* (Cambridge, Cambridge University Press, 1977). A number of shorter works have also been particularly insightful including M. Sayer, 'Norfolk Involvement in Dynastic Conflict 1467–1471 and 1483–1487', *Norfolk Archaeology*, 36 (1977), M. Cherry, 'The Struggle for Power in mid-fifteenth century Devonshire', in *Patronage, the Crown and the Provinces*, ed. R.A.

Griffiths (Stroud, Alan Sutton Publishing, 1981), K. Mertes, 'Aristocracy', in *Fifteenth Century Attitudes: Perceptions of society in late medieval England*, ed. R. Horrox (Cambridge, Cambridge University Press, 1994), C. Carpenter, 'Gentry and Community in Medieval England', *Journal of British Studies*, 33 (1994), Carpenter, 'The Stonor Circle in the Fifteenth Century', in *Rulers and Ruled in Late Medieval England: Essays presented to Gerald Harriss*, ed. R.E. Archer and S. Walker (London, The Hambledon Press, 1995), *Kingsford's Stonor Letters and Papers, 1290–1483*, ed. C. Carpenter (Cambridge, Cambridge University Press, 1996), and S. Payling, 'The politics of family: late medieval marriage contracts', *The McFarlane Legacy: Studies in Late Medieval Politics and Society*, ed. R.H. Britnell and A.J. Pollard (Stroud, Alan Sutton Publishing, 1995).

CHAPTER 3: POLITICS AND 'THE POWERS THAT BE'

The topic is richly served by numerous works such as C.L. Scofield, *The Life and Reign of Edward the Fourth, King of England and of France and Lord of Ireland* (2 vols, London, rev. edn, Frank Cass and Company Limited, 1967) which offers a detailed narrative, while C. Ross, *The Wars of the Roses* (London, Book Club Associates, 1976), A.J. Pollard, *The Wars of the Roses* (London, Macmillan Education Ltd, 1988), J. Gillingham, *The Wars of the Roses* (London, Weidenfeld and Nicolson, 1981), J. Goodman, *The Wars of the Roses* (London, Routledge and Kegan Paul, 1981) and Carpenter, *The Wars of the Roses* all provide illuminating guides to the period. P.W. Hammond, *The Battles of Barnet and Tewkesbury* (Stroud, Alan Sutton Publishing, 1990) and P.A. Haigh, *The Military Campaigns of the Wars of the Roses* (Gloucester, Alan Sutton Publishing, 1995) are also informative studies. Works which should not be missed include K.B. McFarlane, 'Bastard Feudalism', reprinted in *England in the Fifteenth Century* (London, The Hambledon Press, 1981), C. Richmond, 'After McFarlane', *History* (1983), G.L. Harriss, 'The Dimensions of Politics', in *The McFarlane Legacy*, ed. R.H. Britnell and A.J. Pollard (Stroud, Alan Sutton Publishing, 1995), M. Hicks, *Bastard Feudalism* (London, Longman Group Limited, 1995) and Carpenter, *The Wars of the Roses*, bibliographical notes to chapter 1: Sources and Historiography. See, in general, the collection of essays in M. Hicks, *Richard III and his Rivals: Magnates and their Motives in the Wars of the Roses* (London, The Hambledon Press, 1991).

CHAPTER 4: ALLIES AND ENEMIES

The key primary sources for this fascinating but complex period are *The Crowland Chronicle Continuations 1459–1486*, ed. N. Pronay and J. Cox (London, Alan Sutton Publishing, 1986) and *Dominic Mancini, The Usurpation of Richard III*, ed. C.A.J. Armstrong (Oxford, Clarendon Press, 1969). Helpful detail is found in *The Coronation of Richard III: the Extant Documents*, ed. A.F. Sutton and P.W. Hammond (Stroud, Alan Sutton Publishing, 1983). Among the most stimulating acccounts of Richard's coup, his mounting opposition and Buckingham's defection are Ross, *Richard III* and Bennett, *The Battle of Bosworth*. Other useful studies include R.A. Griffiths and S. Thomas, *The Making of the Tudor Dynasty* (Gloucester, Alan Sutton Publishing, 1985), A.J. Pollard, *Richard III and the Princes in the Tower* (Gloucester, Alan Sutton Publishing, 1991) and Horrox, *Richard III* which discusses the reasons for Richard's coup among other thorny issues. Thought-provoking insights are found in M.K. Jones and M.G. Underwood, *The King's Mother: Lady Margaret Beaufort, Countess of Richmond and Derby* (Cambridge, Cambridge University Press, 1992) and R.A. Griffiths, *Sir Rhys ap Thomas and his family: a study in the Wars of the Roses and early Tudor politics* (Cardiff, University of Wales Press, 1993), which provides a Welsh perspective on the Duke of Buckingham's position in 1483. See also Carpenter, *The Wars of the Roses* and R. Britnell, *The Closing of the Middle Ages? England, 1471–1529* (Oxford, Blackwell Publishers Ltd, 1997) for pertinent observations.

CHAPTER 5: BUCKINGHAM'S REBELLION

A useful starting point for the rebellion is *Rotuli Parliamentorum*, ed. J. Strachey (6 vols, London, Record Commissioners, 1767–83), vol. 6, pp. 244–51, which lists the attainted rebels; other traitors are recorded in *Harleian MS 433* and in two indictments taken at Bodmin and Exeter. Sources which enable a bald reconstruction of the the revolt include *Extracts from the Municipal Records of the City of York during the Reigns of Edward IV, Edward V and Richard III*, ed. R. Davies (Gloucester, rev. edn, Trowbridge and Esher, 1976) and *Household Books of John Duke of Norfolk*, ed. J.P. Collier (London, 1844), while useful snippets are found in *The Stonor Letters and Papers 1290–1483*, ed. C.L. Kingsford (2 vols, Camden Society, third series, 1919) and *Plumpton Correspondence*, ed. T. Stapleton (Camden Society, old series, 1839). The best guide to Richard's movements and, by default, the rebels', is *The Itinerary of Richard III*, ed. R. Edwards (London, Alan Sutton Publishing, 1983). For Henry Tudor's Breton-backed expedition Griffiths and Thomas, *The Making of the Tudor Dynasty* provides a wonderfully rich reconstruction, while A.E. Conway, 'The Maidstone Sector of Buckingham's Rebellion, October 18, 1483', *Archaeologia Cantiana*, being *Transactions of the Kent Archaeological Society*, 37 (1925) is important for the Kentish rising. *Harleian MS 433* is crucial for an understanding of the impact of the revolt on the country and the continuing unrest, while Horrox, *Richard III*, chapter 3, is far and away the leading work on the rebellion, providing first an assessment of continuity of service under Richard, followed by ample evidence of, and insights into, the size, duration and extent of the revolt.

CHAPTER 6: RICHARD'S RESPONSE

The official record material is crucial in terms of the crown's response to the rebellion. Of most value is *Harleian MS 433* for the forfeits and redistribution of rebels' lands to Richard's northern affinity, and of the locals' reaction to their new landlords. Other material which passed under the great and privy seals and the signet is found in the patent, close and pardon rolls which detail the punishment dealt out to the rebels, the rewards granted to the new men, the overall weight of the movement and the political as well as the social changes as a result of the rising. K. Dockray, 'Richard III and the Yorkshire Gentry', in *Richard III: Loyalty, Lordship and Law*, ed. P.W. Hammond (London, 1986) and Pollard, *Richard III and the Princes in the Tower* provide details of the northern affinity, while Griffiths and Thomas, *The Making of the Tudor Dynasty* presents a snapshot of Henry Tudor's community abroad. For general information on grants of pardon see R.L. Storey, *The End of the House of Lancaster* (Gloucester, rev. edn, Alan Sutton Publishing, 1986), Appendix II.

CHAPTER 7: THE POLITICS OF DISAFFECTION

For an overview of disaffection through 1484–85 and both the rebels' and Richard's preparations for the fight, Griffiths and Thomas, *The Making of the Tudor Dynasty*, Bennett, *The Battle of Bosworth* and especially Horrox, *Richard III* provide useful information. Additional detail is found in W.E. Hampton, *Memorials of the Wars of the Roses* (Gloucester, Alan Sutton Publishing, 1979), R. Virgoe, 'Sir John Risley 1443–1512: Courtier and Councillor', *Norfolk Archaeology*, 38 (1982), C.S.L. Davies, 'Bishop John Morton, the Holy See and the Accession of Henry VII', *EHR*, 102 (1987) and Davies, 'The Alleged "Sack of Bristol": International Ramifications of Breton Privateering, 1484–5', *Historical Research*, 67 (1994).

CHAPTER 8: TO CLAIM THE CROWN

Materials for the History of the Reign of Henry VII, ed. W. Campbell, Rolls Series (2 vols, London, HMSO, 1873–77) lists Henry's grants of patronage after Bosworth and is important for an understanding of the composition of the court and the household. For the role of the exiles in the new régime the following works are essential reading: D. Luckett, 'Crown Office and Licensed Retinues in the Reign of Henry VII', *Rulers and Ruled in Late Medieval England: Essays Presented to Gerald Harriss*, ed. R.E. Archer and S. Walker (London, The Hambledon Press, 1995), Luckett, 'Crown Patronage and Political Morality in Early Tudor England: The Case of Giles, Lord Daubenay', *EHR*, 110 (1995), and S.J. Gunn, 'The Courtiers of Henry VII', *EHR*, 108 (1993). More generally, useful material is found in Jones and Underwood, *The King's Mother: Lady Margaret Beaufort, Countess of Richmond and Derby*, chapter 3; while for the role of the 1483 rebels in a military context under Henry, see M.J. Bennett, 'Henry VII and the Northern Rising of 1489', *EHR*, 105 (1990).

CHAPTER 9: 1483 IN PERSPECTIVE

For a broader perspective on fifteenth-century kingship, see J. Watts, *Henry VI and the Politics of Kingship* (Cambridge, Cambridge University Press, 1996) and Carpenter, *The Wars of the Roses*. For the reign of Henry VII, see D. Luckett, 'Crown Office and Licensed Retinues in *Rulers and Ruled in Late Medieval England*, ed. R.E. Archer and S. Walker; Luckett, 'Crown Patronage and Political Morality in Early Tudor England: The Case of Giles, Lord Daubenay', S.J. Gunn, 'The Courtiers of Henry VII', and Gunn, *Early Tudor Government, 1485–1558* (New York, St Martin's Press, 1995), M.J. Bennett, *Lambert Simnel and the Battle of Stoke* (Gloucester, Alan Sutton Publishing, 1987) and Bennett, 'Henry VII and the Northern Rising of 1489'; see also J.M. Currin, 'Persuasions to Peace: The Luxembourg–Marigny–Gaguin Embassy and the State of Anglo-French Relations, 1489–90', *EHR*, 113 (1998), and 'Introduction: The Place of Henry VII in English History', in *The Reign of Henry VII*, ed. B. Thompson, Harlaxton Medieval Studies, 5 (Stamford, Paul Watkins, 1995).

Appendices

(1) CHRONICLE SOURCES AND INDEPENDENT ENGLISH ACCOUNTS

(a) Historical Notes of a Londoner

The chronicle provides a window on 1483 and is the earliest extant English source which links the Duke of Buckingham with the murders of the princes in the Tower.

Date: probably 1485–6.

Source: part of an early sixteenth-century heraldic miscellany most likely the property of Christopher Barker, Suffolk Herald (1514–22), and thought to have been compiled by a London merchant using civic records. Reprinted in R.F. Green, 'Historical notes of a London citizen, 1483–1488', *EHR*, 96 (1981), 588–9. (Spelling modernized.)

> This year King Edward deceased the 8th day of April.
>
> Item: King Edward V should have been crowned the 4th day of May, and the Duke of Gloucester and his lords at Northampton said he should be crowned another time with more honour at London; it was condescended that he should be crowned the 22nd day of June and a parliament should be held at Westminster the 4th day after. And in the meantime there was divers imagined the death of the Duke of Gloucester, and it was aspied and the Lord Hastings was taken in the Tower and beheaded forthwith, the 13th day of June in the year 1483. And the Archbishop of York, the Bishop of Ely and Oliver King the secretary, with others, was arrested the same day and put in prison in the Tower, and the coronation deferred till the 9th day of November . . . and the Duke of Gloucester made protector. And in the same month the Queen's brother, Anthony Woodville, Lord Rivers, and Lord Richard, Queen Elizabeth's son by her first husband, were put to death, with many more. And on St John Baptist's day next following, the Duke of Gloucester in his household took upon him to be King, and on the 3rd day after went to Westminster with all the lords and commonality of London, and there was proclaimed King Richard III. And on Sunday, the 6th of July next after, he was crowned and the Queen, both the same day.
>
> Item: this same year Louis the French King deceased.
>
> Item: this same year the Duke of Buckingham with many other knights, squires, and gentlemen from Kent to St Michael's Mount were rebels against King Richard. And the Bishop

of Ely, the Bishop of Exeter, and the Bishop of Salisbury fled the land with many other gentlemen.

Item: this year King Edward V, late called Prince of Wales, and Richard Duke of York his brother, King Edward IV's sons, were put to death in the Tower of London by the advice of the Duke of Buckingham.

(b) Miscellanous Town Chronicles

Date: compiled on a yearly basis.

Author: a citizen of London.

Text: *London 'Vitellius A XVI': Chronicles of London* (Oxford, 1905), pp. 191–2. (Spelling modernized.)

> In this year many knights and gentlemen of Kent and other places, gathered them together to have gone toward the Duke of Buckingham, being then at Brecon in the March of Wales, which intended to have subdued King Richard . . . as the said King Richard had put to death the lord chamberlain and other gentlemen . . . he also put to death the two children of King Edward, for which cause he lost the hearts of the people. And thereupon many gentlemen intended his destruction. And when the King knew of the Duke's intent . . . he went westward; and there raised his people, whereof the Duke . . . fled, because at that time his people were not come to him. . . . Then the gentlemen which had intended to have gone to him, hearing of his taking, fled sore dismayed.
>
> And upon this beheading of the Duke, King Richard rode to Exeter, where was taken Sir Thomas St Leger knight, and one Thomas Rameney, gentleman, and another . . . which three persons were then beheaded. Also this year was taken Sir George Brown knight, and one Clifford esquire, in Kent . . .

(c) The Great Chronicle

Date: Early sixteenth century.

Text: *The Great Chronicle of London*, ed. A.H. Thomas and I.D. Thornley (London, 1938), p. 234. (Spelling modernized.)

> All the winter season of this mayor's time the land was in good quiet. But after Easter much whispering was among the people that the King had put the children of King Edward to death, and also that he had poisoned the Queen, his wife, and intended with a licence purchased to have married the eldest daughter of King Edward. . . . It was not long after, were it for the aforesaid causes or other, but that the Duke of Buckingham estranged him from the King, and . . . sent for many of his fee'd men and such other as he supposed owed unto him favour, unto his manor of Brecon, whereof King Richard having knowledge, in as secret and possible hasty wise as he might assembled his people and drew towards the Duke. . . . In this while many knights and men of worship as Sir Thomas St Leger, Sir George Brown knights, William Clifford, Thomas Rameney esquires with many other which intended toward the Duke with all the power that they could make, when they heard of the Duke's thus avoiding put from them their companies and shifted for themselves in the best wise that they might . . .

(d) John Rous's Account of Buckingham's Rebellion

Date: *c.* 1490.

Author: John Rous, a Warwickshire priest.

Text: A. Hanham, *Richard III and his Early Historians, 1483–1535* (Oxford, Clarendon Press, 1975), pp. 122–3. (Spelling modernized.)

> And shortly after such rejoicing a great conspiracy was made against the king and a great insurrection. The king rode south with his followers in a great army, and the Duke of Buckingham was taken and led to the king at Salisbury and there beheaded. Then many lords fled from the country, and shortly after the prince died a tragic death.

(e) Polydore Vergil

Date: Composed between 1503 and 1513.

Author: Polydore Vergil of Urbino.

Text: *The 'Anglica Historia' of Polydore Vergil, AD 1485–1537*, ed. D. Hay (Camden Society, new series, 74, 1950), pp. 195–200. (Spelling modernized.)

The history is taken up after the Duke of Buckingham had left Richard III at Gloucester on the first leg of the royal progress, for his estates at Brecon where he unburdened his mind to John Morton, Bishop of Ely. Allegedly moved by his failure to receive from the king his Bohun lands, and his own complicity with Richard in events over the summer, the duke determined to rise against the king and then unite the dynasties of Lancaster and York.

> The Bishop of Ely . . . procured one Reginald Bray, servant to Margaret, Earl Henry's mother, who had married Thomas Lord Stanley, to come unto the duke into Wales, and his pleasure known to return speedily unto the said Margaret, and certify her of all things which had been deliberated between him and the duke concerning common safety . . .
>
> This Margaret for want of health used the advice of a physician named Lewis, a Welshman born, who . . . she was wont oftentimes to confer freely with all, and with him familiarly to lament her adversity. . . . She uttered to Lewis that the time was now come when as King Edward's eldest daughter might be given in marriage to her son Henry, and that King Richard, accounted of all men enemy to his country, might easily be dejected from all honour and bereft the realm, and therefore prayed him to deal secretly with the queen of such affair; for the queen also used his head, because he was a very learned physician. Lewis nothing lingering spoke with the queen . . . [who] was so well pleased with this device, that she commanded Lewis to repair to the Countess Margaret, who remained in her husband's house at London, and to promise in her name that she would do her endeavour to procure all her husband King Edward's friends to take part with Henry her son, so that he might be sworn to take in marriage Elizabeth her daughter, after he shall have gotten the realm, or else Cecily, the younger, if the other should die before he enjoyed the same.
>
> Thus Margaret being brought in good hope appointed Reginald Bray her servitor, a man most faithful and trusted, to be the chief dealer in this conspiracy, and commanded him to draw unto her party, as secretly as might be, some such noble or worshipful men as were wise, faithful and

active, who were able to make help in the cause. Reginald within few days gathered into the society of that conspiracy Giles Daubenay knight, Richard Guildford, Thomas Rameney, John Cheyne, and many more, having taken an oath beforehand of every man particularly.

Margaret the meanwhile took into her family Christopher Urswick . . . to go unto Earl Henry into Brittany, and to signify unto him all that was done with the queen.

But before he began to take his journey behold she was suddenly advertised of the same practice purposed by the Duke of Buckingham . . . which when she knew she altered her intent, staying Christopher at home, and sent Hugh Conway into Brittany unto her son Henry with a good great sum of money . . .

In the meantime in England the heads of the conspiracy went about many matters . . .

Vergil then reports that Richard, who became aware of Buckingham's leadership of the rebellion, summoned the duke to his side. The latter declined, 'alleging infirmity of stomach'. On the king's insistence,

the duke openly denied he would come to his enemy, and withal made ready for war, and persuaded his confederates forthwith . . . to raise the people. So almost at one moment and time Thomas Marquess of Dorset, who was gone out of sanctuary and preserved from all danger by means of Thomas Lovell, in Yorkshire, Edward Courtenay, with Peter his brother, Bishop of Exeter, in Devonshire, Richard Guildford, with certain of great reputation, in Kent, raised up the commons everywhere to armour, and made a beginning of war.

But when his confederates, who had now begun war, knew that the duke was forsaken of his people, and fled no man wist whither, they were suddenly dismayed, every man fled without hope of safety, and other got into sanctuary or wilderness, or assayed to sail over the seas, whereof a great part came safe soon after into Brittany. Amongst that company was Peter Courtenay, Bishop of Exeter, with Edward his brother . . . Thomas Marquess Dorset, with Thomas his son, . . John Bourchier, John Welles, Edward Woodville, a valiant man of war, brother to Queen Elizabeth, Robert Willoughby, Giles Daubenay, Thomas Arundel, John Cheyne, with his two brothers, William Berkeley, William Brandon, with Thomas his brother, Richard Edgecombe, and all these almost of the order of knighthood: also John Halwell, Edward Poynings, chief captain of the army, Christopher Urswick, and John Morton, Bishop of Ely, with many other noble men, transported over about the same very time into Flanders.

(2) OFFICIAL INDICTMENT AGAINST THE REBELS, ISSUED BY RICHARD III AT LEICESTER

Date: 23 October 1483.
Source: *Calendar of Patent Rolls, 1476–1485*, p. 371.

Precept to the sheriff of Devon to issue a proclamation denouncing Thomas Dorset, late Marquess of Dorset, who holds the unshameful and mischievous woman called Shore's wife in adultery, Sir William Norris, Sir William Knyvet, Sir Thomas Bourchier of Barnes, Sir George

Brown, knights, John Cheyne, John Norris, Walter Hungerford, John Rushe and John Harcourt of Staunton, who have assembled the people by the comfort of the great rebel the late Duke of Buckingham and Bishops of Ely and Salisbury, and offering rewards for their capture and pardon for all who withdraw from them.

(3) BUCKINGHAM'S REBELS

(a) From the Official Acts of Attainder

Date: January–February 1484.
Source: *Rotuli Parliamentorum*, ed. J. Strachey (6 vols, London, Record Commissioners, 1767–83), vol. 6, pp. 244–51. See also S.B. Chrimes, *Henry VII* (London, Eyre Methuen, 1972), Appendix B.

(i) The First Act
The rising at Brecon, 18 October:
Henry, Duke of Buckingham, John Morton, Bishop of Ely; Sir William Knyvet; John Rushe, late of London, merchant; Thomas Nandik, late of Cambridge, necromancer. It also includes Henry, Earl of Richmond, and Jasper, Earl of Pembroke, who sailed from Brittany for Plymouth.

The risings in Kent and Surrey, at Maidstone, Rochester, Gravesend, Guildford, and elsewhere between 18 and 25 October, involving twenty-eight persons:
Sir George Brown, Sir Thomas Lewkenor, Sir John Guildford, Sir John Fogge, Edward Poynings esquire, Richard Haute esquire, Richard Guildford esquire, John Pympe esquire, Thomas Fiennes esquire, Nicholas Gaynesford esquire, John Gaynesford esquire, William Clifford esquire, John Darell esquire, Anthony Kene esquire, Thomas Ryder esquire, William Brandon esquire, John Wingfield esquire [listed in the act but who avoided attainder], Alexander Culpepper gentleman, James Horne gentleman, Reginald Pympe gentleman, Robert Brewes gentleman, John Boutayne yeoman of the crown, Richard Potter yeoman of the crown, Richard Fissher yeoman of the crown, William Strode yeoman of the crown, William Loveday yeoman, Roger Long yeoman, John Hoo yeoman.

The rising at Newbury, Berkshire, and elsewhere, 18 October, involving fourteen persons:
Sir Richard Beauchamp (Lord St Amand), Sir William Norris, Sir William Berkeley, Sir Roger Tocotes, Sir William Stonor, Sir Thomas Delamare, Sir William Overay, Sir Richard Woodville, John Harcourt esquire, William Uvedale esquire, Edmund Hampden gentleman, Walter Williams merchant, Roger Kelsale yeoman of the crown, Amyas Paulet.

The rising at Salisbury and elsewhere, 18 October, involving thirty-two persons:
Sir John St Lo, Sir Nicholas Latimer, Sir Giles Daubenay, John Cheyne esquire, Thomas Melbourne esquire, Walter Hungerford esquire, John Trenchard esquire, William Hall gentleman, Michael Skilling gentleman, Humphrey Cheyne gentleman, Robert Cheyne gentleman, John Bevyn gentleman, John Heron gentleman, John Champney gentleman, William Case gentleman, John

Higgons gentleman, William Baskett gentleman, John Fesaunt gentleman, Thomas Brown gentleman, John Melbourne gentleman, William Knight yeoman of the crown, John Shirwell yeoman, Robert Canon yeoman, John Forde yeoman, Walter Cole yeoman, John Averey yeoman, James Worsley yeoman, Robert Bowdon yeoman, William Bampton, Thomas Lynde, John Knolles, John Watts.

The rising at Exeter, 18 October, involving eighteen persons:
The Marquess of Dorset, Sir Robert Willoughby, Sir Thomas St Leger, Sir Thomas Arundel, John Welles esquire, Edward Courtenay esquire, Richard Nanfan esquire, John Halwell esquire, Walter Courtenay esquire, John Treffry esquire, John Trevelyan gentleman, William Bolter gentleman, Thomas Lovell gentleman, William Treffry gentleman, Thomas Pyne gentleman, John Morton gentleman, Richard Cruse yeoman of the crown, William Frost yeoman of the crown.

(ii) The Second Act
Attainder of John Morton, Bishop of Ely, Lionel Woodville, Bishop of Salisbury, and Peter Courtenay, Bishop of Exeter.

(iii) The Third Act
Attainder of Margaret, Countess of Richmond:
Margaret, Countess of Richmond, mother to the king's great rebel and traitor, Henry, Earl of Richmond, has conspired and committed high treason, especially by sending messages, writings and tokens to Henry, stirring him to come into the realm to make war; and has made chevisancez of great sums of money in the City of London and elsewhere to be employed in treason; and has conspired and imagined the destruction of the king and was asserting and assisting Henry, Duke of Buckingham, in treason.

But the king, of his especial grace, remembering the good and faithful service that Thomas, Lord Stanley has done and intends to do to him, and for the good love and trust that the king has in him, and for his sake, remits and forbears the great punishment of attainder of the said countess that she deserves.

It is ordained and enacted that she shall be disabled in the law from having or inheriting any lands or name of estate or dignity, and shall forfeit all estates whatsoever, which shall be to Thomas Lord Stanley for the term of his life and thereafter to the king and his heirs. Any estates she has or are held to her use, of the inheritance of Thomas Lord Stanley, shall be void.

(iv) The Fourth Act
Attainder of Walter Roberd of Cranbrooke, Kent, having levied war at Maidstone, 18 October, and having harboured Sir John Guildford and other traitors on 10 February.

(b) Leading rebels included in Lord Scope's indictment at Torrington

(Only names additional to Act of Attainder)
Date: November 1483.
Source: Devon RO, ECA Book 51.

Sir Thomas Fulford, Sir John Crocker, Sir Hugh Lutterell, Bartholomew St Leger, John Norris, Thomas Greenfield, Robert Burnaby, William Chilson.

(c) Leading rebels included in Lord Scope's indictment at Bodmin

(Only names additional to Act of Attainder)
Date: 13 November 1483.
Source: Royal Institution of Cornwall: MS BV. 1/4.
Ralph Arundel, Geoffrey Beauchamp, Remfry Densell, John Rosogan.

(d) Leading rebels from royal indictments

Date: November 1483–1484.
Source: British Harley MS 433.

Cornwall: Stephen Calmady, James Bonython esquire.
Devon: Richard Edgecombe.
Dorset: Thomas Audley esquire, John Cheverell esquire, William Twynyho esquire, Richard Morton gentleman.
Somerset: William Hody gentleman, Sir Thomas Bourchier.
Buckinghamshire-Bedfordshire: Sir Richard Enderby, Sir John Donne.
Norfolk/Suffolk: Sir William Brandon, William Loveday.
Kent: John Waller esquire, Stephen Gerard, Sir William Haute, William Cheyne, John Wingfield the younger, John Isley, Ralph Tykull, John Alsey, Anthony Brown, Robert Brent, Richard Latimer, Roger Long, John Bale, John Waller esquire, William Tyler.

(e) Names of rebels in exile with Henry Tudor, supplied by Polydore Vergil

Source: *The 'Anglica Historia' of Polydore Vergil, AD 1485–1537*, ed. D. Hay (Camden Society, new series, 74, 1950), p. 200. See also Chrimes, *Henry VII*, Appendix B.

Peter Courtenay, Bishop of Exeter, Thomas Grey, Marquess of Dorset, and his young son, Edward Courtenay, John Bourchier, John Welles, Edward Woodville, Robert Willoughby, Giles Daubenay, Thomas Arundel, John Cheyne and his two brothers, William Berkeley, William and Thomas Brandon, Richard Edgecombe, Evan Morgan, Edward Poynings, John de Vere, Earl of Oxford, James Blount, Sir John Fortescue, Richard Fox.

(f) The chronicle sources

Richard Grafton, *Chronicle* (1568):
Robert Poyntz.
John Stow, *The Annales of England* (1592):
Sir John Scott.

(4) SAMPLE OF FIFTY-FIVE REBELS SELECTED FOR DISCUSSION

Thirty-nine of the following knights, esquires and gentlemen were under sentence of attainder, sixteen were indicted but avoided attainder. Category (i) represents attainted rebels; category (ii), the unattainted.

* represents king's knights and knights and esquires of the body under Edward IV.

Brecon:
(ii) Sir William Knyvet.

Kent:
(i) *Sir George Brown, *Sir John Fogge, Sir John Guildford, Sir Thomas Lewkenor; esquires John Darell, John and *Nicholas Gaynesford, Richard Guildford, *Thomas Fiennes, Richard Haute, Edward Poynings, William Brandon.

(ii) *Sir Thomas Bourchier, Sir John Scott, Sir William Haute, Sir William Brandon; esquire *John Wingfield.

Newbury:
(i) Sir Richard Beauchamp, Lord St Amand, *Sir William Berkeley, Sir Thomas Delamare, *Sir William Norris, *Sir William Stonor, Sir Roger Tocotes; esquires *William Uvedale, John Harcourt; yeoman of the crown Roger Kelsale; gentleman Edmund Hampden.

Salisbury:
(i) *Sir Giles Daubenay, Sir Nicholas Latimer, Sir John St Lo; esquires *Walter Hungerford, *John Cheyne, John Trenchard; gentlemen Humphrey Cheyne, Alexander Cheyne, John Heron.

(ii) * Robert Poyntz.

Exeter:
(i) *Sir Thomas St Leger, Sir Robert Willoughby, *Sir Thomas Arundel; esquires Edward Courtenay, John Halwell, Richard Nanfan, John Trevelyan and John Treffry.

(ii) Sir Thomas Fulford, Sir John Crocker; esquires *Thomas Audley, Thomas Brandon, John Cheverell, Richard Edgecombe, William Twynyho, Richard and Robert Morton, and * John Norris.

Index